CW01290985

Great Perfection

The Essence of Pure Spirituality

Great Perfection

The Essence of Pure Spirituality

Calling the Lama from Afar
The Excellent Path of Supreme Great Bliss

Chatral Rinpoche, Sangye Dorje

•

The Precious Treasury of Phenomenal Space

Longchen Rabjam

•

From the Heart Essence of the Great Expanse
The Most Secret Guru Yoga Having
the Seal of the Essence

Jigme Lingpa

Translations by

Shyalpa Tenzin Rinpoche

Vajra Books

Dedicated to the great Vidyadhara Teachers
of
the Dzogchen Lineage

Published & Distributed by

Vajra Books
Jyatha, Thamel, P.O. Box 21779, Kathmandu, Nepal
Tel.: 977-1-4220562, Fax: 977-1-4246536
e-mail: bidur_la@mos.com.np
www.vajrabooks.com.np

Copyright © 2014 by Shyalpa Tenzin Rinpoche

All rights reserved. This book may not be reproduced in whole or in part, stored in a retrieval system, or transmitted in any form or by any means — electronic, mechanical, or other — without written permission from the publisher, except by a reviewer, who may quote brief passages in a review.

ISBN 978-9937-623-24-7

Printed in Nepal

Contents

Foreword

Great Perfection: The Essence of Pure Spirituality presents precious texts from three of the greatest masters of Dzogpa Chenpo, the Heart Essence of the Vast Expanse. For those who wish to study, contemplate, and recite these sacred verses in English, our Root Guru, His Eminence Shyalpa Tenzin Rinpoche, has orally translated each of them from the original Tibetan texts.

The first, *Calling the Lama from Afar, The Excellent Path of Supreme Great Bliss* is by His Holiness Chatral Rinpoche, Shyalpa Rinpoche's own Root Guru. It is a prayer that sets forth the quintessence of the path of the Great Perfection — unwavering trust, genuine respect, and heartfelt devotion for one's root teacher.

The second text, constituting the core of this book, is perhaps the greatest work ever penned on the nature of mind and phenomena from the viewpoint of Dzogchen, the Great Perfection. Known as *The Precious Treasury of Phenomenal Space,* it was composed by the omniscient Longchen Rabjam. This is considered an expression of Longchenpa's realization and contains the profound essence of the 84,000 teachings of the Buddha. The first nine chapters present the view, the tenth presents the meditation, the eleventh the action, the twelfth the provisional result of the path, and the thirteenth the ultimate result. Many of the greatest masters of past and present have made this "relic of dharmakaya" the heart of their daily practice. Regarding this work, the great Dzogchen master Patrul Rinpoche wrote in *An Exhortation to Read The Seven Treasuries*:

> A fine work like this is a treasury of all the holy Dharma.
> Regarding the ultimate topic of all the teachings of Dharma,
> The primordial wisdom of dharmakaya revealed in nakedness,
> In comparing all other teachings, there would be nothing more
> than this.

The third and final text, *The Heart Essence of the Great Expanse, The Most Secret Guru Yoga Having the Seal of the Essence* by Kunkhyen Jigme Lingpa, is a revealed mind-treasure, a practice of Guru Yoga that unites the mind of the disciple with the enlightened wisdom mind of the perfect Guru.

More than 20 years ago, while living in the United States, His Eminence Shyalpa Tenzin Rinpoche began the task of translating *The Precious Treasury of Phenomenal Space* into English. His Eminence felt that the translation of this spiritual masterpiece from the original Tibetan would greatly benefit countless beings. More recently, as the text was prepared for publication, the translation was refined and polished again and again with great care.

Rinpoche expresses his appreciation to Arthur Mendelbaum, Ives Waldo, Sangye Gyalmo, Zach Larson, and Lou Koval for their invaluable assistance in the translation of these precious texts. A special thanks to Ives Waldo for his work on the glossary, which serves as an excellent reference on Buddhist terminology in the context of Dzogchen, the Great Perfection. Finally, Rinpoche extends sincere thanks to Dr. Marvin Tse for generously sponsoring the printing of this sacred book.

His Eminence Shyalpa Tenzin Rinpoche is pleased to introduce these sublime and sacred texts to the English-speaking world, having no doubt that whoever makes a connection with their unconditional essence will surely reach the state of Samantabhadra!

Paul J. Patrick
Rangrig Yeshe

Preface

The essence of the Buddha's teachings of the three classes[1] and nine
expanses,[2]
The ultimate refinement of the essence, the true realization of learned and
accomplished masters,
Is the supreme direct path of liberation into a luminous body in a single
lifetime.
I bow to the Guru who has great skill in propagating such liberating
teachings for those who are fortunate.

The omniscient lord of victorious ones, Immaculate Rays of Light,[3] was one of the three incarnate Manjushris[4] of the land of snow. The ultimate innermost essence of the 600,000 tantras of Dzogchen, the heart's blood of a hundred thousand dakinis, the ocean of cream, the enlightened heart of omniscient Longchenpa, manifested in the forms of the extensive and great *Seven Treasuries* of the ways of the panditas, the profound tradition of the kusulu yogins[5] that is of the four texts of Nyingthig; the *Trilogy of Comfort and Ease* that teaches the true meaning of the points of both the profound nature and the extent of phenomena, complete and without error; the *Trilogy of Self-liberation*; the *Trilogy of Clearing Away Darkness,* and so on. These relics of dharmakaya that are not different from the words of Vajradhara were composed and bestowed as cherished wealth for those of us of later generations by the omniscient one.

In particular, the quintessence of the great *Seven Treasuries*, this *Precious Treasury of Phenomenal Space*, is a true replica of the omniscient Guru's realization. As Dzogchen Patrul Rinpoche says, this excellent work bestows liberation in a single lifetime on karmically connected fortunate ones of the highest capabilities.

Nowadays, in this extensive realm of Jambuling, externally there are real manifestations of glory and abundant prosperity that spread and increase day by day like the waxing moon. However, internally one's mind is continually tormented by extreme attachment, covetous desire, competitiveness, discord, jealousy, and so forth.

Therefore, in this time of extremely fleeting happiness, His Eminence Shyalpa Tenzin Rinpoche, with exemplary diligence and kindness, for the benefit of supremely fortunate ones, illuminates the innermost secret meaning to be realized with complete understanding within this lifetime. In this way, all beings can pacify the host of negative discursive thoughts and afflictive emotions, moisten the mind with compassion, be enriched by the principle of peace and non-violence, and ultimately actualize the true face of self-awareness—Samantabhadra. Accordingly, the radiant light of peace and happiness will completely pervade the earth.

In particular, when the time of death approaches, by mastering this profound instruction, one will be able to reach the primordial kingdom, pure from the very beginning. Therefore, I truly rejoice in Rinpoche's translation of this most profound and amazing text, *The Precious Treasury of Phenomenal Space*, which is like a priceless wish-fulfilling jewel, and in conclusion, I hope and pray that his wish for all devoted beings to gain extensive temporal and ultimate benefit will be realized.

Arising from the ocean of his compassionate attitude,
This good text, a jewel of space, has been auspiciously translated
And now graciously manifests on the face of the earth.
By this, may the suffering of beings be completely cleared away.

This was written on May 25th, 2014, by one who holds the title of Khenpo, Ogyen Tsering, at the peak of vehicles, Ati Ling Monastery.

༄༅། །ཐུབ་བསྟན་སྙིང་པོ་སྡེ་གསུམ་གླིང་དགུ་ཡི།།
སྙིང་པོའི་ཡང་ཞུན་མཁས་གྲུབ་དགོངས་པའི་བཅུད།།
ཚེ་གཅིག་འོད་སྐུར་གྲོལ་བའི་ཉེ་ལམ་ཆེ།།
ཐར་འདོད་གསོས་སུ་སྤེལ་མཁས་བླ་མར་འདུད།།

དེ་འང་གངས་ལྗོངས་འཛམ་དབྱངས་རྣམ་གསུམ་གྱི་ཡ་གྱལ་༸རྒྱལ་བའི་དབང་པོ་ཀུན་མཁྱེན་དྲི་མེད་འོད་ཟེར་མཆོག་གི་ཐུགས་ཀྱི་འོ་མཚོ་ལས་བྱུང་བའི་རྫོགས་པ་ཆེན་པོའི་རྒྱུད་འབུམ་ཐུག་དྲུག་ཅུའི་ཡང་སྙིང་། མཁའ་འགྲོ་སྙིང་གི་སྙིང་ཁྲག ཀླུ་ཆེ་བ་པཎྜི་ཏའི་ལུགས་མཛོད་ཆེན་བདུན་དང་། ཟབ་པ་ཀུ་སུ་ལུའི་ལུགས་སྙིང་ཐིག་ཡ་བཞི། ཟབ་རྒྱས་གཉིས་ཀྱི་དོན་ཚང་ལ་མ་ནོར་བར་བསྟན་པ་ངེས་དོན་ངལ་གསོ་སྐོར་གསུམ། རང་གྲོལ་སྐོར་གསུམ། མུན་སེལ་སྐོར་གསུམ་སོགས་རྒྱལ་བ་རྡོ་རྗེ་འཆང་གི་བཀའ་དང་གཉིས་སུ་མེད་པའི་ཆོས་སྐུའི་རིང་བསྲེལ་འདི་དག་རང་རེ་ཕྱི་རབས་རྣམས་ལ་གཅེས་ནོར་དུ་བཞག་གནང་ཞིང་། ཁྱད་པར་དུ་མཛོད་ཆེན་བདུན་གྱི་ཡང་སྙིང་ཆོས་དབྱིངས་རིན་པོ་ཆེའི་མཛོད་འདི་ནི་ཀུན་མཁྱེན་བླ་མའི་རྟོགས་པའི་འདྲ་འབག་དངོས་ཡིན་པར་རྫོགས་ཆེན་དཔལ་སྤྲུལ་རིན་པོ་ཆེས་གསུངས་པ་ལྟར། སྐལ་ལྡན་དབང་རབ་ལས་ཅན་རྣམས་ཚེ་གཅིག་ལ་གྲོལ་བར་སྟེར་བའི་གཞུང་བཟང་འདི་ཉིད། དེང་དུས་འཛམ་གླིང་གོ་ལའི་ཁྱོན་འདིར་ཕྱི་དཔལ་འབྱོར་གྱི་དངོས་པོ་ཉིན་རེ་བཞིན་འཕེལ་རྒྱས་ཡར་ཟླ་ལྟར་འགྲོ་བཞིན་ཡོད་ནའང་། ནང་སེམས་རྒྱུད་ལ་ཕན་ཚུན་འགྲན་རྩོད་དང་། འདོད་རྔམས། མགོན་འཛིན་སོགས་ཆགས་སྡང་གིས་རྒྱུན་དུ་མནར་ཏེ་བདེ་བའི་གོ་སྐབས་ཤིན་ཏུ་ཉག་ཕྲ་བའི་སྐབས་འདིར། ༸སྐྱབས་རྗེ་གཞལ་པ་བསྟན་འཛིན་རིན་པོ་ཆེ་མཆོག་ནས་སྐུ་ངལ་ཁྱད་བསད་ཀྱིས་སྐལ་ལྡན་མཆོག་རབ་རྣམས་ཀྱིས་ཚེ་འདིར་ཡང་གསང་ཟབ་མོའི་དགོངས་དོན་ཚུལ་བཞིན་རྟོགས་ཏེ་སྟན་ཐོག་གཅིག་ལ་རང་རིག་ཀུན་ཏུ་བཟང་པོའི་རང་ཞལ་མངོན་སུམ་དུ་མཇལ་བ་དང་། ལས་ཅན་སྐྱེ་འགྲོའི་ཉོན་མོངས་པའི་ཀུན་རྟོག་ངན་པའི་ཚོགས་རྣམས་ཞི་ཞིང་ཐུགས་རྒྱུད་བྱང་ཆུབ་སེམས་ཀྱིས་རབ་ཏུ་བརླན་ཏེ་འཆི་མེད་ཞི་བདེའི་ལྷ་བས་རྒྱུད་ཕྱུག་ཅིང་ས་ཡི་ཁྱོན་འདིར་བདེ་སྐྱིད་འོད་སྣང་དཀར་པོས་ཡོངས་སུ་ཁྱབ་སྟེ། ནམ་ཞིག་འཕོས་ཚེ་ཀ་དག་གདོད་མའི་རྒྱལ་སར་བསྙེག་ཐུབ་པའི་གདམས་ངག་ཟབ་མོར་མངའ་དབང་འབྱོར་བའི་ཆེད་དུ། ཡིད་བཞིན་གྱི་ནོར་བུ་རིན་པོ་ཆེ་ལྟ་བུའི་གཞུང་བཟང་རྨད་དུ་བྱུང་བ་འདི་ཉིད་དབྱིན་ཡིག་ཐོག་ཕབ་བསྒྱུར་གནང་བ་ལ་རྗེས་སུ་ཡི་རང་ཞུ་རྒྱུ་མ་ཟད། ཁོང་གི་ཐུགས་རེ་བཞིན་སྐྱེ་འགྲོ་དད་ལྡན་ཡོངས་ལ་གནས་སྐབས་དང་མཐར་ཐུག་གི་ཕན་འབྲས་རྒྱ་ཆེན་པོ་འབྱུང་བའི་རེ་བ་དང་སྨོན་ལམ་ཟབ་མོ་ཞུའོ།།

གང་གི་ཐུགས་བསྐྱེད་རྒྱ་མཚོ་བསྒྲུབས་པ་ལས།།
ལེགས་པར་འཁྲུངས་པའི་གཞུང་བཟང་ནམ་མཁའི་ནོར།།
འཛམ་གླིང་གོ་ལའི་ངོགས་སུ་ལེགས་འཆར་བས།།
འགྲོ་བའི་དུཿཁའི་མུན་པ་ཀུན་བསལ་ཤོག།

ཅེས་སྤྱི་ལོ་༢༠༡༩ ཟླ་༥ ཚེས་༢༥ ཉིན་མཁན་མིང་འཛིན་པ་ཨོ་རྒྱན་ཚེ་རིང་ནས་ཐེག་རྩེ་ཨ་ཧི་ཏའི་གླིང་དུ་བྲིས།།

Shyalpa Tenzin Rinpoche's Principal Gurus

Top row, left to right: HE Deshung Rinpoche, HH The Dalai Lama,
HH Dilgo Khyentse Rinpoche, HE Trulku Theklo Rinpoche.
Second row, left to right: Very Ven. Khenchen Thrangu Rinpoche, HH Penor Rinpoche,
HH Taklung Shabdrung Rinpoche, HH Dodrupchen Rinpoche, HE Drikung Tokden Rinpoche.
Third row, left to right: Ven. Khenchen Daser Rinpoche, Very Ven. Nyulshol Khen Rinpoche,
HH Sangye Tsering Rinpoche, Ven. Lama Dakpa Gyatso.
Fourth row, left to right: HH Taklung Tsetrul Rinpoche,
His Holiness Chatral Rinpoche, Sangye Dorje (Root Guru), HH Khangsar Tenpo Rinpoche.

[illegible]

Calling the Lama from Afar

The Excellent Path of Supreme Great Bliss

༄༅། །བླ་མ་བརྒྱུད་འདེབས་གསོལ་འདེབས་བདེ་ཆེན་མཆོག་གི་ལམ་བཟང་ཞེས་བྱ་བ་བཞུགས་སོ། །
༄༅། །ན་མོ་གུ་རུ་བྷྱ།

རྒྱུ་འབྲས་ཐེག་པ་ཀུན་ནས་བླ་མ་ནི། །
སངས་རྒྱས་སྤྲུལ་པར་གསུངས་ཕྱིར་དེར་མོས་པས། །
གང་ཞིག་གསོལ་བཏབ་བྱིན་རླབས་བསླུ་མེད་དུ། །
འབྱུང་མོད་གཙོ་བོར་མོས་གུས་ཉིད་ལ་རག།
ཐེ་ཚོམ་དང་དང་ནས་ཁ་ཙམ་བརྒྱུད་འདེབས་ཀྱིས། །
བྱིན་རླབས་དངོས་གྲུབ་ཉེ་རྒྱུར་ག་ལ་འགྱུར། །
བློ་གཏད་ཡིད་བསྐྱུར་ཕུར་ཚུགས་གསོལ་འདེབས་དང་། །
བླ་མ་བརྒྱུད་འདེབས་འདི་ལྟར་བྱ་བ་གཅེས། །

བླ་མ་མཁྱེན།
ཞེས་ལན་གསུམ་བོས་ནས་ཐུགས་རྗེ་ལྷོངས་པར་བྱས་ལ།

ངོ་བོ་ཆོས་སྐུ་ཀུན་ཁྱབ་ནམ་མཁའ་ཡི་དང་ནས། །
རང་བཞིན་ལོངས་སྐུ་འགགས་མེད་ཉི་འོད་ལྟར་གསལ་ཞིང་། །
ཐུགས་རྗེ་སྤྲུལ་སྐུ་འཇའ་ཚོན་ལྟ་བུ་རུ་བཞེངས་པའི། །
སྐུ་གསུམ་དབྱེར་མེད་དགོངས་པ་སྙིང་དབུས་སུ་སད་པར། །
སངས་རྒྱས་ངོ་བོ་རྡོ་རྗེའི་བླ་མ་ཁྱེད་མཁྱེན་ནོ། །

Calling the Lama from Afar
The Excellent Path of Supreme Great Bliss

Chatralwa Sangye Dorje

Homage to the Lama.

Since it is said in all the cause and fruition vehicles that the Lama is an emanation of the Buddha, anyone who supplicates the teacher with devotion will receive blessings without fail. However, this result is above all dependent on one's faith and devotion. If with doubts, you simply utter the words of Calling the Lama from Afar, *how could this be a cause for directly producing blessings and accomplishments?*

With utter trust and complete conviction, ardently supplicate the Lama, and with that it is important to practice Calling the Lama from Afar *as follows:*

Lama, please think of me!
Lama, please think of me!
Lama, please think of me!

Having called like this three times, one awakens the supreme blessing and enters the Lama's compassionate heart.

In the continuum of all-pervading space, dharmakaya,[6] the essence,
There are, without cessation, sambhogakaya,[7] the nature, luminous like the rays of the sun,
And nirmanakaya,[8] compassion, which arises like a rainbow.
To achieve realization of the inseparability of the three kayas in the core of my heart,
I pray to you, the essence of the Buddha, the Vajra Guru, please think of me!

མཐའ་བརྒྱད་སྤྲོས་བྲལ་རྫོགས་ཆེན་ཡེ་གཞིའི་དོན་རྟོགས་ཤིང་།།
ལྟ་སྒོམ་ཤུབས་ནས་དོན་པའི་གསེང་ལམ་གྱི་སྦུབས་ནས།།
བྱ་རྩོལ་ཞེ་འདོད་ཟད་པའི་འབྲས་བུ་ལ་སྦྱོར་བའི།།
གཞི་འབྲས་དབྱེར་མེད་གདོད་མའི་ཆོས་སྐུ་རུ་གྲོལ་བར།།
སངས་རྒྱས་ངོ་བོ་རྡོ་རྗེའི་བླ་མ་ཁྱེད་མཁྱེན་ནོ།།
བརྒྱ་ལ་ལན་གཅིག་རྙེད་པའི་དལ་འབྱོར་གྱི་རྟེན་བཟང་།།
དོན་མེད་སྟོང་ཟད་མ་གཏོང་སྐྱེ་འཆི་དང་བར་དོའི།།
གདམས་ཟབ་རང་བྱན་ཆུད་པའི་སྐྱེལ་མ་དང་འགྲོགས་ནས།།
སྐུ་གསུམ་རང་རྩལ་རྫོགས་པའི་རྟོགས་ཚད་དང་ལྡན་པར།།
སངས་རྒྱས་ངོ་བོ་རྡོ་རྗེའི་བླ་མ་ཁྱེད་མཁྱེན་ནོ།།
ཕྱི་ནང་སྣོད་བཅུད་སྣང་ཅིག་མི་རྟག་པའི་མཚང་རིག།
ཡེ་ནས་མ་བྱུང་མ་སྐྱེས་འཕོ་འགྱུར་དང་བྲལ་བའི།།
བདེ་ཆེན་འདུས་མ་བྱས་ཤིང་ལྷུན་གྲུབ་ཀྱིས་ལ།།
མ་འབད་བཞིན་དུ་སྣང་ཅིག་ད་ལྟ་རང་ཕྱིན་པར།།
སངས་རྒྱས་ངོ་བོ་རྡོ་རྗེའི་བླ་མ་ཁྱེད་མཁྱེན་ནོ།།

To realize reality as the primordial ground, the Great Perfection, free from elaboration of the eight extremes,
And following the hidden way of the direct path, to emerge from the shell of view and meditation,
To join to the fruition, where action, effort, and endeavor are exhausted,
To be liberated in primordial dharmakaya, where ground and fruition are inseparable,
I pray to you, the essence of the Buddha, the Vajra Guru, please think of me!

While I now possess the freedoms and favorable conditions of this excellent human birth, attained but once in a hundred lifetimes,
And I am accompanied and escorted by profound instructions of those who have completely mastered birth, death, and the intermediate state,[9]
May I avoid uselessly squandering these.
So that I may possess the full measure of realization, in which the intrinsic potential of the three kayas is perfected,
I pray to you, the essence of the Buddha, the Vajra Guru, please think of me!

To be aware of the faults of the external world and the beings contained within it,
As they consist of what is momentary and impermanent,
To reach without effort in this present moment,
The unconditioned, spontaneously existing ground of great bliss,
Which, present from the beginning, has never arisen, been born, or changed,
I pray to you, the essence of the Buddha, the Vajra Guru, please think of me!

འཇིགས་རུང་འཁོར་བའི་གཡང་ས་ཡ་ང་འདི་སྐྱོབ་པའི།།
དམ་ཆོས་ཐེག་དགུའི་རྩེ་རྒྱལ་ཨ་ཏི་དང་ཡང་ཏིའི།།
སྨིན་གྲོལ་བདུད་རྩིའི་བཅུད་རོལ་དགའ་སྟོན་གྱི་ངང་ནས།།
འཁོར་བའི་འདམ་ནང་བྱིངས་ལས་ད་ལྟ་རང་ཐར་བར།།
སངས་རྒྱས་ངོ་བོ་རྡོ་རྗེའི་བླ་མ་མཁྱེན་མཁྱེན་ནོ།།
འཁོར་བའི་འཁྲུལ་འཁོར་དཀར་ནག་བདེ་སྡུག་གི་རྩ་བ།།
ལྷན་སྐྱེས་ཀུན་བརྟགས་མ་རིག་ས་བོན་ལ་ཐུག་ཕྱིར།།
བདག་མེད་ཤེས་རབ་རང་བྱུང་རིག་པ་ཡི་སྒྲོན་མེས།།
གཏི་མུག་སྙིང་གི་མུན་པ་རང་མལ་དུ་སངས་པར།།
སངས་རྒྱས་ངོ་བོ་རྡོ་རྗེའི་བླ་མ་མཁྱེན་མཁྱེན་ནོ།།
ཡེ་གྲོལ་རིག་པ་དོན་དམ་གནས་ལུགས་ཀྱི་སྐྱབས་ཡུལ།།
མ་ངེས་ཉི་ཚེའི་སྐྱབས་འགྲོས་མཐར་འབྲས་ནི་མི་ཐོབ།།
བསྐྱབ་བྱ་སྐྱོབ་བྱེད་སྐྱབས་འགྲོ་འཁོར་གསུམ་དང་བྲལ་བའི།།
ཡོངས་གྲུབ་སེམས་ཀྱི་རྡོ་རྗེ་སྐྱབས་མཆོག་ཏུ་རྟོགས་པར།།
སངས་རྒྱས་ངོ་བོ་རྡོ་རྗེའི་བླ་མ་མཁྱེན་མཁྱེན་ནོ།།

So that I may be immediately liberated from sinking in the swamp of samsara,
Through the enjoyment of continuous feast and celebration
Of that which protects from the frightening and terrible precipice of samsara —
The essence of the ripening and liberating nectar of Ati and Yangti,[10] the victorious peak of the nine vehicles of the holy Dharma,
I pray to you, the essence of the Buddha, the Vajra Guru, please think of me!

The root of the mechanism of samsara, black and white, pleasure and pain,
Comes down to the seeds of ignorance — co-emergence and false conceptions.[11]
To be naturally awakened from the darkest heart of ignorance
By egoless knowledge, the self-originated lamp of awareness,
I pray to you, the essence of the Buddha, the Vajra Guru, please think of me!

Primordially liberated awareness of things as they are is the absolute object of refuge.
The final fruition cannot be attained through uncertain or temporal objects of refuge.
To realize the supreme refuge, completely accomplished indestructible mind,
Free from the three-fold object, agent, and action of going for refuge,
I pray to you, the essence of the Buddha, the Vajra Guru, please think of me!

བདག་གཞན་འཁོར་འདས་རེ་དོགས་འཇུར་བུ་ཡིས་བཅིངས་པའི།།
ཡིད་སྨོན་འདུ་བྱེད་སེམས་བསྐྱེད་བཟང་ཞེན་ལས་འདས་ཀྱང་།།
མཐའ་བྲལ་དོན་དམ་བྱང་ཆུབ་སེམས་ཉིད་ཀྱི་གཤིས་ལས།།
ནམ་ཡང་འདའ་བ་མེད་པའི་ཐག་ཆོད་ལ་གནས་པར།།
སངས་རྒྱས་ངོ་བོ་རྡོ་རྗེའི་བླ་མ་ཁྱེད་མཁྱེན་ནོ།།
ཐོག་མེད་དུས་རིང་བརྟག་དཀའི་སྒྲིབ་གཉིས་ཀྱི་མུན་སྟུག།
འོད་གསལ་རིག་པ་ཡེ་ཤེས་མདངས་ལྡན་གྱི་ཉི་མས།།
ཉེས་ལྟུང་བག་ཆགས་དྲི་མ་རང་ངོ་རུ་སངས་ནས།།
དྲི་མེད་དུང་མདོག་མགོན་པོ་བདག་ལ་རང་འགྲུབ་པར།།
སངས་རྒྱས་ངོ་བོ་རྡོ་རྗེའི་བླ་མ་ཁྱེད་མཁྱེན་ནོ།།
གནས་ལུགས་རང་ངོ་ཤེས་པའི་ཚོགས་ཆེན་དེ་རྫོགས་ནས།།
ཁྱེད་ཆོས་དྲུག་ལྡན་ཀུན་བཟང་དགོངས་ཀློང་དུ་ཕྱམ་གདལ།།
འབད་རྩོལ་སྤྲོས་པ་ཀུན་བྲལ་ཨ་ཏི་ཡི་ཐེག་པས།།
ཆོས་སྐུའི་རྒྱལ་སྲིད་ཚེ་འདི་ཉིད་ལ་རང་ཟིན་པར།།
སངས་རྒྱས་ངོ་བོ་རྡོ་རྗེའི་བླ་མ་ཁྱེད་མཁྱེན་ནོ།།

Even if one has gone beyond attachment to the good compassionate attitude
that hopes to attract praise and approval,

Whereby one is bound by knots of self and other, samsara and nirvana,[12] hope
and fear,

Nevertheless, to be able to remain firmly in one's decision never to stray

From the natural state of absolute bodhicitta, which is free from elaboration,

I pray to you, the essence of the Buddha, the Vajra Guru, please think of me!

The thick darkness of the two obscurations, hard to investigate, exists from
beginningless time.

When the luminous sun of awareness, with its radiant primordial wisdom,

Purifies defiled habits that lead to transgressions and downfalls into their own
true nature,

May I be established as an undefiled lord protector, white in color like a
conch shell,

I pray to you, the essence of the Buddha, the Vajra Guru, please think of me!

Once the knowledge of the way things are is attained, the great accumulation is
perfected,

And one dwells in the all-encompassing expanse of Samantabhadra's realization,
with its six unique qualities.[13]

So that, by dwelling there, the kingdom of dharmakaya may be established
within this very life,

Through the Ati vehicle, free from all elaboration, effort, and endeavor,

I pray to you, the essence of the Buddha, the Vajra Guru, please think of me!

གསོལ་འདེབས་མོས་གུས་དྲག་པོའི་ཉེ་རྒྱུ་ལ་བརྟེན་ནས།།
རིག་སྟོང་དོན་གྱི་བླ་མ་སྙིང་དབུས་སུ་མཇལ་ཏེ།།
སེམས་ལ་རིག་པ་རྩལ་གྱི་དབང་ཆེན་དེ་ཐོབ་ཕྱིར།།
མཚོན་བྱ་དོན་གྱི་དགོངས་བརྒྱུད་ད་ལྟ་རང་འཕོ་བར།།
སངས་རྒྱས་ངོ་བོ་རྡོ་རྗེའི་བླ་མ་ཁྱེད་མཁྱེན་ནོ།།
བསགས་སྒྲིབ་རང་སར་དག་ཀྱང་བསོད་ནམས་ཚོགས་མི་གཙོག།
བདག་གཞན་གཉིས་སུ་མེད་ཀྱང་སེམས་བསྐྱེད་རྒྱུན་མི་བཅད།།
རང་སེམས་བླ་མར་ཤེས་ཀྱང་མོས་གུས་ལ་རྟག་འབུང་།།
ལྟ་སྒྲུ་ལོགས་ན་མེད་ཀྱང་རིམ་གཉིས་ལ་བརྩོན་པར།།
སངས་རྒྱས་ངོ་བོ་རྡོ་རྗེའི་བླ་མ་ཁྱེད་མཁྱེན་ནོ།།
མདོར་ན་དབེན་པའི་རི་ཁྲོད་བྲག་ཕུག་དང་སྦྱིལ་བུར།།
གཅིག་ཤེས་ཀུན་གྲོལ་མ་བསྒོམ་སངས་རྒྱས་ལམ་ཉིད་ལས།།
དགོས་མེད་བྱ་བཏང་རྒྱལ་པོའི་བརྟུལ་ཞུགས་དང་འགྲོགས་ཏེ།།
འཁོར་འདས་བར་ལག་འཁྱེལ་ནུས་དེ་ཁོན་འབྱུང་བར།།
སངས་རྒྱས་ངོ་བོ་རྡོ་རྗེའི་བླ་མ་ཁྱེད་མཁྱེན་ནོ།།

Due to the direct cause of strong devotional prayer,
One recognizes the absolute Guru of insight-emptiness in the center of one's heart.
So that the mind may attain the great empowerment of the energy of awareness,
And so that what is indicated, the absolute mind-transmission, may be conferred at this very moment,
I pray to you, the essence of the Buddha, the Vajra Guru, please think of me!

Though accumulation and purification are naturally complete, may accumulation of merit never be abandoned.
Though self and other are not two, may generation of compassionate mind never be curtailed.
Though one's mind is realized as Guru, may the practice of devotion and respect always be performed.
Though the deity's form is not separate from oneself, may I endeavor in the practice of the two stages.[14]
I pray to you, the essence of the Buddha, the Vajra Guru, please think of me!

In brief, in a solitary retreat cave or a simple hut,
By being on nothing other than the path of enlightenment,
By knowing non-meditation, the single thing that liberates all,
And being accompanied by an uninhibited, renounced, and carefree yogic style,
May I truly be able to make samsara and nirvana fall apart.
I pray to you, the essence of the Buddha, the Vajra Guru, please think of me!

རང་དོན་ཆོས་སྐུ་སྐྱེ་མེད་སྤྲོས་བྲལ་གྱི་དབྱིངས་ནས།།
འགག་མེད་གཟུགས་སྐུ་གཞན་དོན་ཕྲིན་ལས་དང་བཅས་པ།།
མངོན་གྱུར་སྲས་བཅས་རྒྱལ་བའི་ཞུལ་ལམ་དེ་སྙོགས་ནས།།
ཁམས་གསུམ་འཁོར་བ་དོང་སྤྲུགས་སྨོན་པ་བཞིན་འགྲུབ་པར།།
སངས་རྒྱས་ངོ་བོ་རྡོ་རྗེའི་བླ་མ་ཁྱེད་མཁྱེན་ནོ།།

ཞེས་པའང་སྙིང་པོའི་རྣལ་འབྱོར་ལ་མོས་པ་ཅན་ཉག་བླ་ཨ་འབའ་ནས་སྲིད་དུ་རིང་བའི་ལྷ་རྫས་རེག་བྱ་དང་ནེ་པཱ་ལའི་སྐོར་བརྒྱ་རྩའི་མཇལ་བཅས་དངོས་དང་ཡི་གེའི་ལམ་ནས་བསྐུལ་ངོ་མ་ལྡོག་པར་དུས་ཞབས་ཀྱི་བྱ་བྲལ་བ་སངས་རྒྱས་རྡོ་རྗེས་ཤིང་གླང་ཟླ་༡ ཚེས་༡༥ དགེ་བར་སྤྲས་ཡུལ་ཡོལ་མོ་གངས་རའི་ནགས་འདབས་སུ་སྦྱར་བ་དགེའོ།། །སརྦ་མངྒ་ལཾ།།

Having benefited oneself in the space of unborn, unelaborated dharmakaya,
Ceaseless forms of Buddha activity are actualized for the benefit of others.
By following in the footsteps of the Buddhas and Bodhisattvas,
May I be able to raise, as I aspire, the three realms of samsara from the depths.
I pray to you, the essence of the Buddha, the Vajra Guru, please think of me!

Entreated with offerings of a mandala[15] *of tangible divine substances, hundreds of Nepali rupees, and the actual written letters of Nyakla Ahbha, one whose interest is in the yoga of the essence, I, Chatralwa of the degenerate age, Sangye Dorje, unable to refuse his request, composed this in the wood ox year, in the virtuous eighth month, fifteenth day, in the hidden land of Yolmo's thick forests and snow mountains. May there be virtue. Sarva Mangalam.*

The Precious Treasury of Phenomenal Space

༄༅། །ཆོས་དབྱིངས་རིན་པོ་ཆེའི་མཛོད་ཅེས་བྱ་བ་བཞུགས།།
རྒྱ་གར་སྐད་དུ། དྷརྨ་དྷཱ་ཏུ་རཏྣ་ཀོ་ཥ་ནཱ་མ།
བོད་སྐད་དུ། ཆོས་དབྱིངས་རིན་པོ་ཆེའི་མཛོད་ཅེས་བྱ་བ།

དཔལ་ཀུན་ཏུ་བཟང་པོ་ལ་ཕྱག་འཚལ་ལོ།།

།གདོད་ནས་ལྷུན་གྲུབ་ངོ་མཚར་རྨད་ཀྱི་ཆོས།
།རང་བྱུང་ཡེ་ཤེས་འོད་གསལ་བྱང་ཆུབ་སེམས།
།སྣང་སྲིད་སྣོད་བཅུད་འཁོར་འདས་འབྱུང་བའི་མཛོད།
།མི་གཡོ་སྤྲོས་དང་བྲལ་ལ་ཕྱག་འཚལ་ལོ།
།ཐེག་པའི་ཡང་རྩེ་རི་རྒྱལ་ཉི་ཟླའི་ཀློང་།
།འོད་གསལ་ལྷུན་གྲུབ་རྡོ་རྗེ་སྙིང་པོའི་ཀློང་།
།རྩོལ་ཞིང་སྒྲུབ་མེད་རང་བཞིན་བབས་ཀྱི་ཀློང་།
།ཡེ་འབྲུམས་རྨད་དུ་བྱུང་བ་བཤད་ཀྱིས་ཉོན།
།ལྷུན་གྲུབ་ཀློང་ལས་ཐམས་ཅད་འབྱུང་བའི་གཞི།
།ངོ་བོ་སྟོང་ལ་རང་བཞིན་མ་འགགས་པས།
།ཅིར་ཡང་མ་གྲུབ་ཅིར་ཡང་འཆར་བ་སྟེ།
།སྐུ་གསུམ་ཀློང་ནས་འཁོར་འདས་རང་ཤར་ཀྱང་།
།དབྱིངས་ལས་མ་གཡོས་ཆོས་ཉིད་བདེ་བའི་ཞིང་།
།སེམས་ཉིད་ཀློང་ཆེན་འགྱུར་མེད་ནམ་མཁའི་དང་།

The Precious Treasury of Phenomenal Space

Longchen Rabjam

1

From *The Precious Treasury of Phenomenal Space*, explaining that samsara and nirvana are not moved from space, the first chapter.

Homage to glorious All-Good![16]

Spontaneously accomplished from the beginning, amazing sublime essence;

Self-originated primordial wisdom, luminously clear compassionate mind;

The treasury that is the source of appearance and existence, the universe and its inhabitants, samsara and nirvana.

Homage to the unwavering state that is free from elaboration.

The highest peak of the vehicles[17] is like the King of Mountains,[18] abiding within the expanse of the sun and moon,[19]

Luminously clear, spontaneously accomplished, the expanse of indestructible essence.

Without searching or striving is the simply natural expanse,

Primordially pervasive and sublime – listen, I will elucidate.

The spontaneously accomplished expanse is the basis for the origination of everything.

Its essence is empty, and its nature is unobstructed,

So that nothing exists, but everything is manifest.

From the expanse of the three kayas,[20] samsara and nirvana are self-arising,

But not moved from space, the nature of phenomena, the field of bliss.

In the sky-like continuum, the unchanging great expanse of mind itself,

།རོལ་པ་ངེས་མེད་ཐུགས་རྗེ་ཆོ་འཕྲུལ་ཀློང་།
།ཐམས་ཅད་དབྱིངས་ཀྱི་རྒྱན་ལས་ལོགས་ན་མེད།
།ཕྱི་ནང་འདུ་འཕྲོ་བྱང་ཆུབ་སེམས་ཀྱི་རྩལ།
།ཅིར་ཡང་མ་ཡིན་ཅིར་ཡང་སྣང་བའི་ཕྱིར།
།ངོ་མཚར་ཆོ་འཕྲུལ་ཡ་མཚན་རྨད་ཀྱི་ཆོས།
།ཕྱི་ནང་སྐྱེ་འགྲོ་གཟུགས་སུ་སྣང་བ་ཀུན།
།དབྱིངས་ཀྱི་རྒྱན་ཏེ་སྐུ་ཡི་འཁོར་ལོར་ཤར།
།མ་ལུས་གྲགས་པའི་སྒྲ་སྐད་ཇི་སྙེད་ཀུན།
།དབྱིངས་ཀྱི་རྒྱན་ཏེ་གསུང་གི་འཁོར་ལོར་ཤར།
།དྲན་རིག་འགྱུ་འཕྲོ་མི་རྟོག་བསམ་ཡས་ཀྱང་།
།དབྱིངས་ཀྱི་རྒྱན་ཏེ་ཐུགས་ཀྱི་འཁོར་ལོར་ཤར།
།འགྲོ་བ་རིགས་དྲུག་སྐྱེ་གནས་བཞི་པོ་ཡང་།
།ཆོས་དབྱིངས་ངང་ལས་གཡོས་པ་རྡུལ་ཙམ་མེད།
།སྣང་སྲིད་ཡུལ་དྲུག་གཟུང་འཛིན་སྣང་བ་ཡང་།
།ཆོས་དབྱིངས་ངང་ན་མེད་སྣང་སྒྱུ་མའི་ཚུལ།
།རྟེན་མེད་སང་སེང་ཡེ་སྟོང་ཡངས་པ་ཆེ།
།རང་གསལ་ཇི་བཞིན་ཆོས་དབྱིངས་རྒྱན་དུ་ཤར།
།ཇི་ལྟར་སྣང་གྲགས་དབྱིངས་ཀྱི་ངང་ཆེན་འདིར།
།ལྷུན་མཉམ་མི་གཡོ་ཆོས་སྐུ་བྱང་ཆུབ་སེམས།

Indeterminate play, the miraculous expanse of compassion,
Is nothing other than adornment of space.
The external and internal, all that dissolves and emanates,[21] are the energy of compassionate mind.
They are nothing at all, but appear as various things;
Therefore, they are amazing, marvelous, wonderful, excellent phenomena.
Externally and internally, all sentient beings appearing in form,
Are ornaments of space arising as the circle[22] of enlightened body.
Without exception, whatever sounds of speech there may be
Are ornaments of space arising as the circle of enlightened speech.
Mental movements and emanations, mindfulness and awareness beyond conceptualization
Are also ornaments of space arising as the circle of enlightened mind.
Beings of the six realms[23] and four types of birth[24]
Are also not separated by even an atom's distance from the continuum of phenomenal space.
Appearance and existence, whatever appears as grasper and grasped[25] in the six realms,
Are also not existent in the continuum of phenomenal space,[26] yet appear in the manner of an illusion.
Unsupported immaculate clarity, primordially void great vastness,
Arises as it is, as the naturally clear ornament of phenomenal space.
Whatever is seen or heard in this great continuum of space
Is spontaneously even, not moving from dharmakaya, compassionate mind.

།ཡེ་བབས་རང་སྟོང་འཕོ་དང་འགྱུར་མེད་པས།
།ཅིར་སྣང་ཆོས་ཉིད་རང་བྱུང་ཡེ་ཤེས་དང་།
།བྱ་དང་རྩོལ་མེད་བདེ་ཀློང་གཅིག་ཏུ་འཁྱིལ།
།རང་གསལ་མི་གཡོ་ཡོངས་སྤྱོད་རྫོགས་པ་ནི།
།གང་སྣང་ཉིད་ནས་རང་བཞིན་ལྷུན་གྱིས་གྲུབ།
།བཅོས་ཤིང་བསྒྱུར་མེད་ལྷུན་མཉམ་གདལ་བའོ།
།སྣ་ཚོགས་མ་འདྲེས་རོལ་པའི་འཆར་ཚུལ་ལས།
།སྤྲུལ་པ་རང་བྱུང་ཡ་མཚན་འཕྲུལ་གྱི་དོན།
།བྱ་བྲལ་ཀུན་ཏུ་བཟང་ལས་གཡོས་པ་མེད།
།གཡང་ས་མེད་པའི་བྱང་ཆུབ་སེམས་ཉིད་ལ།
།རྩོལ་བ་མེད་པའི་སྐུ་གསུམ་ལྷུན་རྫོགས་ཀྱང་།
།དབྱིངས་ལས་མ་གཡོས་ལྷུན་གྲུབ་འདུས་མ་བྱས།
།སྐུ་དང་ཡེ་ཤེས་ཕྲིན་ལས་ལྷུན་རྫོགས་ཀྱང་།
།ཚོགས་ཆེན་ཡེ་རྫོགས་ཡེ་ཤར་ཆེན་པོའི་ཀློང་།
།ཡེ་ནས་ལྷུན་གྲུབ་འཕོ་འགྱུར་མེད་པའི་ཞིང་།
།ཆོས་དབྱིངས་དང་ལས་ཆོས་ཉིད་གཟིགས་པ་ཡང་།
།མཁྱེན་པ་མ་འགགས་དབྱིངས་ཀྱི་རྒྱན་དུ་ཤར།
།བྱས་ཤིང་སྒྲིབ་མེད་ཡེ་ནས་གནས་པ་ཉིད།
།ཉི་མ་མཁའ་བཞིན་ཧེ་ངོ་མཚར་རྨད་ཀྱི་ཆོས།
།ཡེ་ནས་ལྷུན་གྱིས་གྲུབ་པའི་དབྱིངས་རུམ་འདིར།
།འཁོར་བ་ཀུན་བཟང་མྱ་ངན་འདས་པ་བཟང་།
།ཀུན་བཟང་ཀློང་ན་འཁོར་འདས་ཡེ་ནས་མེད།

Since primordial simplicity, empty of self, is without transformation or change,

Whatever arises is the nature of phenomena, and is self-originated in the continuum of primordial wisdom,

Without effort or endeavor, pooling in the single, blissful expanse.

Self-luminous, unchanging perfection of qualities[27]

Is spontaneously accomplished from the moment that it naturally appears.

Therefore, unalterable by fabrication, it is encompassed in equanimity and spontaneity.

The display[28] appears in a way that is various yet distinct.

Such naturally arising emanation, the truth of miraculous illusions,

Is not removed from All-Good, so there is nothing to do.

As to compassionate mind itself that has no precipice,[29]

Without striving, all three kayas are spontaneously perfected.

However, it is unmoved from space, spontaneously accomplished and uncompounded.

The kayas, wisdoms, and virtuous activities are spontaneously perfected;

Moreover, within the great expanse of primordial dawn, the supreme accumulations[30] are completed from the beginning,

Spontaneously perfected from the beginning, in the field of the unchanging and free from transformation.

Realizing the nature of phenomena in the continuum of phenomenal space

Is also unobstructed knowledge arising as the ornament of space.

Nothing can be accomplished by deeds. This primordially exists by itself.

Like the sun in the sky, it is amazing, wonderful reality,

Spontaneously accomplished from the beginning in the womb of space.

Samsara is All-Good, nirvana is All-Good.

In the expanse of All-Good, there is no samsara and no nirvana from the beginning.

།སྣང་བ་ཀུན་བཟང་སྟོང་པ་ཀུན་ཏུ་བཟང་།
།ཀུན་བཟང་གློང་ན་སྣང་སྟོང་ཡེ་ནས་མེད།
།སྐྱེ་ཤི་ཀུན་བཟང་བདེ་སྡུག་ཀུན་ཏུ་བཟང་།
།ཀུན་བཟང་གློང་ན་བདེ་སྡུག་སྐྱེ་ཤི་མེད།
།བདག་གཞན་ཀུན་བཟང་རྟག་ཆད་ཀུན་ཏུ་བཟང་།
།ཀུན་བཟང་གློང་ན་བདག་གཞན་རྟག་ཆད་མེད།
།མེད་ལ་ཡོད་པར་འཛིན་པས་འཁྲུལ་པར་བཏགས།
།རྟེན་མེད་རྨི་ལམ་འདྲ་བའི་རང་བཞིན་ལ།
།འཁོར་འདས་རང་མཚན་ཞེན་པ་མཚར་རེ་ཆེ།
།ཐམས་ཅད་ཀུན་བཟང་ལྷུན་གྲུབ་ཆེན་པོ་ནི།
།མ་འཁྲུལ་མི་འཁྲུལ་འཁྲུལ་པར་མི་འགྱུར་བས།
།སྲིད་པ་མིང་ཙམ་ཡོད་མེད་མཐའ་ལས་འདས།
།སུ་ཡང་གང་དུ་སྣང་ཡང་མ་འཁྲུལ་ལ།
།ད་ལྟ་མི་འཁྲུལ་སླད་ཀྱིས་འཁྲུལ་མི་འགྱུར།
།འདི་ནི་སྲིད་གསུམ་ཀ་དག་དགོངས་པའོ།
།འཁྲུལ་བ་མེད་པས་མ་འཁྲུལ་ཆོས་སུ་མེད།
།ཡེ་ནས་ལྷུན་གྲུབ་རང་བྱུང་རིག་པ་ཆེ།
།མ་གྲོལ་མི་གྲོལ་གྲོལ་བར་མི་འགྱུར་ལ།
།འདས་པ་མིང་ཙམ་སུ་ཡང་གྲོལ་མ་མྱོང་།
།གྲོལ་བར་མི་འགྱུར་བཅིངས་པ་ཡེ་ནས་མེད།
།མཁའ་བཞིན་རྣམ་དག་རྒྱ་ཆད་ཕྱོགས་ལྷུང་བྲལ།
།འདི་ནི་ཡོངས་གྲོལ་ཀ་དག་དགོངས་པའོ།

Appearance is All-Good, emptiness is All-Good.

Appearance and emptiness are non-existent from the beginning in the expanse of All-Good.

Birth and death are All-Good, happiness and unhappiness are All-Good.

In the expanse of All-Good there is no happiness and no suffering, no birth and no death.

Self and others are All-Good, eternalism and nihilism are All-Good.

In the expanse of All-Good, there is no self and no others, no permanence and no nothingness.[31]

Grasping existence where there is none is called confusion.

Because they lack true existence, like a dream,

Attachment to samsara and nirvana as independent reality is very surprising!

Everything is All-Good, the great, spontaneous accomplishment.

It was not deluded, is not deluded, nor will it be deluded.

Thus existence is just a name for what is beyond the limitations of existence and non-existence.

No one anywhere in the past has been deluded;

Presently no one is deluded, nor will there be any delusion in the future.

This is the principle of the primordially pure three existences.[32]

There is no delusion; therefore, there are no undeluded phenomena.

From the beginning, great awareness is self-originated and spontaneously perfected.

It was not liberated, is not liberated, nor will it be liberated.

Nirvana is just a name; no one has ever experienced liberation.

Nor will there be liberation, because there has been no bondage from the beginning.

Like the sky, totally pure, free from partiality and bias,

This is the principle of completely liberated, primordial purity.

།མདོར་ན་ལྷུན་གྲུབ་ཡངས་པའི་དབྱིངས་རུམ་ནས།
།རོལ་པའི་རྩལ་གྱི་འཁོར་འདས་ཅི་ཤར་ཡང་།
།ཤར་ཙམ་ཉིད་ནས་འཁོར་འདས་ཡོད་མ་གྲྭོང་།
།གཉིད་ཀྱི་རྩལ་ལས་རྨི་ལམ་ཅི་ཤར་ཡང་།
།དོན་ལ་མེད་དེ་རང་རིག་བདེ་བའི་མལ།
།ལྷུན་མཉམ་ཡངས་པ་ཆེན་པོར་ཁྱུམ་གདལ་ལོ།

།ཆོས་དབྱིངས་རིན་པོ་ཆེའི་མཛོད་ལས། འཁོར་འདས་དབྱིངས་ལས་མ་གཡོས་པར་བསྟན་པའི་ལེའུ་སྟེ་དང་པོའོ།།

In brief, from the spontaneously accomplished, vast womb of space,
Whatever display of energy arises as samsara or nirvana,
Even as it arises, there are never any such things as samsara or nirvana.
From the potency of sleep, whatever dream arises has no reality.
Furthermore, the resting place of blissful self-awareness
Is spontaneously even, completely encompassing in the great vastness.

From *The Precious Treasury of Phenomenal Space*, explaining that samsara and nirvana are not moved from space, the first chapter, is completed.

།དབྱིངས་ཀྱི་རང་བཞིན་གདོད་ནས་ལྷུན་གྲུབ་ལ།
།ཕྱི་དང་ནང་མེད་ཀུན་ཏུ་ཁྱབ་པར་གདལ།
།མཐའ་ཡི་མུ་མེད་སྟེང་འོག་ཕྱོགས་མཚམས་འདས།
།ཡངས་དོག་གཉིས་མེད་རིག་པ་མཁའ་ལྟར་དག
།དམིགས་བསམ་སྤྲོ་བསྡུ་བྲལ་བའི་ཀློང་ཉིད་དུ།
།སྐྱེ་མེད་དབྱིངས་ལས་སྐྱེ་བའི་ཆོ་འཕྲུལ་རྣམས།
།ཅིར་ཡང་མ་ངེས་གར་ཡང་རྒྱ་ཆད་མེད།
།འདི་ཞེས་མི་མཚོན་དངོས་པོ་མཚན་མ་མེད།
།ཕྱོགས་འབྱམས་ནམ་མཁའ་འདྲ་བའི་རང་བཞིན་ལ།
།སྐྱེ་མེད་ལྷུན་གྲུབ་སྔ་ཕྱི་ཐོག་མཐའ་བྲལ།
།འཁོར་འདས་ཀུན་གྱི་ངོ་བོ་བྱང་ཆུབ་སེམས།
།མ་བྱུང་མ་སྐྱེས་མ་ངེས་ལྷུན་གྲུབ་ནི།
།གང་ནས་མ་འོངས་གར་ཡང་སོང་བ་མེད།
།སྔ་ཕྱི་རིས་མེད་བྱང་ཆུབ་སེམས་ཀྱི་ཀློང་།
།འགྲོ་དང་འོང་མེད་ཀུན་ཏུ་ཁྱབ་པར་གདལ།
།ཐོག་མཐའ་དབུས་མེད་ཆོས་ཉིད་དེ་བཞིན་ཉིད།
།ཁྱམ་གདལ་མཁའ་མཉམ་དག་པའི་རང་བཞིན་ལ།
།ཐོག་མཐའ་མེད་དེ་སྔ་ཕྱིའི་ཡུལ་ལས་འདས།
།སྐྱེ་འགག་མེད་དེ་དངོས་པོ་མཚན་མ་མེད།
།འགྲོ་འོང་མེད་དེ་འདི་ཞེས་མཚོན་དང་བྲལ།

2

From *The Precious Treasury of Phenomenal Space*, showing that appearance and existence arise as a pure land,[33] the second chapter.

The nature of space is spontaneously accomplished from the beginning.
Without inside or outside, all-pervading and all-encompassing,
Without limited boundaries, beyond divisions of above, below, and every direction,
Without duality of wide and narrow, awareness is as clear as the sky.
The expanse itself, free from imagination and concept, is without diffusion or absorption.
All miracles are born from unborn space.
They are nothing certain and have no restrictions at all.
They cannot be characterized as this or that, since there is nothing substantial to characterize.
Their self-nature is expansive in all directions, like the sky,
Unborn, spontaneously perfected, free from beginning and end, past and future.
The nature of all samsara and nirvana is compassionate mind.[34]
The unoriginated, unborn, uncertain, and spontaneously accomplished
Has not come from anywhere and has never gone anywhere.
There is no division of past and future in the expanse of compassionate mind.
Not coming, not going, all-pervading and all-encompassing;
Without beginning, middle, or end, the nature of phenomena is suchness.[35]
The equally pervading, equal to the sky, pure in self-nature,
Has neither beginning nor end and is beyond the objects of past and future.
Unborn, unceasing, without substantial characteristics,
Beyond coming or going, it cannot be characterized as "this."

།རྩོལ་ཞིང་སྒྲུབ་མེད་བྱ་བའི་ཆོས་ཀྱིས་སྟོང་།
།ཕྱོགས་ཆ་དབུས་མེད་དེ་བཞིན་ཉིད་ཀྱི་གཞི།
།དམིགས་མེད་རྒྱུན་ཆད་མེད་དེ་མཉམ་པའི་ཀློང་།
།ཐམས་ཅད་ཆོས་ཉིད་མཉམ་པའི་རང་བཞིན་ལས།
།མཉམ་པའི་ཀློང་ན་མི་གནས་གཅིག་ཀྱང་མེད།
།གཅིག་མཉམ་ཀུན་མཉམ་བྱང་ཆུབ་སེམས་ཀྱི་ངང་།
།མ་སྐྱེས་མཁའ་མཉམ་ཡངས་པར་ཕྱམ་གདལ་བས།
།མཉམ་ཉིད་ངང་ལ་རྒྱུན་ཆད་མེད་པའི་ཕྱིར།
།ལྷུན་གྲུབ་ཕྱོགས་མེད་ཀུན་ཁྱབ་གདལ་བའི་རྫོང་།
།སྟེང་འོག་བར་མེད་ཡེ་ཀློང་ཡངས་པའི་རྫོང་།
།ཕྱོགས་མེད་ཀུན་ཤོང་སྐྱེ་མེད་ཆོས་སྐུའི་རྫོང་།
།མི་འགྱུར་ལྷུན་གྲུབ་རིན་ཆེན་གསང་བའི་རྫོང་།
།སྣང་སྲིད་འཁོར་འདས་ཡེ་རྫོང་ཕྱམ་གཅིག་རྫོགས།
།ཕྱོགས་མེད་ཀུན་ཁྱབ་གདལ་བའི་ས་གཞི་ལ།
།འཁོར་འདས་རིས་མེད་བྱང་ཆུབ་སེམས་ཀྱི་མཁར།
།ཆོས་ཉིད་ཀློང་ཡངས་རྩེ་མོ་ལྷུན་མཐོ་ཞིང་།
།མ་བྱས་རང་བཞིན་ཕྱོགས་བཞི་ཡངས་པའི་དཀྱིལ།
།རིམ་རྩོལ་བྲལ་བའི་འཇུག་སྒོ་ཤིན་ཏུ་ཡངས།
།ལྷུན་གྲུབ་འབྱོར་པའི་བཀོད་པས་བརྒྱན་པ་དེར།
།རང་བྱུང་ཡེ་ཤེས་རྒྱལ་པོ་གདན་ལ་བཞུགས།
།འདུ་འཕྲོར་སྣང་བ་ཡེ་ཤེས་རྩལ་རྣམས་ཀུན།
།བློན་པོར་གྱུར་པས་ཡུལ་ལ་དབང་བསྒྱུར་ཞིང་།

It cannot be attained by effort. There is no such thing as action.
Partless, directionless, centerless is the ground of suchness,
Unimaginable, uninterrupted, a uniform expanse.
In the nature of phenomena, everything is of the nature of equanimity.
There is not even one unsettling thing in the expanse of equanimity.
Equanimity, one and all, in the continuum of compassionate mind.
Since all-pervading vastness, equal to the sky, is unborn,
It is free from discontinuity in the continuum of equanimity itself.
It is therefore a spontaneously accomplished, directionless, all-pervading fortress.[36]
Without top, bottom, or middle, the primordial fortress of the expanse of space
Is the directionless, all-containing, unborn fortress of dharmakaya.
Unchanging, spontaneously accomplished, precious secret fortress,
Appearance and existence of samsara and nirvana are perfected all at once in the primordial fortress.
On the basis of the directionless, completely all-pervading ground,
Whether there is samsara or nirvana is of no concern in the space of compassionate mind.
There, the nature of phenomena is the peak, the highest vast expanse, spontaneously accomplished,
Naturally uncreated, the mandala of the four vast directions.
The entranceway of the non-gradual and effortless is wide open.
Spontaneously accomplished, ornamented by an array of wealth,
There, self-originated primordial wisdom is seated as the victorious king.
Dissolved and emanated appearances, all the energies of primordial wisdom,
Are like the ministers who rule the land.

།རང་གནས་བསམ་གཏན་བཙུན་མོ་དམ་པ་དང་།

།དགོངས་པ་རང་ཤར་སྲས་དང་བྲན་གཡོག་བཅས།

།བདེ་ཆེན་ཀློང་དཀྱིལ་རང་གསལ་རྟོག་པ་མེད།

།མི་གཡོ་བསམ་བརྗོད་བྲལ་བའི་ངང་ཉིད་ལས།

།སྣང་སྲིད་སྣོད་བཅུད་ཀུན་ལ་མངའ་དབང་བསྒྱུར།

།ཆོས་དབྱིངས་ཡངས་པའི་ཡུལ་ཁམས་རྒྱ་ཆེའོ།

།ཡུལ་དེར་གནས་ན་ཐམས་ཅད་ཆོས་ཀྱི་སྐུ།

།རང་བྱུང་ཡེ་ཤེས་གཅིག་ལས་མ་གཡོས་པར།

།མ་བྱས་ཡེ་ཟིན་རྩོལ་སྒྲུབ་འདས་པ་ཉིད།

།གྲྭ་ཟུར་མེད་པའི་ཐིག་ལེ་ཟླུམ་པས་ན།

།ཇི་བཞིན་དབྱེ་བསལ་མེད་པའི་ཀློང་དུ་འཁྱིལ།

།འགྲོ་དྲུག་གནས་དང་སངས་རྒྱས་ཞིང་ཁམས་ཀུན།

།གཞན་ན་མེད་དེ་ཆོས་ཉིད་ནམ་མཁའི་ངང་།

།རང་གསལ་བྱང་ཆུབ་སེམས་སུ་རོ་གཅིག་པས།

།རིག་པའི་ངང་དུ་འཁོར་འདས་འུབ་ཆུབ་བོ།

།ཐམས་ཅད་ཀུན་འབྱུང་ཆོས་དབྱིངས་མཛོད་འདི་ནི།

།འདས་པ་མ་བཙལ་ཡེ་ནས་ལྷུན་གྲུབ་པས།

།ཆོས་སྐུ་མི་འགྱུར་ཡུལ་མེད་ཀུན་འབྱམས་ལ།

།ཕྱི་ནང་སྣོད་བཅུད་སྣང་བ་ལོངས་སྤྱོད་རྫོགས།

།གཟུགས་བརྙན་ལྟ་བུར་རང་ཤར་སྤྲུལ་པའི་སྐུ།

།སྐུ་གསུམ་རྒྱན་དུ་མ་རྫོགས་ཆོས་མེད་པས།

།ཐམས་ཅད་སྐུ་གསུང་ཐུགས་ཀྱི་རོལ་པར་ཤར།

Naturally existing concentration is the sacred queen,

And self-arising vision is all the princes and servants.

They all merge together in the expanse of the great, blissful mandala, natural luminosity beyond thought.

In the natural continuum, unmoving, beyond conception or expression,

Ruling over all appearance and existence, the universe and its inhabitants,

The field of phenomenal space is completely vast and wide.

If it remains in that place, all is dharmakaya,

Not moving from the self-originated primordial wisdom.

This is effortlessly accomplished from the beginning without trying.

Since, without corners or edges, the essence[37] is circular,

It is spiraling in the expanse of non-separation and non-distinction.

Neither the places of the six realms nor the pure lands of Buddha

Exist separately from that continuum of the sky-like nature of phenomena.

Because they are of one taste in self-luminous compassionate mind,

In the continuum of awareness, samsara and nirvana are perfectly included.

As for this treasury of phenomenal space, source of everything,

Nirvana does not need to be sought; it is primordially, spontaneously perfected.

Therefore, the appearances of external and internal, the universe and its inhabitants, are the perfection of enjoyments.[38]

Like a reflection is the self-arisen nirmanakaya.

Since there are no phenomena in which the three kayas are not perfected as ornaments,

Everything arises as a display of enlightened body, speech, and mind.

།བདེ་གཤེགས་ཞིང་ཁམས་མ་ལུས་གྲངས་མེད་ཀྱང་།
།ཉིད་ལས་བྱུང་བའི་སེམས་ཉིད་སྐུ་གསུམ་ཀློང་།
།འཁོར་བའི་རང་བཞིན་འགྲོ་དྲུག་གྲོང་ཁྱེར་ཀྱང་།
།ཆོས་དབྱིངས་དང་ལས་གཟུགས་བརྙན་ཤར་བ་ཙམ།
།སྐྱེ་ཤི་བདེ་སྡུག་སྣ་ཚོགས་སྣང་བ་ཡང་།
།སེམས་ཉིད་ཀློང་འདིར་སྤྲུལ་པའི་ལྟད་མོ་བཞིན།
།མེད་ལ་ཡོད་ལ་སྣང་ལ་གཞི་མེད་པས།
།མཁའ་ལ་སྤྲིན་བཞིན་གློ་བུར་རྐྱེན་བྱུང་ཙམ།
།ཡོད་མིན་མེད་མིན་རང་བཞིན་མཐའ་འདས་པས།
།སྤྲོས་བྲལ་ཐིག་ལེའི་ངང་དུ་འུབ་ཆུབ་པོ།
།སེམས་ཉིད་བྱང་ཆུབ་སེམས་ཀྱི་རང་བཞིན་ནི།
།མཁའ་ལྟར་དག་པས་སྐྱེ་ཤི་བདེ་སྡུག་མེད།
།དངོས་པོ་རིས་མེད་འཁོར་འདས་ཆོས་ལས་གྲོལ།
།འདི་ཞེས་མི་མཚོན་མཁའ་ཀློང་རབ་ཡངས་པས།
།མི་འགྱུར་མི་འཕོ་ལྷུན་གྲུབ་འདུས་མ་བྱས།
།འོད་གསལ་རྡོ་རྗེ་སྙིང་པོར་སངས་རྒྱས་པས།
།ཐམས་ཅད་ཀུན་ཀྱང་རང་བྱུང་བདེ་བའི་ཞིང་།
།ལྷུན་མཉམ་བྱང་ཆུབ་མཆོག་གི་ངང་ཉིད་དོ།

།ཆོས་དབྱིངས་རིན་པོ་ཆེའི་མཛོད་ལས། །སྣང་སྲིད་ཞིང་ཁམས་སུ་ཤར་བའི་ལེའུ་སྟེ་གཉིས་པའོ།།

The countless pure lands of the sugatas, without exception,
Are also mind itself, naturally originated, in the expanse of the three kayas.
The self-nature of samsara, the six-realmed city,
Also just arises as a reflection from the continuum of phenomenal space.
Various appearances of birth and death, happiness and unhappiness,
Are also like magic shows in the expanse of mind itself.
Existence and non-existence, all appearances, have no basis;
Just like clouds in the sky, they arise incidentally from conditions.
The nature, neither existing nor non-existing, is beyond extremes,
Perfected all at once in the continuum of the unelaborated essence.
Mind itself, the nature of compassionate mind,
Is pure like the sky, so there is no birth or death, no happiness or suffering.
Things are impartial, liberated from the phenomena of samsara and nirvana.
They cannot be characterized as "this." The expanse of the sky is vast;
So freedom from transformation, unchanging, is spontaneously accomplished and uncompounded,
Completely awakened in the clearly luminous indestructible essence.
Therefore, all and everything, the self-originated fields of bliss,
Are of the nature of the continuum of spontaneously even, supremely compassionate mind itself.

From *The Precious Treasury of Phenomenal Space,* showing that appearance and existence arise as a pure land, the second chapter, is completed.

།ཐམས་ཅད་ཀུན་འདུས་བྱང་ཆུབ་སེམས་སུ་འདུས།
།བྱང་ཆུབ་སེམས་ལས་མ་གཏོགས་ཆོས་མེད་པས།
།ཆོས་ཀུན་བྱང་ཆུབ་སེམས་ཀྱི་རང་བཞིན་ནོ།
།བྱང་ཆུབ་སེམས་ཀྱི་མཚོན་དཔེ་ནམ་མཁའ་འདྲ།
།སེམས་ལ་རྒྱུ་མེད་སྐྱེ་བའི་ཡུལ་མེད་པས།
།མི་གནས་བརྗོད་འདས་བསམ་ཡུལ་འདས་པ་ཉིད།
།ནམ་མཁའི་དབྱིངས་ཞེས་དཔེ་རུ་མཚོན་པ་ཙམ།
།མཚོན་དཔེ་ཉིད་ཀྱང་འདི་ཞེས་བྱར་མེད་ན།
།མཚོན་དཔེའི་དོན་ལ་བསམ་བརྗོད་ག་ལ་སྲིད།
།འདི་ནི་རང་བཞིན་དག་པའི་དཔེར་ཞེས་བྱ།
།དོན་ནི་རང་རིག་མཁའ་མཉམ་བྱང་ཆུབ་སེམས།
།བསམ་པའི་ཡུལ་མིན་མཚོན་བརྗོད་འདས་པ་སྟེ།
།རང་གསལ་མི་གཡོ་འོད་གསལ་ཡངས་པའི་ཀློང་།
།མ་བྱས་ལྷུན་གྲུབ་ཡངས་དོག་མཐོ་དམན་མེད།
།ཆོས་སྐུ་བྱང་ཆུབ་སྙིང་པོའི་དཀྱིལ་ཡངས་སོ།
།རྟགས་ནི་རྩལ་ལས་ཅིར་ཡང་འཆར་བ་སྟེ།
།ཤར་བའི་དུས་ན་ཤར་ས་ཤར་མཁན་མེད།
།ཤར་ཞེས་མིང་ཙམ་དཔྱད་ན་ནམ་མཁའ་འདྲ།
།རིས་མེད་མཉམ་པ་ཆེན་པོར་འུབ་ཆུབ་པས།
།ཕྱམ་གདལ་གཟུང་འཛིན་མེད་པའི་ཀློང་ཉིད་དོ།

3

From *The Precious Treasury of Phenomenal Space*, showing examples that indicate compassionate mind, the third chapter.

All and everything together is contained in compassionate mind.
Outside of compassionate mind there are no phenomena;
So all phenomena have the nature of compassionate mind.
The simile of compassionate mind is "like the sky."
Mind has no cause and no birthplace,
So it is non-existent, beyond expression, beyond objects of thought themselves.
"The space of the sky" is just a symbolic example.
If even the symbolic example is inexpressible as "this,"
How can the true meaning of the example be imagined or expressed?
One ought to know that this is the example of pure self-nature.
The meaning is self-awareness equal to the sky, compassionate mind.
Not an object of thought, it is beyond symbolic expression,
Self-luminous, unmoving, clear light, vast expanse —
Uncreated, spontaneously perfected, neither wide nor narrow, neither high nor low.
Dharmakaya, the essence of enlightenment, is vast space.
Moreover, everything arises from the potency[39] as signs.
Yet, when there is arising, there is no place to arise and nothing that arises.
So-called "arising" is just a name. If analyzed, it is like the sky,
Without partiality, completely contained in great equanimity.
So equally pervading, without grasper or grasped, is the expanse itself.

།རང་བྱུང་ཡེ་ཤེས་ཆོས་ཉིད་ཕྱོགས་ཡན་ལ།
།དཔེ་དོན་རྟགས་ཀྱི་ངེས་པའི་མཚོན་དཔེ་བསྟན།
།མཁའ་མཉམ་གཞིར་ཆེན་གསུམ་གྱི་བདག་ཉིད་དུ།
།ཐམས་ཅད་ཀུན་འདུས་རང་བཞིན་དབྱེ་བསལ་མེད།
།ཕྱམ་མཉམ་ཡངས་པ་ཆེན་པོའི་དབྱིངས་རུམ་ན།
།ཐམས་ཅད་ཡེ་མཉམ་སྔ་ཕྱི་བར་གསུམ་མེད།
།ཀུན་བཟང་རྡོ་རྗེ་སེམས་དཔའི་དགོངས་པའོ།
།བྱང་ཆུབ་སེམས་ནི་ཉི་མའི་སྙིང་པོ་འདྲ།
།ངང་གིས་འོད་གསལ་ཡེ་ནས་འདུས་མ་བྱས།
།སྒྲིབ་པའི་ཆོས་མེད་ཟང་ཐལ་ལྷུན་གྱིས་གྲུབ།
།སྤྲོས་པའི་ཚོགས་མེད་མི་རྟོག་ཆོས་ཉིད་ངང་།
།སྟོང་པས་ཆོས་སྐུ་གསལ་བས་ལོངས་སྤྱོད་རྫོགས།
།ཟེར་ལྡན་སྤྲུལ་པ་སྐུ་གསུམ་འདུ་འབྲལ་མེད།
།ཡེ་ནས་ཡོན་ཏན་ལྷུན་གྱིས་གྲུབ་ཟིན་པས།
།སྐྱོན་དང་ཉེས་ཚའི་མུན་པས་བསྒྲིབས་པ་མེད།
།སྔ་ཕྱི་དུས་གསུམ་འཕོ་འགྱུར་མེད་པར་གཅིག
།སངས་རྒྱས་སེམས་ཅན་ཀུན་ལ་ཁྱབ་པར་གཅིག
།འདི་ནི་རང་བྱུང་བྱང་ཆུབ་སེམས་ཞེས་བྱ།
།དེ་ཡི་རྩལ་ནི་ཅིར་ཡང་འཆར་བ་སྟེ།
།རྟོག་དང་མི་རྟོག་སྣང་སྲིད་སྣོད་བཅུད་དང་།
།སྐྱེ་འགྲོའི་སྣང་བ་སྣ་ཚོགས་ཇི་སྙེད་དོ།
།འདི་ཀུན་ཤར་ཡང་རང་བཞིན་འགག་མེད་དེ།
།སྨིག་རྒྱུའི་ཆུ་དང་རྨི་ལམ་སྒྲ་བརྙན་བཞིན།
།སྤྲུལ་པ་གཟུགས་བརྙན་དྲི་ཟའི་གྲོང་ཁྱེར་དང་།
།མིག་ཡོར་ཇི་བཞིན་མེད་པ་གསལ་སྣང་དུ།

As to limitless, self-originated primordial wisdom, suchness itself,

It is ascertained through example, sign, and meaning as symbolic indications.

Equal to the sky in the self-nature of these three great nails,[40]

The nature into which all and everything is gathered is without separation or distinction.

In this even equality, the great, vast womb of space,

Everything is primordially equal, without before, later, or in between.

This is the principle of All-Good, Indestructible Enlightened Mind.[41]

Compassionate mind is like the essence of the sun,

Natural, luminously clear, primordially uncompounded.

There are no phenomena that can obscure it — direct and spontaneously accomplished.

In the continuum of the nature of phenomena there is no host of elaborations and no thoughts.

Due to voidness it is dharmakaya; due to clarity it is sambhogakaya;

Due to having rays it is nirmanakaya — the three kayas are beyond gathering or separating.

From the beginning, these qualities are spontaneously perfected;

Therefore, not obscured by the darkness of flaws and faults,

The three times of past, present, and future are all equally unmoving and unchanging.

Pervading all buddhas and sentient beings alike,

This is known as self-originated compassionate mind.

The energy of this appears in various ways,

Conceptualization and non-conceptualization, appearance and existence, the universe and its inhabitants,

And all the various appearances of beings.

།གཞི་མེད་རྟེན་མེད་གློ་བུར་སྣང་བ་ཙམ།
།བར་སྣབས་རེ་འགའི་ཆོས་སུ་རྟོགས་པར་བྱ།
།ལྷུན་གྲུབ་བྱང་ཆུབ་སེམས་ཀྱི་རང་བཞིན་ལས།
།རོལ་པ་མ་འགགས་འཁོར་འདས་ཆོ་འཕྲུལ་འབྱུང་།
།ཆོ་འཕྲུལ་དེ་ཀུན་དབྱིངས་སུ་འུབ་ཆུབ་པས།
།གདོད་མའི་ངང་ལས་གཡོས་པ་མེད་ཞེས་བྱ།
།འདིར་ནི་ཐམས་ཅད་བྱང་ཆུབ་སེམས་ཀྱི་ངང་།
།གཅིག་རྫོགས་ཀུན་རྫོགས་མ་བྱས་དོན་ཀུན་རྫོགས།
།རང་བཞིན་ལྷུན་རྫོགས་རང་བྱུང་ཡེ་ཤེས་སོ།
།བྱང་ཆུབ་སེམས་ནི་སྣང་དང་མི་སྣང་ལས།
།འཁོར་འདས་ཕྱི་ནང་ཆོས་སུ་མེད་ན་ཡང་།
།དེ་ཡི་རྩལ་ལས་གཡོས་པའི་རང་བཞིན་གྱིས།
།སྣང་སྲིད་འཁོར་འདས་སྣ་ཚོགས་རོལ་པར་ཤར།
ཤར་ཙམ་ཉིད་ནས་རང་བཞིན་སྟོང་པའི་གཟུགས།
།སྐྱེ་བ་མེད་ལས་སྐྱེ་བར་སྣང་བ་སྟེ།
།སྣང་དུས་ཉིད་ནས་སྐྱེས་པ་འགའ་ཡང་མེད།
།འགག་པ་མེད་པ་འགག་པར་སྣང་ན་ཡང་།
།འགག་པ་མེད་དེ་སྒྱུ་མ་སྟོང་པའི་གཟུགས།

Even as all this arises, its nature is unobstructed.
Like a mirage, a dream, an echo,
Like an emanation, a reflection, a gandharva city,[42]
Like an optical illusion, it does not exist.
Clear appearance, without a basis or support, is mere, instantaneous manifestation.
In any event, one must understand that such things are unreliable phenomena.
From the self-nature of spontaneously perfected, compassionate mind,
Unobstructed display gives rise to the miracles of samsara and nirvana.
All these miracles are perfect together in space,
Therefore, understand that nothing has moved from the primal continuity.
In this, everything is in the continuum of compassionate mind.
Perfect in one, perfect in all, everything is perfect without deed.
Spontaneously perfected self-nature is self-originated primordial wisdom.
Compassionate mind is neither apparent nor not apparent.
Externally or internally, it does not exist as phenomena of samsara or nirvana;
Nevertheless, from the movement of energy of the self-nature,
The variety of appearance and existence, samsara and nirvana, arises as a display.
From the moment of their arising, forms are by nature empty.[43]
From the unborn, they appear to be born,
But from the very time they appear, nothing has been born.
The unobstructed, that which appears to be obstructed, is also not obstructed;
It is the illusory form of emptiness.

།གནས་པ་ཉིད་ནས་གནས་པའི་ཆོས་མེད་དེ།
།གནས་མཁན་གཞི་མེད་འགྲོ་འོང་མེད་པའི་ངང་།
།ཇི་ལྟར་སྣང་བ་དེ་ལྟར་མ་གྲུབ་པས།
།རང་བཞིན་མེད་ཅེས་བཏགས་པ་ཙམ་དུ་ཟད།
།སྣང་བ་དེ་ཡང་རྒྱལ་ལས་རང་ཤར་བས།
།རྟེན་འབྲེལ་ཉིད་ཅེས་རང་བཞིན་བརྫ་ཙམ་བརྗོད།
།རྒྱལ་ལས་ཤར་བར་སྣང་བའི་རང་དུས་ནས།
།ཤར་དང་མ་ཤར་ཕྱོགས་དང་རིས་མེད་པས།
།རྒྱལ་ཡང་བརྫ་ཙམ་ངོ་བོ་འགག་མེད་པས།
།ཐམས་ཅད་རྟག་ཏུ་འཕོ་འགྱུར་མེད་པའི་ངང་།
།བྱང་ཆུབ་སེམས་ལས་གཡོས་པ་རྡུལ་ཙམ་མེད།

།ཆོས་དབྱིངས་རིན་པོ་ཆེའི་མཛོད་ལས། །བྱང་ཆུབ་སེམས་ཀྱི་མཚོན་དཔེ་བསྟན་པའི་ལེའུ་སྟེ་གསུམ་པའོ།།

From the time that they exist, there are no existent phenomena.
What exists has no ground in the continuum of no coming or going,
Not existing as it appears.
Therefore, saying that they have no self-nature is merely labeling.
Since appearances also are self-arisen from the potential,[44]
Their so-called interdependence is by nature a mere symbolic expression.
From the very moment these manifestations arise from the potential,
Since there is no bias or partiality as to arising or non-arising,
The potential, also just an expression, has no essence at all.
Thus, everything is always in the continuum of the unmoving and unchanging,
Not moving even an atom from compassionate mind.

From *The Precious Treasury of Phenomenal Space,* showing examples that indicate compassionate mind, the third chapter, is completed.

།ཀུན་འདུས་བྱང་ཆུབ་སེམས་ཀྱི་རང་བཞིན་ནི།
།སྣང་བ་མ་ཡིན་སྣང་བའི་ཆོས་ལས་འདས།
།སྟོང་པ་མ་ཡིན་སྟོང་པའི་ཆོས་ལས་འདས།
།ཡོད་པ་མ་ཡིན་དངོས་པོ་མཚན་མ་མེད།
།མེད་པ་མ་ཡིན་འཁོར་འདས་ཀུན་ལ་ཁྱབ།
།ཡོད་མེད་མ་ཡིན་ལྷུན་མཉམ་གདོད་མའི་དབྱིངས།
།ཕྱོགས་དང་རིས་མེད་གཞི་རྩ་དངོས་པོ་མེད།
།རྒྱུན་ཆད་མེད་པས་རིག་པ་བྱང་ཆུབ་ཀློང་།
།འཕོ་དང་འགྱུར་མེད་མཁའ་དབྱིངས་ཡེ་ནས་གདལ།
།རང་བྱུང་ཡེ་ཤེས་ཡེ་བླ་མེད་པའི་དོན།
།མི་སྐྱེ་མི་འགག་ཐིག་ལེ་གཅིག་ཏུ་འདུས།
།མ་ངེས་ཀུན་ཁྱབ་ཕྱོགས་མཐའ་ཡོངས་ཀྱིས་མེད།
།ལྷུན་མཉམ་མི་གཡོ་རྡོ་རྗེ་སྙིང་པོའི་གདུང་།
།འདུ་འབྲལ་མེད་པའི་དབྱིངས་མཆོག་རབ་འབྱམས་འདི།
།ཚིག་གིས་མཚོན་པའི་སྤྱོད་ཡུལ་མ་ཡིན་ཏེ།
།ཤེས་རབ་ཀློང་རྡོལ་སོ་སོ་རང་རིག་ཡུལ།
།བསམ་བརྗོད་སྤྲོས་དང་བྲལ་བའི་རྣལ་འབྱོར་པས།
།མཚོན་དང་མི་མཚོན་མེད་པར་ཐག་བཅད་དེ།
།སྒོམ་དང་བསྒོམ་པར་བྱ་བ་མ་རྙེད་པས།
།བྱིང་རྨོད་རྣམ་རྟོག་དགྲ་བོ་བསད་མ་དགོས།

4

From *The Precious Treasury of Phenomenal Space*, showing the self-nature of compassionate mind, the fourth chapter.

The nature of all-inclusive, compassionate mind,
Is not appearance; it is beyond appearance of phenomena.
It is not emptiness; it is beyond emptiness of phenomena.
It is not existent; it is without substance or characteristics.[45]
It is not non-existent; it pervades all samsara and nirvana.
It is neither existent nor non-existent, spontaneously equal, primordial space.
Directionless and impartial, it has neither base, nor root, nor substance.
Since it is uninterrupted, it is the expanse of perfect awareness.
It is not transformable and it is changeless, encompassing the space of the sky from the beginning.
The primordial, incomparable meaning of self-originated wisdom
Is unborn and unceasing, gathered into a single essential sphere,
Indefinite, all-pervading, completely directionless, and without boundaries,
Spontaneously equal, unmoving, the lineage of the indestructible essence.
This perfect, infinite space of no gathering and no dispersing[46]
Is beyond the scope of verbal expression.
Perfect wisdom, which is coming forth from the expanse, is the realm of distinct self-awareness.
The yogin of the unelaborated, beyond thought or expression,
Deciding that there are neither characteristics nor no characteristics,
Finds no meditation and nothing to meditate on;
So it is unnecessary to slay the enemies, dullness and discursive thoughts.

།ཡེ་ནས་སྤྱི་བླུགས་གནས་པའི་ཆོས་ཉིད་ལ།
།བདག་དང་གཞན་དུ་རྟོག་པ་མི་མངའ་བས།
༎ཁམས་གསུམ་འདི་ཉིད་རང་བཞིན་མཉམ་པའི་ཞིང་།
།དུས་གསུམ་རྒྱལ་བ་རང་སྣང་དག་པ་སྟེ།
།སྤྱང་བླང་མེད་པར་ཐམས་ཅད་ཁྱམ་གཅིག་པས།
།གཞན་ནས་ཐོབ་པར་བྱ་བ་རྡུལ་ཙམ་མེད།
།ཆོས་ཀུན་སེམས་ཉིད་ཀློང་ཆེན་དེར་གསལ་ལ།
།མཉམ་པའི་དོན་ལས་གཡོས་པ་ཙུང་ཟད་མེད།
།ཕྱི་དང་ནང་མེད་འཆར་ནུབ་རྙོག་པ་མེད།
།མཐའ་ཡི་མུན་སེལ་རྩ་བ་བྱང་ཆུབ་སེམས།
།གང་ཡང་མ་སྤྱངས་གོལ་ས་ཞུགས་ལ་ཆོད།
།འགྲོ་བའི་སྣང་ཚུལ་སྣ་ཚོགས་འཇིག་རྟེན་དང་།
།དག་པའི་སངས་རྒྱས་སྐུ་དང་ཡེ་ཤེས་ཀྱང་།
།རྟོགས་དང་མ་རྟོགས་རྩལ་ལས་ཤར་བ་ཡི།
།རོལ་པ་མ་འགགས་ནམ་མཁའི་དབྱིངས་ཁྱབ་ཀྱང་།
།ཆོས་དབྱིངས་ངང་ལ་རྟོགས་དང་མ་རྟོགས་ཙམ།
།རྟོགས་པས་བདེ་གཤེགས་དག་པའི་སྣང་བ་དང་།
།མ་རྟོགས་མ་རིག་གཟུང་འཛིན་བག་ཆགས་ལས།
།སྣ་ཚོགས་སྣང་ཡང་དབྱིངས་ལས་གཡོས་པ་མེད།
།བྱང་ཆུབ་སེམས་ནི་ཀུན་གྱི་དངོས་གཞི་སྟེ།
།མཚན་ཉིད་མ་འགགས་སྣ་ཚོགས་ཅིར་ཤར་ཡང་།
།རང་གསལ་ཆོས་ཉིད་དག་པའི་དབྱིངས་སུ་གསལ།

Existing from the beginning as the crown anointment[47] is suchness itself.
It possesses no thoughts of self and other;
Thus the three realms themselves are a field of natural equanimity.
The natural perfect vision of the conquerors of the three times,
Without accepting or rejecting, is completed all at once.
There is nothing to obtain from another, not even an atom.
All phenomena are clear in the great expanse of mind itself,
Not even a speck away from the meaning of equanimity.
Neither external nor internal, neither rising nor setting, without disturbance,
Compassionate mind is the root that clears away the darkness of limitations.
Without renouncing anything, the possibility for error is cut through as a matter of course.
The various ways in which sentient beings perceive the ordinary world,
As well as the pure bodies of enlightened ones and primordial wisdom,
Are respectively a matter of not realizing or realizing that all arises from the potential.
Unobstructed display pervades the space of the sky,
But in the continuum of phenomenal space there is just simply realizing or not realizing.
Through realization there come a sugata[48] and the appearance of purity.
Through non-realization there is ignorance and habituated grasper and grasped.
Though variety appears, it is unmoved from space.
Compassionate mind is the actual basis of all things.
However, its intrinsic characteristics appear unceasingly and in various ways.
It is the self-luminous clear space of pure Dharma nature.

།དབྱེ་བསལ་མེད་དོ་རྒྱ་ཡན་རིག་པའི་འགྲོས།
།ཟང་ཐལ་ཡེ་ཤེས་རང་བྱུང་ཀློང་ཡངས་ཤིང་།
།མ་བསྒྲིབས་ཕྱི་ནང་མེད་པར་འོད་གསལ་བས།
།རང་རིག་སེམས་ཀྱི་མེ་ལོང་འོད་པོ་ཆེ།
།འདོད་འབྱུང་ནོར་བུ་རིན་ཆེན་ཆོས་ཀྱི་དབྱིངས།
།བཙལ་བ་མེད་པ་ཐམས་ཅད་རང་བྱུང་བས།
།རང་བྱུང་ཡེ་ཤེས་འདོད་དགུར་འབྱུང་བའི་དཔལ།
།ཆེ་བའི་ཡོན་ཏན་རྣམ་གྲངས་ཇི་སྙེད་པ།
།དབྱིངས་ལས་དབྱིངས་བྱུང་ཐབས་མཆོག་མ་འགགས་ཤར།
།ཐམས་ཅད་སྐྱེ་མེད་དབྱིངས་སུ་ལྷུན་རྫོགས་པས།
།དངོས་པོ་ཟིལ་གནོན་སྟོང་ཉིད་བྱང་ཆུབ་ཀློང་།
།སྟོང་པ་ཟིལ་གནོན་བྱང་ཆུབ་རང་རིག་ཀློང་།
།བྱང་ཆུབ་སེམས་ལ་སྣང་སྟོང་ཡེ་ནས་མེད།
།གཉིས་མེད་མཉེན་བསམ་ཡས་ཆོ་འཕྲུལ་འབྱུང་།
།དུས་གསུམ་དུས་མེད་སྐྱེ་མེད་ཆོས་ཀྱི་དབྱིངས།
།མི་འགྱུར་མི་ཕྱེད་འདུས་མ་བྱས་པའི་ཀློང་།
།དུས་གསུམ་སངས་རྒྱས་རིག་པ་ཡེ་ཤེས་དབྱིངས།
།གཟུང་འཛིན་ཟིལ་གནོན་རང་རིག་བྱང་ཆུབ་ཀློང་།
།ཕྱི་དང་ནང་མེད་ཆོས་ཉིད་ལྷུན་ཡངས་སོ།

།ཆོས་དབྱིངས་རིན་པོ་ཆེའི་མཛོད་ལས། །བྱང་ཆུབ་སེམས་ཀྱི་རང་བཞིན་བསྟན་པའི་ལེའུ་སྟེ་བཞི་པའོ།།

Without clear distinction, the manner of awareness is without boundaries.

Direct primordial wisdom, self-originated in the vast expanse,

Is unobscured, clear luminosity, without outside or inside;

Therefore, self-awareness, the mirror of mind, is great light,

A wish-fulfilling precious gem, the space of phenomena.

Without searching, everything is self-originated;

So self-originated primordial wisdom is the glorious wish-fulfilling source.

However many the number of these great qualities,

They are space arising from space, the supreme method ceaselessly arising.

Everything is unborn, spontaneously perfected in space;

So substantiality is suppressed by splendor; in the expanse of emptiness everything is perfect.

Emptiness is suppressed by splendor; in the expanse of natural realization everything is perfect.

Compassionate mind has no appearance and no emptiness from the beginning.

Not fixating on non-duality, inconceivable miracles occur.

The three times beyond time are unborn phenomenal space.

Unchanging, indivisible, this is the uncompounded expanse.

The buddhas of the three times are the primordial wisdom space of awareness.

With grasper and grasped suppressed by splendor, the perfected expanse of self-awareness is without outside or inside.

The nature of phenomena is spontaneously vast.

From *The Precious Treasury of Phenomenal Space,* showing the self-nature of compassionate mind, the fourth chapter, is completed.

།སེམས་ཉིད་བྱང་ཆུབ་སེམས་ཀྱི་ངོ་བོ་ལ།
།ལྟ་བ་བསྒོམ་མེད་སྤྱོད་པ་སྤྱད་དུ་མེད།
།འབྲས་བུ་བསྒྲུབ་མེད་ས་ལམ་བགྲོད་དུ་མེད།
།དཀྱིལ་འཁོར་བསྐྱེད་མེད་བཟླས་བརྗོད་རྫོགས་རིམ་མེད།
།དབང་ལ་བསྐུར་མེད་དམ་ཚིག་བསྲུང་དུ་མེད།
།ཡེ་ནས་ལྷུན་གྲུབ་དག་པའི་ཆོས་ཉིད་ལ།
།བློ་བུར་རིམ་རྩོལ་རྒྱུ་འབྲས་ཆོས་ལས་འདས།
།འདི་དག་བྱང་ཆུབ་སེམས་ཀྱི་ངོ་བོ་སྟེ།
།ཉི་མ་སྤྲིན་དང་མུན་པས་མ་བསྒྲིབས་ལ།
།བློ་བུར་མ་བྱས་དབྱིངས་ན་དང་གིས་གསལ།
།རྩོལ་ཞིང་སྒྲུབ་པའི་ཆོས་བཅུ་གང་བསྟན་པ།
།རྩལ་ལས་བློ་བུར་འཁྲུལ་ངོར་གསུངས་པ་ཉིད།
།རིམ་རྩོལ་དབང་པོའི་རིམ་པས་འཇུག་པའི་ཐབས།
།ཨ་ཏི་ཡོ་ག་རྡོ་རྗེ་སྙིང་པོའི་དོན།
།ཇི་བཞིན་རྣལ་དུ་འབྱོར་ལ་བསྟན་པ་མིན།
།རིམ་འཇུག་རྩོལ་བ་ཅན་གྱི་གང་ཟག་རྣམས།
།ཆོས་ཉིད་གདོད་མའི་དབྱིངས་སུ་དྲང་བའི་ཕྱིར།
།ཉན་ཐོས་རང་རྒྱལ་བྱང་ཆུབ་སེམས་དཔའི་ཐེག
།རྒྱུད་དུ་གསུམ་ལ་བསྟན་པའི་རིམ་པ་སྟེ།
།ཀྲི་ཡ་ཨུ་པ་ཡོ་ག་རྣམ་པ་གསུམ།
།འབྲིང་པོ་གསུམ་ལ་རང་བཞིན་བབས་ཀྱིས་གྲུབ།

5

From *The Precious Treasury of Phenomenal Space*, showing what is beyond endeavor, accomplishment, and cause and effect, the fifth chapter.

Mind itself, the nature of compassionate mind,
Has no view, no meditation, and no action to conduct.
There is no result to attain. There are no grounds and paths to traverse.
There is no visualized mandala to generate. It is beyond recitation and the completion stage.
There is no empowerment to confer. There is no samaya[49] to protect.
Spontaneously accomplished from the beginning, the dharma nature of purity
Is beyond incidental phenomena of cause and effect involving gradual effort.
All these are the essence of compassionate mind.
The sun itself cannot be obscured by clouds or darkness,
Nor is it created incidentally; it always naturally shines in the continuum of space.
The ten virtues[50] of effort and endeavor that have been taught
Are expressed to those who are momentarily deluded by what comes forth from the potential;
These are taught as a means for those who enter through gradual effort.
Ati yoga, experienced as it is, the truth of the indestructible essence,
Does not need to be shown to those who have already entered into actuality.
To draw those who enter gradually with endeavor
Into primordial space, the nature of phenomena,
There are the Shravaka,[51] Pratyekabuddha,[52] and Bodhisattva[53] vehicles,
The three lesser stages of the teachings.
Kriya, Upa, Yoga, these three, are naturally accomplished by the middling ones.[54]

།མ་ཧཱ་ཨ་ནུ་ཨ་ཏི་རྣམ་པ་གསུམ།
།ཆེན་པོ་གསུམ་ལ་གདོད་ནས་སྣང་བ་སྟེ།
།རྒྱུ་འབྲས་ཐེག་པའི་ཆོས་ཀྱི་སྒོ་དབྱེ་བས།
།སྐལ་ལྡན་འགྲོ་བ་བྱང་ཆུབ་གསུམ་ལ་འདྲེན།
།ཀུན་ཀྱང་མཐར་ཐུག་རྡོ་རྗེ་སྙིང་པོའི་དོན།
།གསང་ཆེན་རྨད་དུ་བྱུང་འདིར་འཇུག་དགོས་པས།
།ཀུན་གྱི་རྩེ་མོ་འོད་གསལ་མཆོག་མི་འགྱུར།
།མངོན་པར་བྱང་ཆུབ་སྙིང་པོའི་ཐེག་པར་གྲགས།
།ཆོས་ཀྱང་གཉིས་ལས་བླང་དོར་བྱ་རྩོལ་ཅན།
།རྩལ་ལས་རོལ་པར་ཤར་བའི་རང་བཞིན་གྱི།
།སེམས་དང་སེམས་བྱུང་བག་ཆགས་སྦྱོང་ཕྱིར་བསྟན།
།དེ་དག་སེམས་ལས་ཡེ་ཤེས་དག་པར་འདོད།
།བླང་དོར་བྱ་རྩོལ་མེད་པའི་ཆོས་ཆེན་ནི།
།རང་བྱུང་ཡེ་ཤེས་བྱང་ཆུབ་སེམས་ཉིད་ཀྱི།
།ངོ་བོ་ཐད་དྲང་དང་ལས་མ་གཡོས་པར།
།མངོན་དུ་བྱེད་པས་གཞན་དུ་རྩོལ་མི་དགོས།
།རང་ལ་བཞག་ནས་གཞན་དུ་འཚོལ་མི་བྱེད།
།འདི་ནི་ཉི་མའི་ངོ་བོ་དེ་ཉིད་དོན།
།རང་གཞག་འོད་གསལ་མི་གཡོ་གནས་པར་འདོད།
།གཞན་ནི་སྤྲིན་དང་མུན་སེལ་རྩོལ་སྒྲུབ་ཀྱིས།
།ཉི་མ་གདོད་སྒྲུབ་བྱེད་དང་མཚུངས་པར་བསྟན།

From the outset, Maha, Anu, and Ati, these three,[55]
Appear to those who are great.
By opening the dharma doors of the causal and resultant vehicles,
Fortunate beings are guided to the three perfections.[56]
Ultimately all must enter into the truth of the indestructible essence,
The great marvelous secret,
So it is the peak of all, unchanging, the supreme clear lucency.
Therefore, it is known as the vehicle of the actualized enlightened essence.
However, of these two kinds of teachings, the one with effortful acceptance and rejection
Is taught to cleanse habitual patterns of mind and its contents,
Even though these naturally arise as the display of energy.
These teachings endorse pristine original wisdom as purer than mind.
The great teaching, free from accepting and rejecting, action and effort,
Is self-originated primordial wisdom, compassionate mind itself,
Unmoved from the continuum of the directly present nature.
Having actualized it, you do not need to seek it elsewhere.
Do not search for it elsewhere, leaving behind what is within you.
This is the essence of the sun, the truth of suchness,
Accepted as self-settled clear lucency, remaining without moving.
Other teachings are trying to recreate the primordial sun
By removing clouds and darkness with effort and endeavor.
Therefore, the above two have a huge difference, like that of earth and sky.

།དེས་ན་འདི་གཉིས་ཁྱད་པར་གནམ་ས་བཞིན།
།དིང་སང་ཨ་ཏིར་རློམ་པའི་གླང་ཆེན་དག   །
།འགྱུ་འཕྲོའི་རྟོག་ཚོགས་བྱང་ཆུབ་སེམས་ཡིན་ལོ།
།རྨོངས་པ་འདི་ཀུན་སྨུན་པའི་གློང་ཉིད་དུ།
།རང་བཞིན་རྫོགས་པ་ཆེན་པོའི་དོན་ལ་རིང་།
།རྩལ་དང་རྩལ་ལས་ཤར་བའང་མི་ཤེས་ན།
།བྱང་ཆུབ་སེམས་ཀྱི་ངོ་བོ་སྨོས་ཅི་དགོས།
།འདིར་ནི་གདོད་ནས་དག་པའི་བྱང་ཆུབ་སེམས།
།དོན་དམ་དབྱིངས་ཀྱི་ཆོས་ཉིད་བདེན་པ་ནི།
།སྨྲ་བསམ་འདས་པས་ཤེས་རབ་ཕ་རོལ་ཕྱིན།
།ངང་གིས་མི་གཡོ་རང་བཞིན་འོད་གསལ་ཞིང་།
།འགྱུར་འཕྲོའི་སྤྲོས་དང་ཡེ་ནས་བྲལ་བ་ལ།
།ངོ་བོ་ཞེས་བརྗོད་ཉི་མའི་སྙིང་པོ་འདྲ།
།དེ་ཡི་རྩལ་ནི་འཆར་ཚུལ་མ་འགགས་པའི།
།རིག་པ་ཟང་ཐལ་རྟོག་དཔྱོད་གཉིས་དང་བྲལ།
།སལ་གྱིས་གསལ་ཡང་གཟུང་འཛིན་མེད་པ་ཡིན།
།རྩལ་ལས་ཤར་བའི་རིག་པ་སྤྲོས་པའི་བློ།
།དེས་བསྐྱེད་གཟུང་འཛིན་བག་ཆགས་སྣ་ཚོགས་ཅན།
།ཡུལ་མེད་ཡུལ་དུ་གཟུང་བའི་ཡུལ་ལྔ་དང་།
།བདག་མེད་བདག་ཏུ་འཛིན་པའི་ཉོན་མོངས་ལྔ།
།ཕྱི་ནང་སྣོད་བཅུད་འཁྲུལ་སྣང་ཇི་སྙེད་དེ།
།འཁོར་བར་སྣང་བ་རྩལ་ལས་ཡང་ཤར་བ།

Nowadays old, ox-like, conceited Ati practitioners[57]

Think that the movements of thought are compassionate mind.

All such confusion is the expanse of darkness itself,

Far away from the truth of the natural Great Perfection.

If they do not even understand the potential, or arising from the potential,

Need we mention the essence of compassionate mind?

Here primordially pure compassionate mind,

The absolute truth, the space that is the nature of phenomena,

Is beyond expression and conception, so it is transcendental wisdom.[58]

Naturally unmoved, its nature is clear lucency,

Primordially free from the elaboration of movements and emanations.

This is called the "essence" like the essence of the sun.

The way of arising of its energy is unobstructed, directly present awareness,

Free from conception and analysis.

Although vividly clear,[59] it is free from grasper and grasped.

Awareness that arises from the potential, elaborated mind,

Generates the various habits of grasper and grasped.

By grasping an absence of objects as objects, there are the five objects.[60]

And by clinging to the selfless as self, there are the five afflictions.[61]

The outer and inner, the universe and its inhabitants, are manifestations of confusion;

These appearances of samsara arise from the potential.

།མ་རྟོགས་ལོག་པར་གཟུང་བའི་སྣང་བ་ཉིད།
།གང་ནས་མ་འོངས་གང་དུ་མ་སོང་ལ།
།གར་ཡང་མི་གནས་ཆོས་ཉིད་ཀློང་ཆེན་དུ།
།རྟོགས་པས་ཁམས་གསུམ་ཡོངས་གྲོལ་དགོངས་པ་ཞེས།
།ཨ་ཏི་ལྷུན་གྲུབ་རྡོ་རྗེ་སྙིང་པོའི་ལུང་།
།ཀུན་བཟང་ཡངས་པ་ཆེན་པོའི་ཀློང་ནས་ཤར།
།རྣམ་དག་བྱང་ཆུབ་སེམས་ཀྱི་ངོ་བོ་ལ།
།ལྟ་བའི་ཡུལ་མེད་ལྟ་བའི་ཆོས་སུ་མེད།
།བལྟ་བར་བྱ་དང་བྱེད་པ་རྡུལ་ཙམ་མེད།
།སྒོམ་པའི་བློ་མེད་བསྒོམ་བྱའི་ཆོས་ཀྱང་མེད།
།སྤྱོད་དང་སྤྱོད་པ་གཉིས་མེད་ལྷུན་གྲུབ་པས།
།བསྒྲུབ་པར་བྱ་བའི་འབྲས་བུ་རྡུལ་ཙམ་མེད།
།མེད་པའི་ཆོས་ལ་བགྲོད་པའི་ས་མེད་པས།
།ཕྱིན་པར་བྱ་བའི་ལམ་ཡང་ཡེ་ནས་མེད།
།འོད་གསལ་ཐིག་ལེ་ཆེན་པོར་གྲུབ་ཟིན་པས།
།རྣམ་རྟོག་འཕྲོ་འདུས་བསྐྱེད་པའི་དཀྱིལ་འཁོར་དང་།
།སྔགས་དང་ཁ་ཏོན་དབང་དང་དམ་ཚིག་མེད།
།རིམ་སྔུད་ལ་སོགས་མི་དམིགས་རྫོགས་རིམ་མེད།
།ཡེ་ནས་གྲུབ་ཟིན་སྐུ་དང་ཡེ་ཤེས་ལ།
།འདུས་བྱས་གློ་བུར་རྐྱེན་བྱུང་རྒྱུ་འབྲས་མེད།
།འདི་དག་ཡོད་ན་རང་བྱུང་ཡེ་ཤེས་མིན།

Just appearances wrongly grasped because of non-realization,

They came from nowhere, they go nowhere, and they settle nowhere.

If one realizes this as the great expanse of the true nature of phenomena,

What is called the enlightened view of all three realms thoroughly liberated,

Ati, the spontaneously accomplished, the great indestructible essential teaching,

Arises from the expanse of All-Good, great vastness.

As to the essence of totally pure compassionate mind,

There is neither an object of a view nor any teaching of a view.

There is nothing to view, nor any viewing, not even a speck.

There is no thought of meditation, nor is there any phenomenon to meditate on.

Neither is there acting, nor any action to perform; accomplishment is spontaneous;

So there is no result to achieve, not even a single mote.

As phenomena are non-existent, there is no ground to traverse;

So from the beginning there is no path to travel.

This clear lucency, the great sphere, is already accomplished;

So there is no mandala to generate by emanating and gathering thoughts,

And there is no mantra,[62] no recitation, no empowerment, and no samaya.

There is no idea of stages, no gathering in, and so on, so there is no completion phase.

As to the primordially accomplished kayas and wisdoms,

There are no compounded, incidental circumstances of cause and result.

If these were present, there would be no self-originated primordial wisdom.

།འདུས་བྱས་ཉིད་ཕྱིར་འཇིག་པ་ཉིད་དང་ནི།
།ལྷུན་གྲུབ་འདུས་མ་བྱས་ཞེས་གང་སྨྲད་མཚོན།
།དེ་ཕྱིར་དོན་དམ་དབྱིངས་ཀྱི་ངོ་བོ་ལ།
།རྒྱུ་འབྲས་ལས་འདས་རང་བཞིན་རྣམ་བཅུ་མེད།
།རྩོལ་དང་སྒྲུབ་མེད་སེམས་ཉིད་རྣལ་མའི་དོན།
།ཡོད་མེད་སྤྲོས་ཀུན་ཞི་བར་མཁྱེན་འཚལ་ལོ།

།ཆོས་དབྱིངས་རིན་པོ་ཆེའི་མཛོད་ལས། །རྩོལ་སྒྲུབ་རྒྱུ་འབྲས་ལས་འདས་པའི་ལེའུ་སྟེ་ལྔ་པའོ།།

If it were conditional, it would be subject to destruction;

So how could it be characterized as unconditional and spontaneously accomplished?

Therefore, as to the essence of absolute space,

There is no cause and effect, and it does not have the ten natures.[63]

The original truth, mind itself, is beyond endeavor or accomplishment.

Please know this as completely free from the elaborations of existence and non-existence.

From *The Precious Treasury of Phenomenal Space,* showing what is beyond endeavor, accomplishment, and cause and effect, the fifth chapter, is completed.

།ཉི་མའི་སྙིང་པོར་འོད་རྣམས་འདུས་པ་ལྟར།
།ཆོས་ཀུན་རྩ་བ་བྱང་ཆུབ་སེམས་སུ་འདུས།
།སྣང་སྲིད་སྣོད་བཅུད་མ་དག་འཁྲུལ་པ་ཡང་།
།གང་བྱུང་རྟེན་དང་གནས་པའི་དབྱིངས་བརྟགས་པས།
།གཞི་མེད་ཡེ་གྲོལ་སེམས་ཀྱི་ངང་དུ་འདུས།
།ཆོས་ཉིད་ཡེ་ཀློང་ཡངས་པ་ཆེན་པོའི་ངང་།
།འཁྲུལ་དང་མ་འཁྲུལ་མིང་དོན་འདས་པར་འདུས།
།དག་པའི་རང་སྣང་སྐུ་དང་ཞིང་ཁམས་དང་།
།ཡེ་ཤེས་ཕྲིན་ལས་ངོ་མཚར་རོལ་པ་ཡང་།
།རང་བྱུང་ངང་ལ་འདུ་འབྲལ་མེད་པར་འདུས།
།སྣང་སྲིད་འཁོར་འདས་ཀུན་འདུས་བྱང་ཆུབ་སེམས།
།ཉི་མཁའ་བཞིན་དུ་སྟོང་གསལ་འདུས་མ་བྱས།
།གདོད་ནས་རང་བྱུང་ཡེ་ཀློང་ཡངས་པ་ཡིན།
།སེམས་ཉིད་ཀློང་ཆེན་འགྱུར་མེད་ནམ་མཁའི་ངང་།
།རོལ་པ་ངེས་མེད་བྱང་ཆུབ་སེམས་ཀྱི་རྩལ།
།འཁོར་འདས་ཐེག་པ་ཀུན་ལ་དབང་བསྒྱུར་བའི།
།བྱེར་མེད་གཅིག་གིས་ཐམས་ཅད་ཟིལ་གྱིས་མནན།
།མཐའ་རུ་གྱུར་པའི་ཡུལ་གཞན་ལོགས་ན་མེད།
།ཆོས་ཉིད་བྱང་ཆུབ་སེམས་ལས་གར་མ་གཡོས།

6

From *The Precious Treasury of Phenomenal Space,* showing that everything is included in compassionate mind, the sixth chapter.

As all its rays are gathered in the essence of the sun,
All phenomena are gathered in the root, compassionate mind.
When appearance and existence, the universe and its inhabitants, and impure delusions are examined,
Along with the support from which they arise and the space in which they exist,
They are all without base, subsumed in the primordially liberated continuum of mind.
In this continuum of the great vast primordial expanse, the nature of phenomena,
Delusion and non-delusion are united beyond labels and meanings.
Also, self-appearance of purity, kayas, pure lands,
Primordial wisdom, buddha activity, and amazing display
Are subsumed without separation or union in the continuum of the naturally arising.
Appearance and existence of samsara and nirvana, all together in compassionate mind,
Like the sky and the sun, uncompounded emptiness and clarity,
Are from the beginning the self-originated vast primal expanse.
Mind itself, great expanse, unchangeable continuum of space,
Is unpredictable in its display. Since the energy of compassionate mind
Masters all the vehicles of samsara and nirvana,
Non-action alone suppresses everything by splendor.
With no other country to border it,
Nothing moves from the nature of phenomena, compassionate mind.

།ཐམས་ཅད་ཀུན་བཟང་ལྷུན་གྲུབ་གཅིག་ཤར་བས།
།མ་ལུས་ཀུན་འདུས་འགྲན་ཟླ་བྲལ་བའི་མཆོག
།ཆེ་བའི་ཆེ་བ་ཀུན་བཟང་ཆོས་ཀྱི་དབྱིངས།
།རྒྱལ་པོ་ལྷ་བུར་ཐམས་ཅད་ཀུན་འདུས་པས།
།འཁོར་འདས་ཀུན་ལ་དབང་བསྒྱུར་གར་མ་གཡོས།
།ཐམས་ཅད་ཀུན་བཟང་མི་བཟང་གཅིག་མེད་པས།
།བཟང་ངན་མེད་པར་ཀུན་ཏུ་བཟང་པོར་གཅིག
།གྲུབ་དང་མ་གྲུབ་ཐམས་ཅད་དབྱིངས་གཅིག་པས།
།ཐམས་ཅད་ལྷུན་གྲུབ་མི་གཡོ་མཉམ་པར་གཅིག
།གཅིག་ལས་ཀུན་ཤར་མ་ལུས་ཆོས་ཀྱི་དབྱིངས།
།བྱུར་མེད་ངང་ལ་སྒྲུབ་མེད་བཙལ་དུ་མེད།
།རྩོལ་སྒྲུབ་རང་གི་དབྱིངས་ལས་གཞན་མེད་པས།
།གང་ལས་རྩོལ་ཞིང་གང་དུ་སྒྲུབ་པར་བྱེད།
།བཙལ་བས་ཡུལ་མེད་བསྒོམས་པས་མཐོང་བ་མེད།
།བསྒྲུབ་པའི་གནས་མེད་གཞན་ནས་འོང་བ་མེད།
།འགྲོ་འོང་མེད་པས་མཉམ་ཉིད་ཆོས་ཀྱི་སྐུ།
།ལྷུན་རྫོགས་ཐིག་ལེ་ཆེན་པོའི་དབྱིངས་སུ་འདུས།
།ཉན་ཐོས་རང་རྒྱལ་བྱང་ཆུབ་སེམས་དཔའི་ལུང་།
།བདག་དང་བདག་གི་མེད་པར་ཐག་བཅད་ནས།
།སྤྲོས་བྲལ་ནམ་མཁའ་འདྲ་བར་དགོངས་དོན་གཅིག

Since everything is All-Good, a single manifestation of spontaneous accomplishment,

All-inclusive, supremely incomparable,

All-Good phenomenal space is the greatest of the great.

As if by a king, everything is unified;

So, unmoved, it rules over all samsara and nirvana.

Everything is All-Good. There is not even one non-good.

So, without good or bad, all is one in the All-Good.

Since all that is accomplished and unaccomplished is in the same space,

Everything is one in spontaneously accomplished, unwavering equanimity.

From one, everything arises without exception, the space of phenomena.

In the continuum of non-activity, there is nothing to accomplish and nothing to look for.

Since endeavor and accomplishment are not other than one's own space,

What purpose is there for endeavor, and what could be accomplished?

There is no object to seek and nothing to be seen in meditation.

There is no place of accomplishment. Nothing comes from another.

Since there is no coming or going, equanimity, dharmakaya,

Is spontaneously complete and perfected in the great essence.

The teachings of the Shravakas, Pratyekabuddhas, and Bodhisattvas

Resolve the non-existence of both "me" and "mine,"

As one intended meaning, sky-like freedom from elaboration.

།ཨ་ཏི་མཆོག་གསང་རྣལ་འབྱོར་ཆེན་པོའི་ལུང་།
།བདག་གཞན་དབྱེར་མེད་ཡངས་པའི་ནམ་མཁའ་ལ།
།རང་བྱུང་ཡེ་ཤེས་ཇི་བཞིན་རྣལ་འཇོག་པས།
།དགོངས་དོན་དེ་ཀུན་སྙིང་པོའི་མཆོག་འདིར་འདུས།
།ཀྲི་ཡ་ཨུ་པ་ཡོ་ག་རིགས་གསུམ་ཡང་།
།བདག་དང་ལྷ་དང་ཏིང་འཛིན་མཆོད་སྦྱིན་ལས།
།སྒོ་གསུམ་རྣམ་དག་དངོས་གྲུབ་འདོད་པར་གཅིག
།རྡོ་རྗེ་རྩེ་མོ་ལུང་ཀྱུལ་གསང་བ་ཡང་།
།སྣང་གྲགས་རིག་པ་རྣམ་དག་ཡེ་ནས་ལྷ།
།སྒོ་གསུམ་རྣམ་དག་དངོས་གྲུབ་མངོན་གྱུར་པས།
།དགོངས་པ་དེ་ཀུན་སྙིང་པོའི་མཆོག་འདིར་འདུས།
།མ་ཧཱ་ཨ་ནུ་ཨ་ཏི་རྣམ་གསུམ་ཡང་།
།སྣང་སྲིད་སྣོད་བཅུད་ལྷ་དང་ལྷ་མོའི་ཞིང་།
།དབྱིངས་དང་ཡེ་ཤེས་རྣམ་དག་དབྱེར་མེད་པས།
།ཆོས་ཉིད་མི་གཡོ་རང་བྱུང་ཡེ་ཤེས་འདོད།
།མཆོག་གསང་རབ་འདིར་ཐམས་ཅད་རྣམ་དག་པས།
།མ་བྲུས་གཞལ་ཡས་ཡེ་ཀློང་བདེ་བའི་ཞིང་།
།ཕྱི་དང་ནང་མེད་ཀུན་ཁྱབ་གདལ་བ་ལས།
།བླང་དོར་བྱ་རྩོལ་མཚན་མའི་ཆོས་མེད་པར།
།ཐམས་ཅད་ཡེ་འབྱམས་ཆོས་སྐུའི་ཀློང་དུ་གྲོལ།
།དགོངས་པ་དེ་ཀུན་གསང་ཆེན་སྙིང་པོར་འདུས།

In the teachings of the great yogins of the supreme secret, Ati,
Within the sky of vast inseparability of self and other,
Self-originated primordial wisdom, as it is, remains naturally.
So all their intended meanings are included within this supreme essence.
The three families of Kriya, Upa and Yoga, moreover,
Agree that through oneself, deity, samadhi, and clouds of offerings,
Accomplishment comes from complete purity of the three doors.[64]
However, in the indestructible peak, the secret king of transmissions,
Appearance, sound, and awareness are totally pure, divine from the beginning.
With complete purity of the three doors, accomplishment is actualized;
So all their intended meanings are gathered within this supreme essence.
Maha, Anu, Ati, these three, also believe
That appearance and existence, the universe and its inhabitants, are the field of gods and goddesses.
Space and primordial wisdom are totally pure and inseparable.
Therefore, it is maintained that the nature of phenomena is unwavering, self-originated primordial wisdom.
In this, the great supreme secret, everything is totally pure,
So that the field of the blissful primordial expanse is uncreated and immeasurable,
Without outer or inner, all-pervading and all-encompassing.
Therefore, there are no characterized phenomena of rejecting or accepting, effort or endeavor;
Everything is primordially encompassed and liberated in the expanse of dharmakaya;
So all their intended meanings are gathered within this supreme essence.

།གཅིག་རྫོགས་ཀུན་རྫོགས་ཆོས་ཀུན་འདུས་པའི་ཀློང་།
།ཡེ་བབས་རང་གསལ་ལྷུན་གྲུབ་ཆེན་པོར་འདུས།

།ཆོས་དབྱིངས་རིན་པོ་ཆེའི་མཛོད་ལས། །ཐམས་ཅད་བྱང་ཆུབ་སེམས་སུ་འདུས་པར་བསྟན་པའི་ལེའུ་སྟེ་དྲུག་
པའོ།།

Complete in one, complete in all, all phenomena are gathered in the expanse.
The original state, self-luminous, is gathered in the great spontaneous accomplishment.

From *The Precious Treasury of Phenomenal Space*, showing that everything is included in compassionate mind, the sixth chapter, is completed.

།རང་བཞིན་ལྷུན་གྲུབ་བྱང་ཆུབ་སེམས་ཀྱི་ལུང་།
།མ་བྱས་དོན་གྲུབ་རི་རྒྱལ་རྩེ་མོ་ནི།
།ཀུན་ལས་འཕགས་སོ་ཐེག་མཆོག་རྒྱལ་པོ་ཆེ།
།ཇི་ལྟར་རི་རྒྱལ་རྩེ་མོར་ཕྱིན་པ་ན།
།དམའ་བའི་ལུང་རྣམས་དུས་གཅིག་མཐོང་བ་སྟེ།
།ལུང་གི་རྩེ་མོའི་རང་བཞིན་མཐོང་དང་བྲལ།
།དེ་བཞིན་ཨ་ཏི་རྡོ་རྗེ་སྙིང་པོ་ནི།
།ཐེག་པའི་ཡང་རྩེ་དོན་ཀུན་གསལ་བར་མཐོང་།
།འོག་མའི་ཐེག་པས་འདི་དོན་མཐོང་བ་མེད།
།དེ་ཕྱིར་ལྷུན་གྲུབ་རྩེ་མོར་གྱུར་པའི་རྩེ།
།ཇི་ལྟར་ཡིད་བཞིན་ནོར་བུ་ཆེན་པོ་ལ།
།གསོལ་བ་བཏབ་ན་འདོད་དགུ་ངང་གིས་འབྱུང་།
།ཕལ་པའི་དངོས་ལ་དེ་ལྟ་མ་ཡིན་ནོ།
།རྡོ་རྗེ་སྙིང་པོ་སྐུ་གསུམ་ལྷུན་གྲུབ་པས།
།རང་གཞག་དབྱིངས་ལས་སངས་རྒྱས་རང་ལ་འགྲུབ།
།རྩོལ་ཞིང་སྒྲུབ་མེད་ཆེ་བ་དེ་ཉིད་དོ།
།འོག་མའི་ཐེག་པས་བླང་དོར་འབད་བྱས་ཀྱང་།
།བསྐལ་པར་མི་འགྲུབ་ཆི་ཆད་ནད་དུ་ཆེ།
།ཡེ་ནས་ལྷུན་མཉམ་རིག་པ་བྱང་ཆུབ་སེམས།

7

From *The Precious Treasury of Phenomenal Space*, demonstrating that everything is primordially and spontaneously accomplished in compassionate mind, the seventh chapter.

The field of natural spontaneous accomplishment, compassionate mind,
Where all activities are accomplished without action, is the summit of the highest mountain,
Elevated above all, the great king that is the supreme vehicle.
If one reaches the peak of the highest mountain,
One can see all the valleys below at once;
But, from the valleys below, the nature of the peak cannot be seen;
Like that, Ati, the indestructible essence,
Is the summit of all vehicles, where all meanings are clearly seen.
Lower vehicles cannot ever see the meaning of this.
That is why, when the spontaneously accomplished becomes the peak,
All of one's wishes are naturally granted,
Just as when one prays to a great, wish-fulfilling jewel;
But ordinary substances are not like this.
Since the indestructible essence, the three kayas, is spontaneously accomplished
In the space of the naturally settled state, one achieves enlightenment.
This great state cannot be achieved through effort or endeavor.
The lower vehicles endeavor to reject or accept;
However, they cannot achieve anything for eons, which is hopeless and immeasurably painful.
Primordial, spontaneously equal awareness, compassionate mind,

ཇི་བཞིན་རང་བབས་ཆོས་ཉིད་ཡངས་པ་ནི།
།རང་བཞིན་ཆོས་སྐུ་མཉམ་ཉིད་གདོད་མའི་ཀློང་།
།ཀུན་ལ་ཡོད་དེ་སྐལ་ལྡན་འགའ་ཡི་ཡུལ།
ཇི་བཞིན་བཞག་ན་དང་དེར་བབས་ཀྱིས་འགྲུབ།
།ཁྱབ་གདལ་རང་གསལ་ལྷུན་གྲུབ་ལོངས་སྤྱོད་རྫོགས།
།ཀུན་ལ་ཡོད་ཀྱང་མཐོང་བ་འགའ་ཡི་ཡུལ།
།གང་སྣང་རང་གཞག་བྱ་རྩོལ་བྲལ་ན་མངོན།
།མ་འགགས་རོལ་པ་སྤྲུལ་སྐུ་གདལ་བའི་ཀློང་།
།ཀུན་ལ་ཡོད་དེ་འཆར་བའི་དུས་ན་གསལ།
།ཡིད་བཞིན་ཡོན་ཏན་ཕྲིན་ལས་ཆོ་འཕྲུལ་ཡང་།
།གཞན་ན་མེད་དེ་རང་རིག་དག་པའི་ཀློང་།
།ཆུ་དང་རྙོག་བཞིན་རང་དྭངས་བཞག་ན་གསལ།
།བཙལ་བས་མི་རྙེད་གདོད་ནས་དག་པའི་ཆོས།
།སངས་རྒྱས་བྱང་ཆུབ་རང་བྱུང་ཀློང་ན་གསལ།
།སྔར་གྲུབ་ཟིན་པས་ད་གཟོད་བསྒྲུབ་མི་དགོས།
།ཆེ་བ་རང་གནས་དགོངས་པ་ཆོས་ཉིད་ཀློང་།
མི་འགྱུར་ལྷུན་གྱིས་གྲུབ་ལ་རྩོལ་མི་བྱེད།
།ཡེ་གཞི་བབས་གཞི་བྱང་ཆུབ་སྙིང་པོའི་གཞི།
།རང་བཞིན་དང་ལས་གཡོས་པ་འགའ་མེད་པས།
།ཀློང་གསལ་རིག་པའི་དོན་ལས་མ་གཡོ་ཞིག
།ཐམས་ཅད་བཞག་པས་འགྲུབ་པའི་རྒྱུ་མཚན་ཡང་།
།མི་འགྱུར་ཀུན་འགྲོ་ཁྱབ་བདག་ཡེ་ཤེས་ལྷ།

The natural state as it is, the nature of phenomena, is vast.
It is natural dharmakaya, the primordial expanse of great equanimity.
It exists in all, but is only experienced by some fortunate ones.
If that continuum is left as it is, it will be naturally accomplished.
All-pervading, self-luminous, spontaneously accomplished,
Sambhogakaya exists in all, but only some can perceive it.
If whatever appears is left alone, without endeavor, it will be visible.
Unobstructed display, all-encompassing expanse of nirmanakaya,
Exists in all, but only when it arises is it evident.
Wish-fulfilling qualities, buddha activities, and miraculous magic,
Do not exist elsewhere but in self-realization, the pure expanse.
As with water and sediment, natural purity appears when they are left alone.
By searching, primordially pure phenomena will not be found.
Perfect enlightenment is clear in the self-originated expanse.
Already actualized, it need not be accomplished now.
The great, self-existing principle is the expanse of the nature of phenomena.
Do not strive for what is unchanging and spontaneously accomplished!
The primordial ground, the natural ground, the ground of perfect essence,
Is unmoved from the continuum of self-nature,
So do not move from the meaning of the clear expanse of awareness!
The reason why everything is accomplished when it is left alone
Is because it is the unchanging and all-pervading universal lord;

།སྐུ་ལྷ་གསུང་ལྷ་ཐུགས་ལྷ་ཡོན་ཏན་ལྷ།
།ཕྲིན་ལས་ལྷ་སྟེ་དང་པོའི་སངས་རྒྱས་ཀྱང་།
།ཐོག་མཐའ་མེད་པའི་ཀློང་འདིར་ལྷུན་གྲུབ་པས།
།གཞན་དུ་མ་འཚོལ་རང་བཞིན་ཡེ་ནས་གྲུབ།
།སངས་རྒྱས་ཀུན་གྱི་ཆོས་སྐུ་བྱང་ཆུབ་ཀྱང་།
།མི་འགྱུར་མཉམ་པའི་དོན་ལས་གཞན་དུ་མེད།
།དེ་ཡང་རང་བྱུང་དང་འདིར་ལྷུན་གྲུབ་པས།
།མ་ཚོལ་མ་སྒྲུབས་རེ་དོགས་ལྷུན་གྱིས་ཞོག
།སེམས་ཅན་ཀུན་གྱི་རང་བྱུང་ཡེ་ཤེས་ཀྱང་།
།མ་བྱས་མ་བཙལ་ཆོས་སྐུར་ལྷུན་གྲུབ་པས།
།སྤང་བླང་མ་འཛིན་ཆོས་དབྱིངས་དང་འདིར་ཞོག
།མི་གཡོ་མི་བསམ་ལྷུན་མཉམ་ངོ་བོ་ལ།
།མ་བྱས་དོན་གྲུབ་གཞི་ཀློང་ཡངས་པ་ཡིན།
།མི་འགྱུར་ཀུན་འགྲོ་སྐུ་དང་ཡེ་ཤེས་བདག
།རྒྱལ་ཐབས་སྤྱི་བླུགས་རང་བྱུང་ཆེན་པོའི་དབང་།
།སྣང་སྲིད་སྣོད་བཅུད་ཡེ་གྲོལ་ལྷུན་གྲུབ་པས།
།བྱ་རྩོལ་མི་དགོས་རང་བཞིན་ལྷུན་གྱིས་གྲུབ།
།ཐམས་ཅད་ཀུན་གྲུབ་ལྷུན་གྲུབ་ཆེན་པོར་རྒྱས།

།ཆོས་དབྱིངས་རིན་པོ་ཆེའི་མཛོད་ལས། །ཐམས་ཅད་བྱང་ཆུབ་ཀྱི་སེམས་སུ་ཡེ་ནས་ལྷུན་གྱིས་གྲུབ་པར་བསྟན་པའི་ལེའུ་སྟེ་བདུན་པའོ།།

The five primordial wisdoms, and the five aspects each of enlightened body, speech, mind, qualities, and activity,

Are the first Buddha,[65] which is also spontaneously accomplished

In the expanse which is free from beginning or end.

Therefore, do not search elsewhere. Your true nature is primordially accomplished.

The perfect dharmakaya of all the buddhas

Is also none other than the meaning of changeless equanimity;

And since it is also spontaneously accomplished in this self-originated continuum,

Don't search. Don't strive. Spontaneously abandon hope and fear!

The self-originated, primordial wisdom of all sentient beings

Is also uncreated, unsought for, spontaneously accomplished in dharmakaya,

So do not be attached to rejecting or accepting. Remain in the continuum of phenomenal space.

The unmoving, unthinking essence of spontaneous evenness,

Accomplished without striving, is the vast expanse of the ground.

The unchanging and all-pervading lord of the kayas and primordial wisdoms,

Victorious method, crown anointment, the great self-originated empowerment,

The primordial liberation of appearance and existence, the universe and its inhabitants, is spontaneously present;

So it is naturally, spontaneously accomplished, without effort or endeavor.

All and everything is accomplished, blossoming in the great spontaneous accomplishment.

From *The Precious Treasury of Phenomenal Space*, demonstrating that everything is primordially and spontaneously accomplished in compassionate mind, the seventh chapter, is completed.

།ཐམས་ཅད་དབྱིངས་གཅིག་རང་བྱུང་ཡེ་ཤེས་ལ།
།གཉིས་སུ་མེད་པ་ངོ་བོའི་འདུག་ཚུལ་ཏེ།
།གཉིས་སྣང་མ་འགགས་རྩལ་ལས་རོལ་པར་ཤར།
།སྣང་བཏགས་གཉིས་མེད་བྱང་ཆུབ་སེམས་ཞེས་བྱ།
།འཕོ་འགྱུར་མེད་པའི་རིག་པ་བྱང་ཆུབ་ལ།
།སྤྱངས་ཐོབ་མེད་པའི་སྣང་སྲིད་འཁོར་འདས་ཤར།
།གཟུང་འཛིན་མེད་པའི་རྣལ་འབྱོར་ངོ་ཁ་ལ།
།མེད་ལ་སྣང་འདི་ཡ་མཚན་དགོད་པོ་འཚོར།
།སྣང་བར་མེད་ལ་སྣ་ཚོགས་སྣང་བར་ཤར།
།སྟོང་པར་མེད་ལ་མཐའ་དབུས་ཁྱབ་པར་གདལ།
།གཟུང་འཛིན་མེད་ལ་ང་བདག་སོ་སོར་ཞེན།
།གཞི་རྩ་མེད་ལ་ཚེ་རབས་བརྒྱུད་མར་སྣང་།
།དགག་སྒྲུབ་མེད་ལ་བདེ་སྡུག་བླང་དོར་བྱེད།
།ཕར་བལྟས་སྐྱི་འགྲོའི་སྣང་བ་མཚར་རེ་ཆེ།
།མི་བདེན་བདེན་པར་ཞེན་པས་བདེན་བདེན་འདྲ།
།མ་འཁྲུལ་འཁྲུལ་པར་ཞེན་པས་འཁྲུལ་འཁྲུལ་འདྲ།
།ངེས་མེད་ངེས་པར་བཟུང་བས་ངེས་ངེས་འདྲ།
།ཡིན་མིན་ཡིན་པར་བཟུང་བས་ཡིན་ཡིན་འདྲ།
།མི་འཐད་འཐད་པར་བཟུང་བས་འཐད་འཐད་འདྲ།

8

From *The Precious Treasury of Phenomenal Space*, showing how compassionate mind has no duality, the eighth chapter.

Everything in one space, self-originated primordial wisdom, is free from duality,
And that is the natural way.
The appearance of duality is ceaseless display arising from the potential.
With neither appearance nor labeling, it is known as compassionate mind.
As to perfect awareness, which is free from transformation and change,
Appearance and existence of samsara and nirvana arise without accepting or rejecting.
Present to a yogin who has no grasper and grasped,
This appearance of what does not exist is so amazing that it is laughable!
There is nothing to appearance; nonetheless, variety arises as appearance.
There is nothing to emptiness; nonetheless, it widely pervades from center to border.
There is no existence of grasper and grasped; nevertheless, the self is grasped as an individual identity.
There is no basic root; nevertheless, a succession of lives appears.
There is nothing to negate or assert; nevertheless, happiness and suffering are accepted and rejected.
Looking outward, the appearance of sentient beings is a great surprise!
By attachment to what is untrue as true, it seems to be truly true.
By attachment to non-delusion as delusion, it seems to be truly deluded.
By attachment to what is not certain as certain, it seems to be certainly certain.
By grasping to what is not so as so, it seems to be very much so.
By grasping to the unsuitable as suitable, it seems to be truly suitable.

།སྣ་ཚོགས་ཅོལ་ཆུང་ཡུལ་གྱིས་སེམས་ཁྲིད་ནས།
།དོན་མེད་རིག་པ་སྐད་ཅིག་བརྒྱུད་མར་མཐུད།
།ཉིན་ཞག་ཟླ་བ་ལོ་དང་མི་ཚེ་འདས།
།གཉིས་མེད་གཉིས་སུ་བཟུང་བས་འགྲོ་བ་བསླུས།
།རྣལ་འབྱོར་དག་པའི་སེམས་ལ་ཚུར་བལྟས་པས།
།རྟེན་གཞི་མེད་པའི་རིག་པ་མིང་དང་བྲལ།
།མཚོན་བརྗོད་མ་མཐོང་ལྟ་སྒོམ་ཁྲིགས་ཆགས་བུད།
།ཁྱལ་བ་ལྷུག་པ་ཡངས་པ་ཁྱམ་གདལ་བས།
།ཉམས་ལེན་མ་ཤེས་ཐུན་མཚམས་ཕྱོགས་རིས་མེད།
།ཐམས་ཅད་རྒྱུ་ཡན་ཁྱམ་ཁྱམ་བར་མཚམས་བྲལ།
།ལུས་དང་ཡུལ་དང་སྣང་བའི་གཏད་མེད་པར།
།ནམ་མཁའི་ཀློང་ཡངས་མཉམ་པར་ཁྱམ་གདལ་བས།
།ནང་གི་ཆོས་ཞེས་བདག་ཏུ་འཛིན་པ་མེད།
།ཕྱི་རོལ་སྣང་བའི་ཡུལ་ལ་ཕར་བལྟས་པས།
།ཐམས་ཅད་སང་སེང་འལ་འོལ་ཟང་མ་ཐལ།
།ར་རི་ཟབ་ཟེབ་གཟའ་གཏད་ཆོས་དང་བྲལ།
།སྣང་གྲགས་དྲན་རིག་སྐྱོང་ཚོར་སྤྱར་བཞིན་མེད།
།འདི་ཅི་རང་བཞིན་སྐྱོན་པའི་སྣང་བའམ།
།རྨི་ལམ་ནང་བཞིན་རང་ལ་དགོད་པོ་འཆོར།
།དགྲ་གཉེན་ཆགས་སྡང་ཉེ་རིང་འདུ་ཤེས་བྲལ།
།ཉིན་མཚན་རིས་མེད་མཉམ་པར་ཁྱམ་གཅིག་པས།
།དམིགས་གཏད་མཚན་མར་འཛིན་པའི་འཁོར་བ་སངས།

The mind, led by various silly things,
Pointlessly links instantaneous awareness into a succession.
The days, months, years, and human lives pass by.
By grasping to non-duality as duality, sentient beings have been deceived.
Looking inward to the pure natural mind, groundless awareness is free from labels.
Without finding expressions or characterizations, structured view and meditation drop away.
The evenly level, naturally relaxed, extensively vast is completely pervasive.
So, with no practice to be found, one is without partiality about sessions and breaks.
Everything is at ease, completely even, beyond interruption.
Without reference point of body, object, or appearance,
The wide expanse of the sky is completely and evenly pervasive,
So there are no so-called inner phenomena that could be grasped as a self.
By looking outward to external objects of appearance,
Directly present, clear yet elusive,
Without reference points of faulty and hollow phenomena,
Appearance, sound, memories, awareness, experience, and emotions are not as they were before.
What is this? Is it appearance of the nature of madness?
Or is it really a dream? It is truly laughable!
Free from perception of enemy or friend, attachment or aversion, closeness or distance,
There is no partiality to day or night, equally complete in one.
So one is awakened from samsara, grasping to characteristics as reference points.

།རང་བྱུང་ཡེ་ཤེས་དང་ཤེས་མི་རྟོག་པས།
།སླང་དོར་སྤང་གཉེན་གཟེབ་ལས་འདས་པ་ཡིན།
།འདི་ལྟར་རྟོགས་ན་གཉིས་མེད་ཡེ་ཤེས་ཏེ།
།རང་བྱུང་ཀུན་ཏུ་བཟང་པོའི་དགོངས་པར་ཕྱིན།
།ལྡོག་པའི་གནས་མེད་ཟད་པའི་སར་ཕྱིན་ཏེ།
།རང་བྱུང་དང་ནས་མཉམ་ཉིད་མ་རྟོགས་པར།
།གཉིས་མེད་ཉིད་ཅེས་ཚིག་ལ་མངོན་ཞེན་ནས།
།ཅི་ཡང་མི་དམིགས་ཡིད་དཔྱོད་གདེང་འཆའ་བ།
།ལོག་རྟོག་ཉིད་དེ་མ་རིག་མུན་པའི་གློང་།
།དེ་ཕྱིར་རང་བྱུང་འཕོ་འགྱུར་མེད་པ་ལ།
།བསམ་རྫོགས་རྒྱལ་པོ་གཉིས་སུ་མེད་པར་སྦྱོང་།
།ཁམས་གསུམ་ཡོངས་གྲོལ་འཁོར་འདས་གཉིས་མེད་དོན།
།རང་བཞིན་ཁོང་ནས་རང་ཤར་ཆོས་སྐུའི་རྫོང་།
།མཁའ་ལྟར་རྣམ་དག་དཔེ་ལས་འདས་པ་འབྱུང་།
།འདི་དང་འདི་ཞེས་སོ་སོར་ཞེན་པའི་བར།
།གཉིས་སུ་གནས་པས་རང་གཞན་འཁྲུལ་པའི་གཟེབ།
།གང་ཚེ་འདི་ཞེས་ཐ་དད་རིས་མེད་ཅིང་།
།ཐམས་ཅད་ཕྱམ་མཉམ་དམིགས་གཏད་མེད་པ་ན།།
།གཉིས་མེད་རྟོགས་ཞེས་རྡོ་རྗེ་སེམས་དཔས་གསུངས།

།ཆོས་དབྱིངས་རིན་པོ་ཆེའི་མཛོད་ལས། །བྱང་ཆུབ་ཀྱི་སེམས་ལ་གཉིས་སུ་མེད་པར་བསྟན་པའི་ལེའུ་སྟེ་བརྒྱད་པའོ།།

By not conceptualizing "the continuum of self-originated primordial wisdom,"
One is not trapped by accepting or rejecting, antidotes or renouncing.
If there is realization like this, there is non-dual primordial wisdom,
Having reached the principle of self-originated All-Good,
With no place to turn back, having gone to the field of exhaustion.
However, not realizing equanimity in the continuum of natural origination,
Becoming attached to the word "non-duality" itself,
And placing confidence in the mental analysis of "not conceiving of anything at all,"
Constitutes wrong understanding itself, the expanse of dark ignorance.
Nevertheless, there is self-origination, free from transformation and change.
The wish-fulfilled king is purified in non-duality.
The totally liberated three realms are the meaning of the non-duality of samsara and nirvana;
From within the nature, the self-arising dharmakaya fortress,
There arises complete sky-like purity, in a manner beyond example.
As long as there is attachment to so-called "this" and "that" individually,
By existing as two, self and other are trapped in the cage of delusion.
When there is no distinction of "this" as separate,
When everything is completely equal, without reference point,
As said by Vajrasattva, "This is non-dual realization."

From *The Precious Treasury of Phenomenal Space*, showing how compassionate mind has no duality, the eighth chapter, is completed.

།རང་བཞིན་ཡངས་པ་ཆེན་པོའི་ཀློང་གཅིག་ལ།
།མཁའ་མཉམ་བྱང་ཆུབ་སེམས་ཀྱི་གནམ་གཟེར་ནི།
།གནད་དུ་དྲིལ་ཏེ་བསྟུད་དུ་སྦྱུང་བ་ནི།
།ཆེ་བའི་ཆེ་བ་ཀུན་བཟང་ཡངས་པའི་ཐུགས།
།རང་གི་ངོ་བོས་སྤྱི་རྒྱ་རླབས་ཀྱིས་བཅད།
།ཀློང་ཆེན་གཅིག་ལ་རྟོགས་དང་མ་རྟོགས་དང་།
།གྲོལ་དང་མ་གྲོལ་གཉིས་མེད་མཉམ་པ་ཆེ།
།སྒོ་ངའི་ནང་ནས་འདབ་གཤོག་རྒྱས་པའི་བྱ།
།རྒྱ་དང་བྲལ་བས་ནམ་མཁའི་ཀློང་ན་གནས།
།ཀླུ་རྣམས་ཟིལ་གནོན་གཡངས་ཤུགས་ཀྱིས་ཆོད།
།ཐེག་པའི་ཡང་རྩེ་རྡོ་རྗེ་སྙིང་པོ་ཡང་།
།ཇི་བཞིན་རྟོགས་པའི་རྣལ་འབྱོར་སྐལ་བ་ཅན།
།ཐེག་དམན་ཟིལ་གནོན་འཁོར་བའི་གཡང་ས་ཆོད།
།ཀུན་གྲོལ་མཉམ་པ་ཆེན་པོར་གནས་པ་དེ།
།རྒྱུ་འབྲས་རྩོལ་སྒྲུབ་ཅན་ལ་མི་རིགས་ཀྱང་།
།ཐེག་མཆོག་མི་གཡོ་མཉམ་པའི་དོན་ལ་འཐད།
།ཐམས་ཅད་བདེ་ཆེན་མཁའ་མཉམ་ཆོས་སྐུའི་ཀློང་།
།ཆོས་སྐུའི་ཀློང་དུ་མ་གྲོལ་འགའ་ཡང་མེད།
།ཆོས་ཉིད་རང་བཞེངས་རྡོ་རྗེ་སྙིང་པོའི་སྐུ།

9

From *The Precious Treasury of Phenomenal Space*, showing that all phenomena are free from limitation in the expanse of compassionate mind, the ninth chapter.

As to the single great naturally vast expanse,
The nail of space, equal to the sky, is compassionate mind;
The summation of the key points and distillation of the essence
Is the vast heart of the All-Good, the greatest of the great.
The essential nature forcefully envelops the entire environment.
The single great expanse has neither realization nor non-realization;
Therefore, without the duality of liberation and non-liberation, it is the great equality.
The bird[66] that has fully grown its wings and feathers inside the egg,
When freed from confinement, abides in the expanse of the sky,
Suppresses the nagas by splendor, and powerfully crosses abysses.
Likewise, the fortunate yogin who realizes what is,
The peak of the vehicles, the indestructible essence,
Also suppresses by splendor lesser paths and cuts off the abyss of samsara.
This liberation of everything, abiding in the great equanimity,
Is unsuitable for those who strive and endeavor with cause and effect;
However, it accords with the truth of equanimity, the unwavering, the supreme vehicle.
All is great bliss, equal to space, the expanse of dharmakaya.
In the expanse of dharmakaya, there is nothing that is not liberated.
The naturally manifest nature of phenomena is the vajra essence body.

།བག་ཆགས་ལུས་ལ་སྙིང་པོའི་རྩལ་རྫོགས་ཏེ།
།སྐྱེ་ཤི་བར་དོ་སྲིད་པའི་ལུས་པོར་ནས།
།རིག་པ་གཅིག་པུ་ཀུན་དང་དབྱེར་མེད་ཅིང་།
།ལྷུན་གྲུབ་ས་ལ་རྒྱལ་བའི་སྲིད་ཟིན་ནས།
།རྒྱུ་ཆད་མེད་པར་སྤྲུལ་པ་འབྱུང་བ་དང་།
།ཐོགས་པ་མེད་པར་ཀུན་ལ་འཇུག་པ་ནི།
།ཐུར་མེད་ལྷུང་ཞེན་རྣལ་འབྱོར་སྤྱོད་ཡུལ་ཏེ།
།དམན་པའི་ཐེག་པ་ཀུན་ལ་མི་རིགས་ཀྱང་།
།ཨ་ཏིས་རིགས་པར་སྟོན་པ་འབྲས་བུའི་གནད།
།སྐྱེ་མེད་སྐྱེ་བའི་ཆོ་འཕྲུལ་འབྱུང་བ་ལ།
།རྒྱུ་འབྲས་མཚན་མར་འཛིན་པ་འཁྲུལ་པའི་བློ།
།ཨ་ཏིས་རྒྱུ་རྐྱེན་མེད་པར་བསྟན་པ་སྟེ།
།འོག་མ་རྣམས་ལ་མི་རིགས་རིགས་པའི་གནད།
།སངས་རྒྱས་སེམས་ཅན་དགོངས་སྤྱོད་དབྱེར་མེད་ལ།
།འཁོར་འདས་གཉིས་སུ་འཛིན་པ་འཁྲུལ་པའི་བློ།
།ཨ་ཏིས་གཉིས་སུ་མེད་པར་བསྟན་པ་དེ།
།འོག་མ་རྣམས་ལ་མི་རིགས་རིགས་པའི་གནད།
།རྟོགས་དང་མ་རྟོགས་མེད་པར་གྲོལ་བ་ལ།
།རྟོགས་ནས་གྲོལ་བར་འདོད་པ་ཉམས་པའི་དགྲ།
།ཨ་ཏིས་མཉམ་ཉིད་གཅིག་ཏུ་བསྟན་པ་དེ།
།འོག་མ་རྣམས་ལ་མི་རིགས་རིགས་པའི་གནད།

As to the body of habitual inclinations, the energy of the essence is fully perfected.
When abandoning the existing body of birth, death, and the bardo,
Awareness is inseparable from everything.
When victorious rule in the land of spontaneous accomplishment has been established,
Without extent or partiality, emanations arise,
Engaging in everything without hindrance.
This is the style of non-activity of the wind-riding yogin.
This is inappropriate for all the lesser vehicles,
But Ati shows it is appropriate, it is the essence of fruition.
The unborn arises as the miracles of birth.
Grasping cause and effect as real characteristics is deluded thought.
By Ati it is taught that there are neither causes nor conditions.
What is inappropriate for the lower ones is the truly appropriate here.
The intentions and activities of buddhas and sentient beings are inseparable.
Grasping samsara and nirvana as separate is confused mind.
When in Ati these are taught to be non-dual,
What is inappropriate for the lower ones is the truly appropriate here.
Liberation has neither realization nor non-realization,
So those who think they will be liberated after realization are inferior foes.
By Ati showing a single equanimity,
What is inappropriate for the lower ones is the truly appropriate here.
Maintaining that inexpressible realization is unachievable
Without reliance on means of symbolic expression is the thought of a fool.
As Ati teaches inseparability from the absolute,
What is inappropriate for the lower ones is the truly appropriate here.

།མཚོན་བྱེད་ཐབས་ཀྱི་ཁྱད་པར་མ་བསྟེན་པར།
།བརྗོད་མེད་རྟོགས་པར་མི་འདོད་བླུན་པོའི་བློ།
།ཨ་ཏིས་དོན་དམ་དབྱེར་མེད་བསྟན་པ་དེ།
།འོག་མ་རྣམས་ལ་མི་རིགས་རིགས་པའི་གནད།
།རྫོགས་ཆེན་ཡེ་གདལ་གཏིང་མཐའ་མེད་པ་ལ།
།ཐུག་པ་མེད་ཅེས་ཟེར་བ་བླུན་པོའི་བློ།
།ཨ་ཏིས་སྨུ་མེད་ཆིག་ཆོད་བསྟན་པ་དེ།
།འོག་མའི་བློ་ཡུལ་མི་རིགས་རིགས་པའི་གནད།
།ཐིག་ལེ་གཅིག་ལ་རྒྱ་མཚན་གོ་བཟློག་པས།
།འབྲས་བུ་རེ་དོགས་ཆོད་དེ་མཁའ་དང་མཉམ།
།ཡངས་སོ་ཆེ་འོ་མཁའ་མཉམ་རྒྱལ་བའི་ཐུགས།
།སྦྱངས་ཐོབ་མེད་དེ་ཐིག་ལེ་གཅིག་གི་ཀློང་།
།ཡེ་ནས་གྲོལ་ལོ་རྟོགས་དང་མ་རྟོགས་མེད།
།རྣལ་འབྱོར་མཁའ་མཉམ་བྱ་བྲལ་ལམ་དུ་བདེ།
།ཡེ་སངས་རྒྱས་པའི་རིག་པ་ཡུལ་མེད་འདི།
།འཁོར་བར་མི་འཁྲམ་འཁྲུལ་གཞི་ཀུན་ལས་འདས།
།སུ་ཡང་མ་འཁྲུལ་འཁྲུལ་པའི་གནས་མེད་དེ།
།ཐམས་ཅད་ཆོས་དབྱིངས་ཀློང་གསལ་གཅིག་གི་ངང་།
།སྤྱ་ཕྱི་རིས་མེད་མཁའ་མཉམ་ཡངས་པ་ཉིད།
།ཡེ་བབས་ལྷུན་གྲུབ་འཁོར་བ་གདོད་ནས་དག
།གྲོལ་བར་མི་འཚུག་མྱ་ངན་འདས་མི་ལེན།
།མི་འགྱུར་ཀློང་ཆེན་འཁོར་འདས་ཡོད་མ་མྱོང་།

As to the primordially expansive Great Perfection, limitless in depth,
To say it cannot be reached is the thought of a fool.
Ati teaches all-sufficient boundlessness.
What is inappropriate for lesser thought is truly appropriate here.
In the single essence all reasoning is eliminated;
Therefore, one is free from hope, fear, and fruition, equal to the sky.
It is vast. It is great. The Mind of the Conqueror is equal to the sky:
Without attaining or abandoning, the expanse of a single essence,
Primordially liberated, without realization or non-realization.
The yogin, equal to the sky, free from activity, is happy on the path!
This awareness without object, primordially awakened,
Will not roam in samsara, free from the ground of every delusion.
No one has been deluded; there is no place for delusion.
Everything is in the continuum of a single clear expanse of phenomenal space.
There is no distinction of earlier and later, vastness itself, equal to the sky,
The primordial state, spontaneously accomplished, samsara is pure from the beginning.
Not entering into liberation, without accepting nirvana,
This is the changeless great expanse, where samsara and nirvana do not exist at all.

།འདི་ལ་སྤྱངས་ཐོབ་རེ་དོགས་མི་དམིགས་ཤིང་།
།གདོད་ནས་བྱང་ཆུབ་གཞི་ཀློང་ཡངས་པ་ཆེ།
།ཐམས་ཅད་མིང་ཙམ་དོན་ལ་མཚོན་བརྗོད་འདས།
།གྲོལ་དང་འཁྲུལ་མེད་འཁོར་འདས་ལ་ཟློས་པས།
།སུ་ཡང་མ་རྩོལ་བཅོས་བསྒྱུར་མ་བྱེད་ཅིག
།ཡངས་དོག་མཐོ་དམན་མེད་པའི་རིག་པ་ལ།
།རྒྱུ་ཆད་ཕྱོགས་ལྷུང་མེད་ཀྱིས་དམིགས་གཏད་ཤོལ།
།བྱ་བྱེད་འགྲོ་འོང་མེད་པའི་རིག་པ་ལ།
།དུས་དང་གཉེན་པོ་མེད་ཀྱིས་འཛིན་རྩོལ་ཞོག
།ཆེད་དུ་དམིགས་པ་ཡོད་ན་འཆིང་བའི་རྒྱུ།
།གང་ལའང་གཏད་འཛིན་མ་འཆའ་ཀློང་ལ་ཐོང་།
།ཆོས་ཀུན་ཡེ་ནས་གྲོལ་རུང་མ་གྲོལ་རུང་།
།གནས་ལུགས་རང་བཞིན་དག་རུང་མ་དག་རུང་།
།སེམས་ཉིད་སྤྲོས་དང་བྲལ་རུང་མ་བྲལ་རུང་།
།གཉུག་མའི་གཤིས་ལ་གྲུབ་རུང་མ་གྲུབ་རུང་།
།འཁོར་འདས་རང་བཞིན་གཉིས་རུང་མི་གཉིས་རུང་།
།བསམ་བརྗོད་ཀུན་ལས་འདས་རུང་མ་འདས་རུང་།
།དགག་སྒྲུབ་འཁྲུལ་པ་ཞིག་རུང་མ་ཞིག་རུང་།
།རྟོགས་པའི་ལྟ་བ་རྟོགས་རུང་མ་རྟོགས་རུང་།
།ཆོས་ཉིད་དོན་ལ་བསྒོམས་རུང་མ་བསྒོམས་རུང་།
།བླང་དོར་མེད་པས་སྤྱོད་རུང་མ་སྤྱོད་རུང་།

Here, without conception of hope or fear, abandoning or attaining,
This is the primordially perfect, great vast fundamental expanse.
Everything is just a label; in fact, reality is beyond indication or expression.
There is no liberation or delusion, since the passes of samsara and nirvana have been crossed.
No one should endeavor! Do not change or fabricate!
As to awareness without wide or narrow, high or low,
By being without partiality or bias, discard reference points.
Awareness with no doing or anything to be done, no coming or going,
Is without time or antidotes, so abandon grasping and endeavor.
If there is particular intention, it is the cause of being bound.
Don't hold a focus, let go into evenness!
It doesn't really matter whether or not all phenomena are liberated from the beginning.
It doesn't really matter whether or not the intrinsic nature is pure.
It doesn't really matter whether or not mind itself is free from elaboration.
It doesn't really matter whether or not the innate nature is accomplished.
It doesn't really matter whether or not the nature of samsara and nirvana is duality.
It doesn't really matter whether or not all thoughts and expressions are transcended.
It doesn't really matter whether or not the delusion of affirmation and negation is shattered.
It doesn't really matter whether or not the view of realization is realized.
It doesn't really matter whether or not one meditates on the meaning of the nature of phenomena.
Since there is no accepting or rejecting, it doesn't really matter whether or not one acts.

།གནས་ལུགས་འབྲས་བུ་གྲུབ་རུང་མ་གྲུབ་རུང་།
།ས་དང་ལམ་རྣམས་བགྲོད་རུང་མ་བགྲོད་རུང་།
།སྒྲིབ་པ་ཀུན་དང་བྲལ་རུང་མ་བྲལ་རུང་།
།བསྐྱེད་རྫོགས་ཆོས་ཉིད་རྫོགས་རུང་མ་རྫོགས་རུང་།
།ཐར་པའི་འབྲས་བུ་ཐོབ་རུང་མ་ཐོབ་རུང་།
།འགྲོ་དྲུག་འཁོར་བར་འཁྱམས་རུང་མ་འཁྱམས་རུང་།
།རང་བཞིན་ལྷུན་གྱིས་གྲུབ་རུང་མ་གྲུབ་རུང་།
།རྟག་ཆད་གཉིས་འཛིན་བཅིངས་རུང་མ་བཅིངས་རུང་།
།ཆོས་ཉིད་དགོངས་པར་སླེབ་རུང་མ་སླེབ་རུང་།
།གོང་མའི་རྗེས་སུ་སྙོགས་རུང་མ་སྙོགས་རུང་།
།གནམ་ས་འདྲེ་ལྡོག་སྣང་བ་ཅི་ཤར་ཡང་།
།ཁྱལ་བ་ལྷུག་པ་གཞི་མེད་ཟང་ཀ་མ།
།གཏད་མེད་ཟང་ཟིང་བན་བུན་ཆལ་མ་ཆོལ།
།རི་དྭགས་གཉིས་མེད་སྨྱོན་པའི་དང་རྒྱལ་ཅན།
།ལྷ་སྒོམ་རིས་མེད་ཆེད་འཛིན་འདོད་བློ་ཞིག
།ཞེ་འདོད་འཁྲིས་མེད་འདི་ཞེས་རྩོལ་སྒྲུབ་མེད།
།གང་བྱུང་བྱུང་ལ་གང་སྣང་སྣང་དུ་ཆུག
།གང་ཤར་ཤར་ལ་གང་ཡིན་ཡིན་དུ་ཆུག
།གང་ཡང་ཡིན་ལ་གང་ཡང་མིན་དུ་ཆུག

It doesn't really matter whether or not the fruition, the natural state, is accomplished.

It doesn't really matter whether or not the grounds and paths are traversed.

It doesn't really matter whether or not one is free from all the obscurations.

It doesn't really matter whether or not the natures of generation and completion are perfected.

It doesn't really matter whether or not the fruit of salvation is attained.

It doesn't really matter whether or not the beings of the six realms are wandering in samsara.

It doesn't really matter whether or not there is natural, spontaneous accomplishment.

It doesn't really matter whether or not one is fettered by dualistic grasping of eternalism and nihilism.

It doesn't really matter whether or not one has reached the principle of the nature of phenomena.

It doesn't really matter whether or not one is able to follow the forefathers.

Whatever appearances happen, such as heaven and earth seemingly turning upside-down,

All is at ease, even, groundless, just ordinary.

Without duality of hope and fear, one has the natural manner of a madman,

Without reference point, disorderly, scattered, incoherent.

Without partiality to view or meditation, the desiring mind that clings to particulars disintegrates.

Without heartfelt desire, without hesitation, there is no "this" to try to accomplish.

Whatever happens happens; whatever appears, just let it appear.

Whatever arises arises; whatever is, just let it be as it is.

Let whatever is be so; and whatever is not, just let it be so.

།ཀུན་སྤྱོད་ངེས་མེད་རིག་པ་ཐོད་རྒྱལ་དང་།
།ཆོས་དང་ཆོས་མིན་རྩིས་གཞི་འགག་མེད་པས།
།གཏད་མེད་ཟང་ཀ་གྲུབ་མཐའི་གཟེབ་ལས་འདས།
།ཟ་འཆག་ཉལ་འདུག་ཉིན་ཞག་ཕྱམ་གདལ་བས།
།རང་བཞིན་ཆོས་ཉིད་མཉམ་པའི་ངང་ཉིད་དེ།
།མཆོད་པའི་ལྷ་མེད་བརྟུང་བའི་འདྲེ་ཡང་མེད།
།སྒོམ་པའི་ཆོས་མེད་ཐ་མལ་རང་དགའི་ངང་།
།མ་བཅོས་རྒྱལ་པོ་སླེམས་མེད་ཕྱམ་གཅིག་པས།
།ཕྱལ་བ་ལྷུག་པ་ལྷུན་གྲུབ་གཅིག་པུ་ཉིད།
།མ་བྱས་ཡེ་ཟིན་རྩོལ་སྒྲུབ་བྲལ་བས་བདེ།
།ལྟ་བའི་གཞི་མེད་སྒོམ་པའི་ངང་མེད་ལ།
།སྤྱོད་པའི་ཆོས་མེད་བསྒྲུབ་འདོད་འབྲས་བུ་མེད།
།ཐམས་ཅད་རིས་མེད་མཉམ་པར་ཕྱམ་གདལ་བས།
།བྱ་རྩོལ་མ་དགོས་ཡངས་དོག་མེད་པར་བདེ།
།སྐྱོན་པ་མེད་པས་སྒྲུབ་བློའི་ཆོས་ཟད་དེ།
།སྤང་བྱ་མེད་པས་གཉེན་པོའི་འཆིང་ཞེན་འདས།
།གང་ཡིན་ཀུན་ཡིན་ཡིན་མིན་འགག་མེད་པས།
།གང་སྣང་གང་ཤར་འདེམ་ཀ་མེད་པར་གྲོལ།
།མ་གྲོལ་ཡེ་གྲོལ་རང་གྲོལ་ཆོས་མེད་པས།
།ཕྱམ་གཅིག་གཏད་མེད་ལ་བཟླའི་ཆོས་ལས་འདས།

With no certain behavior, in the continuum of direct awareness,

There is no basis for distinguishing what is and is not the teaching.

Just natural, without purpose, beyond traps of doctrine,

Whether eating or walking, whether sleeping or sitting, the whole day is evenly pervasive,

So that the self-nature of phenomena is in the continuum of equanimity itself.

There are no gods to make offerings to and also no demons to subjugate.

There is no Dharma to meditate on, just the continuum of ordinary natural happiness.

The unfabricated king, without arrogance, is an overarching unity;

Therefore, remaining in evenness, being at ease, spontaneously accomplished, and single in nature,

Without activity, primordially captured; blissful, since it is free from effort and achievement.

There is no ground for the view and no continuum to meditate on.

There is no Dharma of action. There is no desire to attain a result.

Everything is impartial, an evenly pervading equanimity,

Blissful, without wide or narrow, so that there is no need for effort or endeavor.

Free from aspiration, thoughts of achieving are exhausted.

There is nothing to abandon; the grasping entanglements of antidotes are transcended.

Whatever there is, that is everything. There is nothing "to be or not to be."

Whatever appears, whatever arises, is choicelessly liberated.

There are no phenomena of non-liberation, primordial liberation, or self-liberation.

There is an overarching unity, without goal, beyond any phenomenon to cross the pass.

།ཀློང་ཡངས་ཀློང་ཡངས་ཀློང་ཆེན་ཡངས་པའི་ངང་།
།ཀློང་ཆེན་རབ་འབྱམས་ཀློང་གསལ་ཀློང་འབྱམས་པས།
།ཀློང་གཅིག་གཉིས་མེད་བདེ་ཀློང་འཁྱིལ་བ་ནི།
།སྣ་ཚོགས་རང་གྲོལ་ཆོས་ཉིད་ཟད་སར་ཕྱིན།
།མི་འགྱུར་ལྷུན་གྲུབ་འདུན་མ་ལེགས་པའི་རྟེ།
།བདག་བཞིན་རྗེས་སུ་འཇུག་པའི་འགྲོ་རྣམས་ཀྱང་།
།འདི་བཞིན་ཡེ་འབྱམས་ཀློང་ཆེན་གཅིག་ཏུ་དྲིལ།
།ཀུན་བཟང་ས་ལ་གཏན་སྲིད་ཟིན་པ་ཡིན།

།ཆོས་དབྱིངས་རིན་པོ་ཆེའི་མཛོད་ལས། །ཆོས་ཐམས་ཅད་བྱང་ཆུབ་སེམས་ཀྱི་ཀློང་དུ་ལ་བཟླ་བར་བསྟན་པའི་ལེའུ་དགུ་པའོ།།

Vast expanse, vast expanse, the continuum of great, vast expanse;

Great universal expanse,[67] luminous expanse, pervasive expanse;

So one single expanse without duality, the swirling blissful expanse,

Is self-liberated variety,[68] which has gone to the ground of exhaustion of the nature of phenomena.

Unchanging, spontaneous accomplishment is the peak of excellent aspirations.

Beings who wish to follow, doing as I did,

Also, in that way, must be enveloped in the single great primordially pervasive expanse.

In the place of All-Good, a permanent kingdom has been forever captured.

From *The Precious Treasury of Phenomenal Space,* showing that all phenomena are free from limitation in the expanse of compassionate mind, the ninth chapter, is completed.

།རང་བཞིན་གདོད་ནས་དག་པའི་བྱང་ཆུབ་སེམས།
།བཏང་གཞག་འགྲོ་འོང་མེད་པའི་ཆོས་ཉིད་ལ།
།བཙལ་བས་མི་འགྲུབ་ཆོས་ཉིད་ནམ་མཁའི་ཀློང་།
།རང་བཞིན་བཞག་པས་འོད་གསལ་ཉི་ཟླ་འཆར།
།ཡུལ་ཀྱང་མི་དགག་སེམས་ཀྱང་མི་གཟུང་བར།
།རང་བཞིན་ལྷུན་གྲུབ་ངང་ལས་མི་གཡོན།
།ཀུན་བཟང་ཡངས་པ་ཆེན་པོའི་དགོངས་པར་ཕྱིན།
།མི་སྤྲོ་མི་བསྡུ་རང་དྭངས་སང་ངེ་བ།
།དྭངས་པའི་རྒྱ་མཚོ་མི་གཡོ་མཉམ་པ་བཞིན།
།ཆོས་ཉིད་གཏིང་གསལ་རང་བྱུང་ཡེ་ཤེས་དང་།
།འབྱུང་འཇུག་རེ་དོགས་བྲལ་བར་གནས་པ་ཡིན།
།ཚིག་གིས་མི་མཚོན་འཇུར་བུའི་སེམས་མེད་པར།
།རང་བབས་གྱིན་འདའ་བཙོས་བསླད་མེད་པ་ནི།
།ཀློང་ཐིམ་ཆོས་ཉིད་མཚན་མ་མེད་པ་སྟེ།
།སྒོམ་དང་བསྒོམ་པར་བྱ་བའི་ཆོས་མེད་པས།
།ཁྲིང་ཀྲོད་རང་ཡན་རང་བྱུང་དགོངས་པར་ཤར།
།སྤྱངས་པས་མི་སྤོང་ཀུན་རྟོག་རིག་པའི་རྩལ།

10

From *The Precious Treasury of Phenomenal Space*, showing that the intention is unmoved from the nature of phenomena, the tenth chapter.

The primordially pure self-nature, compassionate mind,
The nature of phenomena, has no coming or going, sending or receiving;
Therefore, the true nature of phenomena, expanse of space, cannot be accomplished if sought.
By leaving it naturally as it is, the clear light of the sun and moon will arise.
If there is no movement from the continuum of natural, spontaneous accomplishment,
By neither suppressing objects nor fixating mind,
One has gone to the principle of the great vastness, the All-Good.
Without elaborating and dissolving, refreshingly self-clear,
As the clarity of the ocean is even, without fluctuation,
The depth of the nature of phenomena is clear in the continuum of self-originated primordial wisdom.
It abides without originating or engaging, hope or fear.
Without characterization by words and without entangled mind,
The natural ordinary state, without fabrication or adulteration,
Is dissolved in the expanse, the nature of phenomena without characterization.
There is no phenomenon called meditation, no phenomena to meditate on;
So dullness and discursiveness naturally subside, and the principle of self-origination arises.
Thoughts are the energy of awareness. By abandoning, they will not be abandoned.

།ཆོས་ཉིད་ངང་དུ་དབྱེ་བསལ་རིས་མེད་པས།

།བསྒྲུབས་པས་མི་འགྲུབ་ཆོས་ཉིད་དབྱིངས་སུ་ཤར།

།འཁོར་བ་མ་སྤྱངས་རང་བྱུང་ཡེ་ཤེས་སུ།

།ཀློང་ཆེན་རྩལ་གྱི་རྣལ་འབྱོར་དག་པས་མཐོང་།

།ཡེ་ནས་སྣང་སེམས་རང་བབས་ཆོས་ཉིད་ངང་།

།ཏིང་འཛིན་མི་གཡོ་ཆུ་བོའི་རྒྱུན་ཤར་བས།

།རྡོ་རྗེ་རྩེ་མོ་ཀུན་བཟང་ཐུགས་ཀྱི་མཆོག

།ཡངས་པའི་ཆོས་མཆོག་ནམ་མཁའི་མཐའ་དང་མཉམ།

།དབྱེ་བསལ་མེད་པར་ཐམས་ཅད་སྒོམ་པའི་མཆོག

།ཡེ་འབྱམས་རྨད་བྱུང་རྒྱལ་པོར་ལྷུན་གྱིས་གྲུབ།

།ཡེ་ནས་སྤྱི་བླུགས་འོད་གསལ་ཆུ་བོའི་རྒྱུན།

།བཏང་གཞག་མེད་པའི་ངང་འདིར་ལྷུན་གྲུབ་པས།

།འཁོར་འདས་རང་བཞིན་ཆོས་དབྱིངས་དགོངས་པའི་མཆོག

།མི་གཡོ་བརྗོད་འདས་མཁའ་མཉམ་ཀློང་ཆེན་ཉིད།

།འགྲོ་བ་ཀུན་ལ་ཡེ་ནས་བབས་ཀྱིས་གྲུབ།

།བདག་ལས་གཞན་དུ་སྣང་བ་འཁྲུལ་པའི་སེམས།

།བསྒོམ་དང་རྩོལ་བར་འདོད་པ་འཁྲུལ་པའི་སེམས།

།འཁྲུལ་པ་ཆོས་ཉིད་ངང་བཞག་མཉམ་པའི་ཞིང་།

།མི་གཡོ་གདོད་ནས་དག་པའི་རང་བཞིན་ཀློང་།

།བྱ་དང་རྩོལ་མེད་གཞག་དང་མ་བཞག་མེད།

In the continuum of the nature of phenomena, there is no dividing, distinction, or partiality,

So by accomplishing, it will not be accomplished. The nature of phenomena arises in space.

Without abandoning samsara, through the natural enrichment of great expansive energy,

It is seen as self-originated primordial wisdom.

From the beginning, appearance and mind are the continuum of the self-nature, the nature of phenomena.

Unmoving concentration arises like the flow of a river.

The All-Good, indestructible peak, is the supreme mind,

The vast supreme Dharma, equal to the limit of the sky.

Without distinguishing or clearing away, everything is supreme meditation,

Primordially pervasive, spontaneously accomplished as the marvelous king.

From the primordial crown anointment, a river of clear light

Is spontaneously established in this continuum of "not sending" and "not keeping";

So the self-nature of samsara and nirvana is the foremost principle, phenomenal space.

Unmoving, beyond expression, equal to the sky, is the great expanse itself.

From the beginning, it is naturally accomplished within all beings.

Appearance of what is other than the self is confused mind.

Desire to meditate and endeavor is confused mind.

Confusion is the nature of phenomena, and letting it rest in the continuum is the field of equanimity.

The unmoving, natural expanse of primordial purity

Is free from effort and endeavor, without resting or not resting.

།མི་འགྱུར་ལྷུན་གྱིས་གྲུབ་པའི་ཆོས་ཉིད་ལ།
།དམིགས་བསམ་ཚོལ་ཁྲོ་བྲལ་བའི་རང་རིག་གིས།
།ཡང་ཡང་བལྟས་ན་བལྟ་རུ་མེད་པ་མཐོང་།
།བལྟར་མེད་རིག་པ་སྤྱི་བླུགས་ལྟ་བ་ཡིན།
།མ་བསྒོམས་རིག་པ་བཏང་གཞག་བྲལ་བ་ལ།
།ཡང་ཡང་བསྒོམས་ན་བསྒོམ་དུ་མེད་པ་མཐོང་།
།སྒོམ་མེད་རིག་པ་སྤྱི་བླུགས་སྒོམ་པ་ཡིན།
།གཉིས་མེད་བླང་དོར་བྲལ་བའི་གནས་ལུགས་ལ།
།ཡང་ཡང་སྤྱད་ན་སྤྱད་དུ་མེད་པ་མཐོང་།
།སྤྱད་མེད་རིག་པ་སྤྱི་བླུགས་སྤྱོད་པ་ཡིན།
།ཡེ་ཟིན་རེ་དོགས་བྲལ་བའི་ལྷུན་གྲུབ་ལ།
།ཡང་ཡང་བསྒྲུབས་ན་བསྒྲུབ་ཏུ་མེད་པ་མཐོང་།
།བསྒྲུབ་མེད་རིག་པ་སྤྱི་བླུགས་འབྲས་བུ་ཡིན།
།མཉམ་ཉིད་ངང་ལས་ཡུལ་དུ་མི་རྟོག་ཅིང་།
།སེམས་སུ་མི་འཛིན་རེ་དོགས་འབྱུང་འཇུག་ཞི།
།ཡུལ་སེམས་མཉམ་པའི་ངང་དེར་གནས་པ་ནི།
།ཆོས་ཉིད་ཀློང་ལས་ངང་གིས་གཡོས་པ་མེད།
།མཚན་མའི་ཡུལ་ལ་ཡུལ་མེད་སྤྱི་བླུགས་གནས།
།ཡེ་ནས་གཉིས་མེད་རིག་པ་སྤྱི་བླུགས་པས།
།འཁོར་འདས་དབྱེར་མེད་རྫོགས་པ་ཆེན་པོའི་ངང་།
།ཐམས་ཅད་བླང་དོར་མེད་པར་ཕྱམ་གདལ་ལོ།

As to the unchanging, spontaneously accomplished nature of phenomena,
Free from imagination and conceptual processes of seeking,
If one views again and again with self-awareness, one will see that there is nothing to view.
Unviewed awareness is the crown anointment view.
As to non-meditation awareness, free from resting and letting go,
If one meditates again and again, one will see that there is no meditation.
Non-meditation awareness is the crown anointment meditation.
As to non-duality, free from accepting or rejecting, the natural state,
If one acts again and again, one will see non-action.
Non-action awareness is the crown anointment action.
As to primordially achieved, spontaneous accomplishment of freedom from hope and fear,
If one practices again and again, one will see that there is nothing to accomplish.
Unaccomplished awareness is the crown anointment fruition.
In the continuum of equanimity, nothing is apprehended as objects.
Hope, fear, originating, and engaging dissolve, without being grasped as mind.
Remaining in that continuum of equanimity, mind and objects
Are by nature unmoved from the expanse of the nature of phenomena.
There are no objects that are substantial objects. This is the way of the crown anointment.
Non-dual from the beginning, awareness is the crown anointment;
So, in the continuum of the Great Perfection, samsara and nirvana are not differentiated.
Everything, without accepting or rejecting, is evenly pervaded.

།དངོས་དང་དངོས་མེད་དབྱིངས་སུ་མཉམ་པ་དང་།
།སངས་རྒྱས་སེམས་ཅན་དབྱིངས་སུ་མཉམ་པ་དང་།
།ཀུན་རྫོབ་དོན་དམ་དབྱིངས་སུ་མཉམ་པ་དང་།
།སྐྱོན་དང་ཡོན་ཏན་དབྱིངས་སུ་མཉམ་པ་དང་།
།མཐོ་དམན་ཕྱོགས་མཚམས་དབྱིངས་སུ་མཉམ་པའི་ཕྱིར།
།རང་བྱུང་ངང་ལས་རོལ་པ་ཅི་ཤར་ཡང་།
།ཤར་བའི་དུས་ན་མཉམ་ཤར་བཟང་ངན་མེད།
།དེ་ལ་བླང་དོར་གཉེན་པོས་བཅོས་ཅི་དགོས།
།གནས་པའི་ཚེ་ན་མཉམ་གནས་བཟང་ངན་མེད།
།ད་ལྟ་སེམས་ལས་གང་བྱུང་རང་ཞིར་གློད།
།གྲོལ་བའི་ཚེ་ན་མཉམ་གྲོལ་བཟང་ངན་མེད།
།དྲན་པའི་རྗེས་ལ་དགག་སྒྲུབ་འཕྲོ་མ་མཐུད།
།ཐམས་ཅད་གཞི་ཀློང་བྱང་ཆུབ་སེམས་ཉིད་ལས།
།རྩལ་དང་རོལ་པའི་འཆར་ཚུལ་མ་ངེས་པས།
།མཉམ་པར་ཤར་ཡང་གདོད་མའི་ཀློང་ནས་ཤར།
།མི་མཉམ་ཤར་ཡང་མཉམ་པའི་དབྱིངས་ནས་ཤར།
།མཉམ་པར་གནས་ཀྱང་རང་གཞག་ཆོས་ཉིད་ངང་།
།མི་མཉམ་གནས་ཀྱང་མཉམ་པའི་དབྱིངས་ན་གནས།
།མཉམ་པར་གྲོལ་ཡང་རང་བྱུང་ཡེ་ཤེས་ཀློང་།
།མི་མཉམ་གྲོལ་ཡང་མཉམ་པའི་དབྱིངས་སུ་གྲོལ།
།ཐམས་ཅད་ཡེ་མཉམ་རང་བྱུང་རིག་པ་ལ།
།ཤར་དང་མ་ཤར་དབྱིངས་ལ་ཡེ་ནས་མེད།

Substantial and insubstantial are equal in space.

Enlightened beings and sentient beings are equal in space.

Relative and absolute are equal in space.

Faults and virtues are equal in space.

High and low, and the main and intermediate directions,[69] are equal in space.

Therefore, from the self-originated continuum, whatever display arises,

From the moment it arises, it arises equally without good or bad.

Why would it be necessary to alter this with antidotes of accepting and rejecting?

At the time it settles, it settles evenly without good or bad.

At present, whatever originates from mind, let it be released in natural peace.

At the time it is liberated, it is evenly liberated without good or bad.

Don't continually add affirming and denying after mindfulness.

From compassionate mind itself, the ground, expanse of everything,

The manner of arising, the energy, and the display are uncertain;

Therefore, if the arising is even, it is arising from the primordial expanse.

Even if the arising is uneven, it arises unevenly in the space of equality;

If the settling is even, it is self-settled in the continuum of the nature of phenomena.

Even if it settles unequally, it is still settled in the space of equanimity.

Equal liberation is the self-originated expanse of primordial wisdom.

Unequal liberation is also liberation in the space of equanimity.

Everything is primordially equal. For self-originated awareness,

Arising and non-arising do not exist in space from the beginning.

།གནས་དང་མི་གནས་དབྱིངས་ལ་ཡེ་ནས་མེད།
།གྲོལ་དང་མ་གྲོལ་དབྱིངས་ལ་ཡེ་ནས་མེད།
།མི་གཡོ་མཉམ་པ་ཆེན་པོའི་རིག་པ་ལ།
༑ཤར་བའི་དུས་ན་རང་ཤར་རང་ས་ཟིན།
།གནས་པའི་དུས་ན་རང་གནས་རང་ས་ཟིན།
།གྲོལ་བའི་དུས་ན་རང་གྲོལ་རང་ས་ཟིན།
།མི་འགྱུར་སྤྲོས་དང་བྲལ་བའི་རིག་པ་ལ།
༑ཤར་བ་ཡེ་ཤར་གནས་པ་ཡེ་གནས་ལ།
།གྲོལ་བ་ཡེ་གྲོལ་ནམ་མཁའི་རང་བཞིན་ནོ།
༑ཤར་གནས་གྲོལ་གསུམ་ཤར་གྲོལ་རྒྱུན་ཆད་མེད།
།རྒྱུན་ཆད་མེད་པས་རྒྱུ་འབྲས་བར་མ་ཆོད།
།རྒྱུ་འབྲས་མེད་པས་འཁོར་བའི་གཡང་ས་ཆོད།
།གཡང་ས་མེད་པས་གོལ་ས་ག་ལ་ཡོད།
།ཡེ་ནས་མི་འགྱུར་ཀུན་ཏུ་བཟང་པོའི་ཀློང་།
།འཕོ་འགྱུར་མེད་པ་རྡོ་རྗེ་སེམས་དཔའི་ཀློང་།
།གནས་ལུགས་རང་ངོ་ཤེས་པ་ཙམ་ཉིད་ལ།
།སངས་རྒྱས་ཞེས་སུ་མིང་འདི་བཏགས་པར་ཟད།
།འདི་ཉིད་རྟོགས་ནས་བླང་དོར་ཆོས་མེད་པས།
།ཐམས་ཅད་ཆོས་ཉིད་གཅིག་ཏུ་ཐུམ་གདལ་བ།
།གསེར་གླིང་ལྟ་བུར་དབྱེ་བསལ་མེད་པ་ཡིན།
།མཐའ་ཡིས་མ་རེག་གོལ་སྒྲིབ་གདར་ཤ་ཆོད།
།གཡང་ས་མེད་པའི་བྱང་ཆུབ་སེམས་ཉིད་ལ།
།འབད་རྩོལ་མེད་པའི་སྐུ་གསུམ་ལྷུན་རྫོགས་ཀྱང་།
།བསམ་བརྗོད་འདས་ཤེས་མིང་ཙམ་བརྗོད་པར་ཟད།
།སྣང་བ་རྒྱ་ཡན་རིག་པ་རང་བྱུང་གསལ།

Remaining and non-remaining do not exist in space from the beginning.
Liberation and non-liberation do not exist in space from the beginning.
As to the unmoving great equanimity, awareness,
When it is arising, self-arising, it holds its own ground.
When it is remaining, self-remaining, it holds its own ground.
When it is liberated, self-liberated, it holds its own ground.
As to unchanging awareness, free from elaboration,
Arising is primordially arising; remaining is primordially remaining;
Liberation is primordial liberation, nature of the sky.
Arising, remaining, and liberation are uninterruptedly liberated as they arise.
Since this is uninterrupted, there is no gap between cause and effect.
Since there is no cause and effect, the abyss of samsara is cut off.
Since there is no abyss, how could there be a place to go astray?
Primordially unchanging is the expanse of the All-Good,
Unmoving and unchanging is the expanse of Indestructible Enlightened Mind.
As to realizing the self-nature itself,
It is simply called by the name "Buddha."
If this is realized, there are no phenomena of accepting or rejecting;
So all is evenly pervasive as the single nature of phenomena.
As, on an island of gold, there is nothing else to divide or clear away,
Untouched by extremes, errors and obscurations are resolved.
As to compassionate mind itself without abysses,
Without effort or endeavor, the three kayas are spontaneously perfected;

།མ་བསྒྲིབས་ཕྱི་ནང་མེད་པར་ཟང་ཐལ་བས།
།མ་བཅོས་རྣལ་གཞག་ཆོས་ཉིད་ཆེན་པོར་གསལ།
།བློ་བདེའི་མལ་ན་ལུས་སེམས་ཁོང་གློད་དེ།
༼ཤེས་པ་བག་ཡངས་བྱུར་མེད་སྐྱེས་བུ་བཞིན།
།སྒྲིམས་གློད་མེད་པར་ལུས་སེམས་གང་བདེར་གཞག
།ཇི་ལྟར་འདུག་ཀྱང་རང་གི་ངང་ལ་འདུག
།ཇི་ལྟར་གནས་ཀྱང་རང་གི་ངང་ལ་གནས།
།ཇི་ལྟར་འགྲོ་ཡང་རང་གི་ངང་ལ་འགྲོ།
།བྱང་ཆུབ་དབྱིངས་ལ་འགྲོ་འོང་ངང་གིས་མེད།
།འགྲོ་འོང་མེད་པ་རྒྱལ་བ་རྣམས་ཀྱི་སྐུ།
།ཇི་ལྟར་སྨྲས་ཀྱང་རང་གི་ངང་ལ་སྨྲ།
།ཇི་ལྟར་བརྗོད་ཀྱང་རང་གི་ངང་ལ་བརྗོད།
།བྱང་ཆུབ་སེམས་ལ་སྨྲ་བརྗོད་ངང་གིས་མེད།
།སྨྲ་བརྗོད་མེད་པ་དུས་གསུམ་རྒྱལ་བའི་གསུང་།
།ཇི་ལྟར་བསམས་ཀྱང་རང་གི་ངང་ལ་བསམ།
།ཇི་ལྟར་རྟོག་ཀྱང་རང་གི་ངང་ལ་རྟོག
།བྱང་ཆུབ་སེམས་ལ་བསམ་རྟོག་ཡེ་ནས་མེད།
།བསམ་རྟོག་བྲལ་བ་དུས་གསུམ་རྒྱལ་བའི་ཐུགས།
།མེད་ལ་ཅིར་ཡང་འབྱུང་བ་སྤྲུལ་པའི་སྐུ།
།ཉིད་ལ་ཉིད་ལོངས་སྤྱོད་པ་ལོངས་སྤྱོད་རྫོགས།
།དེ་ལ་དངོས་གཞི་མེད་པས་ཆོས་སྐུ་སྟེ།
།འབྲས་བུ་སྐུ་གསུམ་ལྷུན་གྱིས་གྲུབ་པའི་ཀློང་།
།བྱང་ཆུབ་སེམས་ཀྱི་ཀློང་ཆེན་ངང་ཉིད་ལས།
།དྲན་པའི་རྣམ་པར་རྟོག་པ་མི་འབྱུང་སྟེ།
༼ཤེས་པའི་མཚན་མ་ཡིད་ལ་མི་གཡོན།

Nonetheless, "inconceivable and inexpressible" is merely a figure of speech.

Vast limitless appearance, self-originated awareness, is clear.

It is unobscured, clearly direct, without outer or inner.

Therefore, naturally remaining without fabrication, the great nature of phenomena is luminous.

In the bed of peacefulness, body and mind are relaxed,

With carefree consciousness like a person with nothing to do.

Without tightness or looseness, leave body and mind in whatever way is comfortable.

However they stay, they stay in their own nature.

However they exist, they exist in their own nature.

However they go, they go in their own nature.

As to the perfect space, in its own nature, there is no coming or going.

The body of all the conquerors is without coming or going.

Whatever is uttered is uttered in the continuum of the nature.

Whatever is expressed is expressed in the continuum of the nature.

Compassionate mind has no utterance or expression in its continuum.

Unutterable, inexpressible, is the speech of the conquerors of the three times.[70]

Whatever is conceived is conceived in the continuum of the nature.

Whatever is thought is thought in the continuum of the nature.

Compassionate mind has no conception or thought from the beginning.

Free from conception and thought is the mind of the conquerors of the three times.

Everything originating without existing is nirmanakaya.

Natural enjoyment enjoying itself is sambhogakaya.

Since this has no substantial ground, it is dharmakaya.

།དེ་ཉིད་སངས་རྒྱས་ཉག་གཅིག་དགོངས་པ་ཡིན།
།བྱང་ཆུབ་རང་བཞིན་ནམ་མཁའི་དཀྱིལ་ཡངས་འདྲ།
།དྲན་དང་རྟོག་པ་མེད་པ་སྒོམ་པའི་མཆོག
།རང་གི་རང་བཞིན་མ་གཡོས་བཅོས་པ་མེད།
།མི་བསམ་ཡིད་ལ་བྱེད་པ་རྣམ་བྲལ་བ།
།རང་བབས་ཆོས་ཉིད་དུས་གསུམ་འཕོ་འགྱུར་མེད།
།འགྱུར་འཕྲོའི་ཀུན་རྟོག་མེད་ན་སྒོམ་པའི་མཆོག
།དེ་བཞིན་ཉིད་དེར་གང་གནས་དམ་པའི་སེམས།
།སངས་རྒྱས་ཉག་གཅིག་མཆོན་པ་ཀུན་དང་བྲལ།
།མི་གཡོ་ཆོས་དབྱིངས་འཛིན་རྟོག་ཐྲུམ་འདས་པ།
།རྒྱལ་བའི་དགོངས་ཀློང་རང་བཞིན་ཡངས་པའི་མཆོག
།ལུས་སེམས་བཅོས་པའི་འཆིང་བ་རྣམས་སྤངས་ཤིང་།
།གྱེན་འདདའ་ལྷོད་ཆགས་དྲན་བསམ་ཅི་འགྱུས་ཀྱང་།
།གཞི་གཞག་ཆོས་ཉིད་ངང་ལས་མི་གཡོ་ན།
།ཐམས་ཅད་ཀུན་བཟང་དགོངས་ཀློང་ཡངས་པ་ཡིན།
།མ་བཟུང་མ་བཏང་འཛུར་བུའི་སྒྲིམ་གློད་མེད།
།ཇི་བཞིན་རང་བབས་རྒྱ་ཡན་ངང་གིས་ཟིན།
།མི་གཡོ་ཐྲུམ་གདལ་ཡངས་དོག་མེད་པའི་ཀློང་།

The fruition, these three bodies, is in the expanse of spontaneous accomplishment.

From the continuum of compassionate mind, the great expanse itself,

A thought of mindfulness never originates.

When conscious characterization never moves into mind,

That itself is the sole principle of Buddha.

The perfect nature is like vast space.

The supreme meditation is without thought, without mindfulness,

Unmoved from its own nature and not fabricated,

Without conception and free from all mental activity.

The intrinsic state of the nature of phenomena is free from transformation or change of the three times.

The supreme meditation is without moving or emerging thoughts.

Remaining in that suchness is sublime mind.

The sole Buddha, free from all characterizations,

Unmoving phenomenal space, completely transcending thoughts of grasping,

Is the natural, supremely vast expanse of the Conqueror's intention.

When all chains of fabricated mind and body are abandoned,

In natural relaxation, whatever movement of memories and thoughts occur,

If they rest in the ground and don't move from the continuum of the nature of phenomena,

All is the vast intention, expanse of All-Good.

Don't grasp. Don't release. Without loosening or tightening entanglements,

A natural carefree state is achieved as a matter of course.

Unmoving, evenly pervasive, in the expanse of freedom from wide or narrow,

།དྲན་བསམ་ཐམས་ཅད་རང་བྱུང་རང་ཞི་ན།
།རྡོ་རྗེ་སེམས་དཔའ་ནམ་མཁའི་དགོངས་པ་ཡིན།
།མ་བཅོས་ཀློང་དུ་མ་ཡེངས་དང་ལྡན་ན།
།དྲན་རྟོག་ཡུལ་ལ་འཇུག་པའང་ཆོས་ཉིད་དང་།
།ཆེད་དུ་འཇུར་བུས་བཅོས་ན་ཆོས་ཉིད་ཀྱང་།
།མི་རྟོག་མཁའ་ལྟར་ཡངས་ཀྱང་མཚན་མའི་གཟེབ།
།ཉིན་མཚན་སྒོམ་པས་འདའ་ཡང་འཆིང་ཞེན་ཉིད།
།བསམ་གཏན་ལྷ་དང་མཚུངས་པར་རྒྱལ་བས་གསུངས།
།དེ་བས་མ་ཡེངས་འབད་རྩོལ་ཞིག་པའི་སེམས།
།རང་བབས་འཛིན་རྩོལ་འདས་པ་ཤིན་ཏུ་གཅེས།
།རང་བྱུང་ཡེ་ཤེས་ཕྱོགས་དང་རིས་མེད་པས།
།འདི་ཞེས་མི་མཚོན་རང་བཞིན་སྤྲོས་ཀུན་ཞི།
།དེ་བས་ཡིད་ལ་བྱེད་པ་རྣམས་སྤངས་ཏེ།
།གཞི་བྲལ་ཡངས་པ་ཆེན་པོའི་དོན་ལ་བསླབ།
།ཆོས་ཉིད་ཉག་གཅིག་རང་བྱུང་ཡེ་ཤེས་ཏེ།
།ལྟ་བ་ཉག་གཅིག་སྤྲོས་པའི་མཐའ་དང་བྲལ།
།སྒོམ་པ་ཉག་གཅིག་བཏང་གཞག་འགྲོ་འོང་མེད།
།སྤྱོད་པ་ཉག་གཅིག་བླང་དོར་བྱར་མེད་ཅིང་།
།འབྲས་བུ་ཉག་གཅིག་སྤངས་ཐོབ་གཉིས་དང་བྲལ།
།འདི་ནི་རང་བྱུང་ལྷུན་གྲུབ་དགོངས་པ་ཡིན།

When all memories and conceptions are self-originated and self-settled,
That is the principle of the indestructible space of compassionate mind.
If, in the unfabricated expanse, one remains continuously without distraction,
Even memories and thoughts following their objects are in the continuum of the nature of phenomena.
If the nature of phenomena is fabricated by means of entanglements in particulars,
Even though non-conceptualization is as vast as the sky, it is still a trap of characteristics.
Even the passing of day and night in meditation will still be the chain of grasping itself,
Contemplation like that of the gods, as was said by the Conqueror.
Therefore, don't be distracted. With a mind in which effort and endeavor have disintegrated,
It is most important to leave things in the natural state beyond grasping and endeavor.
Since self-originated primordial wisdom has no bias or partiality,
Beyond characterization as "this," it is naturally free from all elaborations.
Therefore, by abandoning all conceptual activities,
Train in the meaning of great vast groundlessness.
Self-originated primordial wisdom is the definitive nature of phenomena.
Free from the limitations of elaboration is the only view.
Neither sending nor keeping, neither coming nor going, is the only meditation.
Neither accepting nor rejecting is the only action.
Free from abandoning or attaining is the only result.
This is the principle of self-originated spontaneous accomplishment.

།སྣང་སྲིད་སྣོད་བཅུད་འཁོར་དང་མྱ་ངན་འདས།
།ཆོས་སོ་ཅོག་ཀུན་ཆོས་ཉིད་གདོད་མའི་ངང་།
།རང་བྱུང་ཡེ་ཤེས་ཉིད་ལས་མ་གཡོས་པས།
།གང་ཡང་གཞི་གཞག་དགོངས་པར་ཤེས་པར་བྱ།
།སྣ་ཚོགས་ཡུལ་དུ་སྣང་བའི་ཆོས་ཉིད་ལ།
།གང་དུ་འདི་ལྟར་འཛོག་ཅེས་མི་རྟོག་པར།
།རང་བབས་སྤྲོ་བསྡུ་བྲལ་བར་ལྷུན་གྱིས་ཞོག
།ཆོས་ཉིད་མཉམ་པའི་ཀློང་དུ་ངང་གིས་གནས།
།དཀར་དམར་ཡུལ་དུ་སྣང་བའི་རྣམ་པ་ལ།
།དབང་པོ་མི་བསྡུ་མིག་ཀྱང་མི་འགྱུལ་བས།
།བདག་ལ་མི་བསམ་གཞན་ལ་མི་རྟོག་པར།
།ཕྱམ་ཕྱལ་ཡངས་པ་ཆེན་པོར་ངང་གིས་ཞོག
།རྒྱུ་བསྐྱེད་དཔང་བསྐྱོད་སྤྲོ་བསྡུ་བྲལ་བའི་སེམས།
།ཀུན་མཉམ་རང་བྱུང་ཡེ་ཤེས་དགོངས་པ་ལ།
།ཕྱི་ནང་བར་མེད་ནམ་མཁའ་འདྲེས་པའི་ཉམས།
།བདེ་གསལ་སྤྲོས་དང་བྲལ་བའི་ཏིང་འཛིན་འཆར།
།གཞི་གཞག་མི་གཡོ་མཉམ་པའི་དགོངས་པ་ལ།
།ཕྱི་དང་ནང་མེད་གཟུང་འཛིན་སྤྲོས་དང་བྲལ།
།ཡུལ་ཞེས་གཞན་དུ་ཞེན་པའི་སེམས་མེད་པས།
།གཟུང་བའི་ཆོས་མེད་སྣོད་བཅུད་སྣང་ཞེན་བྲལ།
།འཁོར་བར་སྐྱེ་བའི་ཡུལ་མེད་ནམ་མཁའ་འདྲ།

Appearance and existence, the universe and its inhabitants, samsara and nirvana —

All that is in the continuum of natural primordial phenomena

Is unmoved from self-originated primordial wisdom itself;

So it should be known that whatever remains in the basic state is the intention.

As to the Dharma nature itself appearing as various objects,

Without thinking of settling anywhere as "this,"

In a natural manner, free from gathering or separating, let it be spontaneous.

The nature of phenomena remains in the continuum of the expanse of equanimity.

As to the appearance of objects as white and red,[71]

Without obstructing the senses, and with the eyes unblinking,

Without conceiving of oneself or thinking of other,

Be in the continuum of the great vast evenness.

Extend it greatly, praise it — mind that is free from emanating and dissolving.

Given the intention of all-equal, self-originated primordial wisdom,

The experience of assimilating with space, without inside, outside, or in between,

Blissful luminous concentration, free from elaboration, will arise.

As to the unmoving, settled ground, the principle of equanimity,

It has no outside or inside, free from elaboration of grasper and grasped.

There is no attached conception to so-called external objects;

So, in freedom from attachment to the appearance of the universe and its inhabitants, there are no phenomena of grasping.

There is no birth of samsaric objects. It is like the sky.

།རང་ཞེས་སེམས་ལ་ནང་དུ་མི་རྟོག་པས།
།འཛིན་པའི་ཆོས་མེད་སྲིད་པའི་ཀུན་རྟོག་ཞི།
།འཁོར་བར་སྐྱེ་བའི་མཁན་པོ་རྩད་ནས་ཆོད།
།དེ་ཆེ་མཁའ་འདྲ་ཕྱི་ནང་འཁྲུལ་པའི་ཆོས།
།གང་ཡང་མི་དམིགས་ཆོས་སྐུའི་དགོངས་པར་ཕྱིན།
།ཟད་པའི་སར་ཐུག་འགྲོ་དང་འོང་མེད་པས།
།ཐམས་ཅད་ཀློང་འབྱམས་ཀུན་ཏུ་བཟང་པོའི་ཞིང་།
།ཆོས་སྐུའི་ཕོ་བྲང་མཆོག་ཏུ་ཕྱིན་པ་ཡིན།
།ད་ལྟའི་རིག་པ་གཞི་ལས་མ་གཡོས་ན།
།དེ་ཉིད་གོམས་ཆས་ཕྱི་མའི་སྲིད་པ་སྟོངས།
།ཡང་སྲིད་ལེན་པའི་ལས་དང་བག་ཆགས་བྲལ།
།རྒྱུ་འབྲས་ལ་བློས་འཁོར་འདས་མཉམ་པར་བརྗོད།
།སྲིད་ཞིར་མི་གནས་བྱང་ཆུབ་སྙིང་པོར་ཕྱིན།
།འདིར་ཡང་ཞི་གནས་རྩེ་གཅིག་ཕྱེད་པ་གཅེས།
།རང་བཞིན་རྫོགས་པ་ཆེན་པོའི་དགོངས་པ་ཡིན།
།ངང་ལས་གཡོས་ན་ཡིད་དཔྱོད་འཁོར་བ་ཉིད།
།དེ་ལ་རྒྱུ་འབྲས་ཉིད་དེ་ལ་མ་བློས།
།ཉོར་བའི་སྐྱེ་བོ་འོག་ནས་འོག་ཏུ་འགྲོ།
།དེས་ན་མཆོག་གསང་རྫོགས་པ་ཆེན་པོ་ནི།
།དབྱིངས་ལས་མ་གཡོས་རྩལ་རྣམས་གཞི་ལ་འཁྱིལ།
།དགོངས་པ་མི་གཡོ་མཉམ་པར་གནས་པ་ཡིན།
།འདི་ཡི་ངང་ལ་རྒྱུ་འབྲས་བྱ་རྩོལ་མེད།

Since mind is not conceived as being an inner "self,"
There are no phenomena to grasp. All possible thoughts of samsaric existence are pacified.
The agent of samsaric birth is cut off at the root;
And at that time, like the sky, without conceiving anything at all,
Internal and external deluded phenomena have reached the principle of dharmakaya.
Reaching the ground of exhaustion, neither coming nor going;
So everything is the infinite expanse, the field of the All-Good,
Reaching the supreme palace of dharmakaya.
If awareness of nowness is unmoved from the ground,
Familiarization with that clears the existence of future lives.
One is free from karma and habits of taking rebirth.
Having crossed the pass of cause and effect is called equality of samsara and nirvana;
Not remaining in samsara or nirvana is reaching the perfect essence.
Here it is also important to notice the difference between this and one-pointed tranquility meditation.[72]
This is the principle of great natural perfection.
If it moves from the continuum, intellectual analysis is samsara itself.
In that case, one has not crossed the pass of cause and effect.
Such a mistaken person will go lower and lower.
That is why the supremely secret Great Perfection
Is unmoved from space. All energies have reached the ground.
The intention is unmoving and settled in equanimity.
In this continuum there is no cause and effect, no effort or endeavor.

།ལྟ་བ་བསྒོམ་དུ་མེད་པ་ལ་སོགས་ཏེ།
།མཐའ་དབུས་གཉིས་མེད་འགོག་པའི་ཚུལ་བརྗོད་ཀྱི།
།གཞན་དུ་དང་ལས་ཕྱིར་འཕྲུལ་རྩལ་ཉིད་ལས།
།རོལ་པ་སྣ་ཚོགས་སྣང་སྲིད་དགུ་འཆར་བས།
།རྒྱུ་འབྲས་མེད་ཅེས་ནམ་ཡང་མ་བརྗོད་ཅིག
།རྟེན་འབྲེལ་རྐྱེན་འབྱུང་འདུས་བྱས་གྲངས་བསམ་འདས།
།འཁོར་བའི་འཁྲུལ་སྣང་ཞི་བདེའང་གྲངས་བསམ་འདས།
།དེ་ཀུན་རྒྱུ་རྐྱེན་ཚོགས་པའི་རྟེན་འབྲེལ་ཉིད།
།གཤིས་ལ་གཞལ་ན་གང་ཡང་མ་གྲུབ་ལྟར།
།ལམ་དུ་བྱེད་པས་གཤིས་ཐོག་མི་གཡོའི་དུས།
།གང་ཡང་མི་དམིགས་དགོངས་པའི་དུས་ན་སྟེ།
།གཤིས་ཐོག་མཐར་ཕྱིན་གང་ཡང་གོས་མི་འགྱུར།
།ཉོན་མོངས་ལས་དང་བག་ཆགས་ཀློང་ཆེན་འདི།
།རྟེན་མེད་སྒྱུ་མས་སྤྲུལ་པའི་རྩེད་མོ་བྱེད།
།འདི་ལས་ཐར་དགོས་རྒྱུ་འབྲས་ལ་བློས་འཚལ།
།དེ་ཡི་ཐབས་ནི་འདི་ལས་མཆོག་གཞན་མེད།
།དེ་ཕྱིར་ཆོས་དབྱིངས་དགོངས་པ་མ་གཡོས་གཅེས།
།འདི་ཉིད་ཕོ་བོའི་སྙིང་གཏམ་ཟབ་མོའི་ཀློང་།
།ཀུན་ཡིན་ཀུན་མིན་ཡིན་མིན་འདས་པ་གཅེས།

།ཆོས་དབྱིངས་རིན་པོ་ཆེའི་མཛོད་ལས། །དགོངས་པ་ཆོས་ཉིད་ལས་མི་གཡོ་བར་བསྟན་པའི་ལེའུ་སྟེ་བཅུ་པའོ།།

There is no view to meditate on, and so forth;

And though the style of cessation is said to be beyond duality of center and border,

At other times, deviating from the continuum, from the energy itself,

Various displays, all appearance and existence arise.

So never say that there is no cause and effect.

Conditional, interdependent circumstances are innumerable and inconceivable.

The delusory appearances of samsara, and those of peace and happiness, are also innumerable and inconceivable.

All of this is the interdependent arising of compounded causes and conditions themselves.

As nothing exists if one measures the nature,

By traversing like this, when one is unmoved from the natural state,
When nothing is conceived, one has reached the natural state,
The essential principle, unstained by anything.

This great expanse of affliction, karma, and habits

Is baseless illusion performing the magical play of phantom games.

One must be freed from this and remember to cross the pass of cause and effect.

There is no other method for doing so better than this;

Therefore, it is extremely important not to move from the intention of phenomenal space.

This itself is the expanse of my heartfelt, profound advice.

It is everything and it is nothing. It is extremely important to go beyond "is" and "is not."

From *The Precious Treasury of Phenomenal Space*, showing that the intention is unmoved from the nature of phenomena, the tenth chapter, is completed.

།ཐམས་ཅད་མཁའ་མཉམ་བྱང་ཆུབ་སེམས་གཅིག་ལ།
།གཉིས་སུ་བཟུང་བས་རྒྱུ་འབྲས་སྲིད་པར་འཁྲུལ།
།འཁྲུལ་སྣང་རྟེན་མེད་སྒྱུ་མའི་སྣང་བ་ལ།
།ཐུག་ཕྲད་རྗེས་མེད་རྩིས་གདབ་བྲལ་བར་སྐྱོང་།
།མི་འདོད་ཐོག་ཏུ་བབ་ལ་དོར་བྱའི་སེམས།
།ཁྲོ་དང་མི་དགའ་ཕྲག་དོག་འཁྲུག་དང་འཚིག
།སྐྱོ་བས་ཡིད་དབྱུང་ན་ཚ་སྡུག་བསྔལ་སེམས།
།འཆི་དང་སྐྱེ་བས་འཇིགས་ལ་སོགས་པ་སྣེ།
།རྩལ་ལས་རོལ་པར་ཤར་དུས་ངོས་བཟུང་ལ།
།མི་སྤོང་མི་སྐྱོང་མི་སྒྱུར་མི་ལེན་ཞིང་།
།མི་ལྟ་མི་སྒོམ་རང་བབས་ཕྱམ་གཅིག་ཏུ།
།དམིགས་བསམ་སྤྲོ་བསྡུ་བྲལ་བར་ལྷུན་གྱིས་ཞོག
།རྗེས་མེད་རང་ཡལ་མཁའ་ཀློང་ཡངས་པའི་སེམས།
།གསལ་དྭངས་ངར་དང་བཅས་པ་ཁོང་ནས་འཆར།
།ཡིན་མིན་མེད་པའི་རིག་པ་ཕྱོགས་ཡན་ལ།
།འདིར་གཏད་མེད་པའི་སྣང་བ་ཐུག་ཕྲད་ཀྱིས།
།འདིར་གཟུང་མེད་པའི་ངང་དེར་རང་བཞག་པས།
།འདིར་ཁྲོལ་མེད་པའི་དགག་སྒྲུབ་རྗེས་མེད་ཡལ།
།འཛིན་ཞེན་མེད་པའི་ཉམས་སྐྱོང་ཁོང་རྗོལ་འབྱུང་།
།འདི་ཉིད་ཇི་བཞིན་དགོངས་ཀློང་ཡེ་ནས་ཡངས།

11

From *The Precious Treasury of Phenomenal Space*, showing that circumstances and appearances are taught to be purity as limitless as space, the eleventh chapter.

As to sole compassionate mind, it is the sky where everything is equal.
By grasping it as duality, there come to be causes and results, the confusion of existence.
As appearance of delusion is without support, in illusory appearance,
When there is nothing to reach, meet, or follow, it is maintained without having to keep track.
When you come upon what isn't wished for, and there is a thought to abandon anger, unhappiness, jealousy, disturbance, intolerance,
Sadness, depression, sickness, unhappy thoughts,
Fear of birth and death, and so forth;
When these arise from the potential as display, recognize them.
Without abandoning, without purifying, without transforming, without accepting,
Without viewing, without meditating, in one perfect natural flow,
Remain in spontaneity without imagining or conceiving, emanating or dissolving.
Traceless self-disappearance, mind of the vast expanse of space,
Is sharp luminous clarity arising from within.
As to boundless awareness of what neither "is" nor "is not,"
Encountering appearances without focusing on them as "this,"
By naturally remaining in that continuum without grasping anything as "this,"
Without liberation of "this," denying and affirming disappear without a trace.
Experience of non-grasping and non-attachment springs forth from within.
This itself, as it is, the intention of the expanse, is vast from the beginning.

།དེ་བཞིན་འདོད་ཅིང་ཡིད་ལ་དགའ་བའི་སེམས།
།གྲུབ་བདེ་གཉེན་དང་གཏམ་སྙན་ལོངས་སྤྱོད་དང་།
།གནས་དང་ཕྱོགས་ནི་ཡིད་དུ་འོང་བ་དེར།
།རང་བཞིན་དགའ་བས་བརྒྱན་པའི་སེམས་ཤར་བ།
།དེ་ཉིད་ངོས་གཟུང་རང་བབས་ཅོག་བཞག་གིས།
།གདོད་མའི་དབྱིངས་སུ་མ་བཅོས་ལྷུན་གྱིས་གྲུབ།
།རང་བཞིན་བར་མ་འགྲོ་འདུག་གྱིན་འདར་གནས།
།དགའ་དང་མི་དགའ་གཉིས་མིན་ཅི་ཤར་ཡང་།
།ཤར་དུས་ངོས་གཟུང་སྤྱང་བླང་མ་བྱས་པས།
།རང་བབས་ཆོས་ཉིད་དབྱེ་བསལ་མེད་པ་ནི།
།གཏི་མུག་འོད་གསལ་ཆེན་པོར་གྲོལ་ཞེས་བྱ།
།མཚན་མོ་ལ་སོགས་གཉིད་ཀྱིས་མྱོས་པ་ནའང་།
།རང་བབས་སྒྲོ་བསྐྱུ་བྲལ་བའི་ངང་ཉལ་བས།
།རགས་པར་སྣང་བ་ནུབ་པས་དེར་འཛིན་ནུབ།
།ཕྲ་བ་ཆེས་ཕྲ་འཛིན་པར་བཅས་ནུབ་པས།
།ཆ་མཉམ་མི་རྟོག་ངང་དུ་རིག་པའི་སེམས།
།འབྱུང་འཇུག་རེ་དོགས་བྲལ་བ་རང་བཞིན་གནས།
།ཀུན་རྟོག་ཆོས་དབྱིངས་གྲོལ་བའི་དུས་ཡིན་པས།
།འཁོར་བ་མྱང་འདས་གྲོལ་ཞེས་བརྗོད་པ་ཡིན།
།གཉིད་ཀྱང་རང་བྱུང་གདོད་མའི་གློང་ཆེན་ཏེ།
།རྨལ་རྣམས་ངོ་བོའི་དབྱིངས་སུ་གཞིར་ཐིམ་པས།
།རོལ་པར་འཛིན་པའི་སྤྲོས་ཀུན་དང་གིས་ཞི།
།བྱུར་མེད་རང་བྱུང་ཡེ་ཤེས་དགོངས་པའོ།
།དེ་ལྟར་འདོད་དང་མི་འདོད་བར་མའི་སེམས།
།དུག་གསུམ་རྩལ་ལས་རོལ་པར་ཤར་ཏོ་ཅོག

Likewise, what is desired and thoughts that make the mind joyful,
Success, happiness, friends, good news, and wealth,
Places and locations that are pleasing to the mind —
With these, thoughts naturally adorned with happiness arise.
Recognize the nature itself, by simply resting in the natural state,
Without fabrication, spontaneously accomplished in primordial space.
As for things whose nature is in between — going, staying, just ordinary existence,
Neither happy nor unhappy, whatever arises —
At the time of arising, by recognizing that, without accepting or rejecting,
There is the natural state, the nature of phenomena, without differentiation or clearing away;
This is called "ignorance liberated in the great luminosity."
At night and so forth, even when intoxicated by sleep,
When one sleeps in the continuum of the natural state, free from emanating and dissolving,
Gross appearance subsides, and so grasping to it subsides.
Subtle and extremely subtle grasping also subsides,
So equally even, thought-free continuity, awareness mind,
Remains naturally without hope or fear, originating or engaging.
Since this is the time of liberation of all thoughts as phenomenal space,
It is called "liberation of samsara and nirvana."
Sleep is also the great expanse of primordial self-origination.
All potential dissolves in the basis of the nature of space.
So all elaborations of grasping to the display are naturally pacified.
This is the principle of non-action, of self-originated primordial wisdom.

།དབྱིངས་ལས་བྱུང་ཞིང་དབྱིངས་ཀྱི་ངང་དུ་ཤར།
།དབྱིངས་སུ་མ་གཏོགས་གཡོས་པ་འགའ་མེད་པས།
།གཟེབ་དང་བཅོས་བསྒྱུར་གང་ཡང་མི་བྱེད་པར།
།དབྱིངས་ཉིད་ངོས་གཟུང་དང་དེར་གཞག་མ་ཐག
།རང་བཞིན་རང་ཡལ་རང་སར་གྲོལ་བ་གནད།
།ཉོན་མོངས་ལས་དང་བག་ཆགས་ཐམས་ཅད་ཀྱང་།
།རྩལ་ལས་རོལ་པར་ཤར་བའི་ཆོ་འཕྲུལ་ལ།
།གཉེན་པོ་བཟང་བྲུས་ཐར་པའི་ལམ་ཉིད་ཀྱང་།
།རྩལ་ལས་རོལ་པར་ཤར་བའི་ཆོ་འཕྲུལ་ཏེ།
།གཉིས་ཀ་རྩལ་ལས་རོལ་པར་ཡེ་ཤར་བས།
།ངོ་ཤེས་དང་དུ་མ་བཅོས་འཛོག་པ་གནད།
།བང་མཉམ་འགྲོས་མཉམ་གཞི་ནས་གཡོས་པར་མཉམ།
།རྐྱེན་བྱུང་འདུས་བྱས་རྒྱུ་འབྲས་མ་འདས་པས།
།རང་གཞག་ཅོག་གཞག་རྒྱུ་འབྲས་ཟློས་པ་གཅེས།
།འདི་ནི་མཆོག་གསང་ཐེག་པའི་ཡང་རྩེ་སྟེ།
།ཟློ་དམན་རྣམས་ལ་མི་སྨྲ་ཤིན་ཏུ་གསང་།
།སྒྲོ་སྐུར་དབང་གིས་སྙིང་པོའི་བསྟན་པ་འཆལ།
།སྒྲོ་འདེབས་ཉིད་དང་དགོངས་པ་ལོག་པར་ཞུགས།
།གསང་སྒོ་འཆོལ་རྣམས་མཐའ་མེད་ངན་འགྲོར་ལྟུང་།
།དེ་བས་རབ་གསང་ཐེག་པ་རྒྱལ་པོའི་གདུང་།
།སྐལ་བཟང་དམ་པ་རྣམས་ལ་བསྟན་ཞིང་གཏད།
།མདོར་ན་གང་སྣང་ཡུལ་སེམས་རྐྱེན་རྣམས་ལ།
།གཉེན་པོ་མི་འཛུག་རྩོལ་བས་མ་སྤྱངས་པར།
།རང་གཞག་ཅོག་གཞག་རང་བབས་རིག་པའི་གནད།

Like that, the mind of desire, dislike, and in between —
Whatever arises as the display of the three poisons from the potential —
Originating from space, arises in the continuum of space.
Since it does not move anywhere besides being in space,
Don't fabricate, make changes, or be trapped.
Right away, remain in the continuum of recognizing space itself.
Pacifying self, self-disappearance, and liberation in one's own ground are the point.
All afflictions, karma, and habitual patterns
Arise from the potential as miraculous display.
Good deeds as antidotes, and the path of liberation itself,
Also arise from the potential as miraculous display.
Since both arise primordially as display from the potential,
The point is to remain without fabrication in the continuum of self-recognition,
Evenly side-by-side, evenly marching, evenly moving from the ground.
Since all conditional circumstances are not beyond cause and effect,
It is important to remain naturally, completely resting, and to cross the pass of cause and effect.
This is the supreme secret, the ultimate pinnacle of the path.
It is extremely secret and should not be expressed to lesser minds.
By exaggeration and deprecation the doctrine of the essence becomes distorted.
By such exaggeration one enters into wrong doctrine.
By inverting the secret door, one will endlessly fall into the lower realms.
Therefore, the lineage of the supremely secret king of yanas
Should be taught and entrusted only to sublime and fortunate heirs.

།བདེ་སྡུག་ཐམས་ཅད་རིག་པའི་འཆར་ཚུལ་ལ།
།བླང་དོར་གཉིས་སུ་བཟུང་བས་སྲིད་པར་འཆིང་།
།གང་སྣང་ཡུལ་མཉམ་དབང་པོའི་ངོར་གསལ་ཙམ།
།གང་ཤར་སེམས་མཉམ་དྲན་རིག་རྗེས་མེད་ཙམ།
།གཉིས་ཀ་འཁྲུལ་མཉམ་དགག་སྒྲུབ་འཆིང་བ་ཙམ།
།དོན་ལ་ཐུག་མཉམ་གཞི་མེད་སྣང་བ་ཙམ།
།ཡུལ་རྣམས་རིས་མཉམ་གཞིག་ན་རྗེས་མེད་ཙམ།
།བློ་རྣམས་ངོར་མཉམ་དཔྱད་ན་ནམ་མཁའ་ཙམ།
།ཡུལ་སེམས་གཉིས་མེད་བར་སྣང་དག་པ་ཙམ།
།དེ་ལྟར་སུས་ཤེས་ཀུན་ཏུ་བཟང་པོའི་གདུང་།
།རྒྱལ་བའི་སྲས་མཆོག་ས་ར་བ་རིག་པ་འཛིན།
།འདི་ལྟར་ཆོས་རྣམས་ཡོད་མཉམ་མེད་མཉམ་ལ།
།སྣང་མཉམ་སྟོང་མཉམ་བདེན་མཉམ་རྫུན་མཉམ་པས།
།སྤང་གཉེན་འབད་རྩོལ་འཆིང་ཞེན་ཀུན་ཐོང་ལ།
།ཡུལ་མེད་མཉམ་པ་ཆེན་པོར་ཐྲུམ་གདོལ་ཅིག
།སེམས་མེད་རིག་པ་ཆེན་པོར་ཐྲུམ་གདོལ་ཅིག
།སྐྱོན་མེད་དག་མཉམ་ཆེན་པོར་ཐྲུམ་གདོལ་ཅིག

།ཆོས་དབྱིངས་རིན་པོ་ཆེའི་མཛོད་ལས། །རྐྱེན་སྣང་མཁའ་མཉམ་དག་པར་བསྟན་པའི་ལེའུ་སྟེ་བཅུ་གཅིག་པའོ།།

In short, whatever appears, object, mind, or circumstances,
Without applying antidotes, without abandoning with endeavor,
But remaining naturally, completely resting in the natural state of awareness, is the point.
All happiness and unhappiness are simply ways of arising of awareness.
By dualistic grasping of accepting and rejecting, one is bound in existence.
Whatever appears is equal as objects, mere appearance to the senses.
Whatever arises is equal as mind, mere traceless, mindful awareness.
Both are instantly equal, simply the bondage of rejection and acceptance,
In truth, ultimately equal, mere groundless appearance.
All objects are equal in pattern, if investigated, merely traceless.
Thoughts are equal in nature, if analyzed, merely sky-like.
There is no duality of object and mind, merely pure space.
Whoever understands this is of the lineage of All-Good,
Supreme heir to the king, an awareness holder of the ultimate ground.
Like that, all phenomena are even in existence and even in non-existence,
Equally appearing, equally empty, equally true, equally untrue.
Therefore, let go of attachment to all rejection, antidotes, effort, endeavor, and bondage.
Be evenly pervasive in objectless great equanimity,
Be evenly pervasive in great awareness without mind,
Be evenly pervasive in faultless great pure equanimity.

From *The Precious Treasury of Phenomenal Space*, showing that circumstances and appearances are taught to be purity as limitless as space, the eleventh chapter, is completed.

།ཆོས་ཀུན་བྱང་ཆུབ་སེམས་སུ་ཡེ་གྲོལ་བས།

།མ་གྲོལ་བ་ཡི་ཆོས་ནི་ཡོད་མ་ཡིན།

།འཁོར་བ་ཡེ་གྲོལ་གདོད་ནས་དག་པར་གྲོལ།

།འདས་པ་ཡེ་གྲོལ་ལྷུན་གྱིས་རྫོགས་པར་གྲོལ།

།སྣང་བ་ཡེ་གྲོལ་གཞི་རྩ་མེད་པར་གྲོལ།

།སྲིད་པ་ཡེ་གྲོལ་བྱང་ཆུབ་སྙིང་པོར་གྲོལ།

།སྤྲོས་པ་ཡེ་གྲོལ་མུ་མཐའ་མེད་པར་གྲོལ།

།སྤྲོས་མེད་ཡེ་གྲོལ་མ་སྐྱེས་དག་པར་གྲོལ།

།བདེ་བ་ཡེ་གྲོལ་ཆོས་ཉིད་ཕྱམ་དུ་གྲོལ།

།སྡུག་བསྔལ་ཡེ་གྲོལ་གཞི་མཉམ་ཡངས་པར་གྲོལ།

།བར་མ་ཡེ་གྲོལ་མཁའ་མཉམ་ཆོས་སྐུར་གྲོལ།

།དག་པ་ཡེ་གྲོལ་དག་གཉིས་སྟོང་པར་གྲོལ།

།མ་དག་ཡེ་གྲོལ་ཡོངས་གྲོལ་ཆེན་པོར་གྲོལ།

།ས་ལམ་ཡེ་གྲོལ་བསྐྱེད་རྫོགས་བྲལ་བར་གྲོལ།

།ལྟ་སྒོམ་ཡེ་གྲོལ་སྤང་བླང་མེད་པར་གྲོལ།

།སྤྱོད་པ་ཡེ་གྲོལ་ཀུན་ཏུ་བཟང་པོར་གྲོལ།

།འབྲས་བུ་ཡེ་གྲོལ་རེ་དོགས་མེད་པར་གྲོལ།

།དམ་ཚིག་ཡེ་གྲོལ་ཆོས་ཉིད་ཆེན་པོར་གྲོལ།

།བཟླས་བརྗོད་ཡེ་གྲོལ་གླེང་བརྗོད་བྲལ་བར་གྲོལ།

12

From *The Precious Treasury of Phenomenal Space*, showing that all phenomena are liberated in the nature of compassionate mind, the twelfth chapter.

Since all phenomena are primordially liberated in compassionate mind,
There are no phenomena that are not liberated.
Samsara is primordially liberated, purely liberated from the beginning.
Nirvana is primordially liberated, liberated in spontaneous perfection.
Appearance is primordially liberated, liberated without ground or root.
Existence is primordially liberated, liberated in the perfect essence of compassion.
Elaboration is primordially liberated, liberated without limit or border.
Non-elaboration is primordially liberated, liberated as unborn purity.
Happiness is primordially liberated, liberated in the evenness of the nature of phenomena.
Suffering is primordially liberated, liberated as the vast, equal ground.
Neutrality is primordially liberated, liberated in dharmakaya, equal to the sky.
Purity is primordially liberated, liberated in the emptiness of the pure state.
Impurity is primordially liberated, liberated in the complete, great liberation.
The grounds and paths are primordially liberated, liberated without generation and completion.
View and meditation are primordially liberated, liberated without accepting or rejecting.
Action is primordially liberated, liberated as the All-Good.
The result is primordially liberated, liberated without hope or fear.
Samaya is primordially liberated, liberated in the great nature of phenomena.
Recitation is primordially liberated, liberated without conversation or expression.

།ཏིང་འཛིན་ཡེ་གྲོལ་བསམ་ཡུལ་མེད་པར་གྲོལ།
།ཡོད་མེད་ཡེ་གྲོལ་མཐའ་ལས་འདས་པར་གྲོལ།
།རྟག་ཆད་ཡེ་གྲོལ་གཞི་རྩ་མེད་པར་གྲོལ།
།ཡང་དག་ཡེ་གྲོལ་དམིགས་བསམ་འདས་པར་གྲོལ།
།ཡང་དག་མིན་གྲོལ་ཕྱོགས་བསམ་འདས་པར་གྲོལ།
།ལས་རྣམས་ཡེ་གྲོལ་གོས་པ་མེད་པར་གྲོལ།
།ཉོན་མོངས་ཡེ་གྲོལ་འཆིང་གྲོལ་མེད་པར་གྲོལ།
།བག་ཆགས་ཡེ་གྲོལ་རྟེན་གཞི་མེད་པར་གྲོལ།
།རྣམ་སྨིན་ཡེ་གྲོལ་སྨྱོང་གཞི་མེད་པར་གྲོལ།
།གཉེན་པོ་ཡེ་གྲོལ་སྤང་བྱ་མེད་པར་གྲོལ།
།སྤང་བླང་གཉིས་མེད་མཁའ་མཉམ་ཡངས་པར་གྲོལ།
།གྲོལ་བ་ཡེ་གྲོལ་བཅིངས་པ་མེད་པར་གྲོལ།
།མ་གྲོལ་ཡེ་གྲོལ་བཅིང་གྲོལ་མེད་པར་གྲོལ།
།སྤྱོད་པ་ཡེ་གྲོལ་སྤྱོད་རྒྱུ་མེད་པར་གྲོལ།
།ཅོག་གཞག་ཡེ་གྲོལ་འཛོག་རྒྱུ་མེད་པར་གྲོལ།
།མདོར་ན་སྣང་ཞིང་སྲིད་པའི་ཆོས་རྣམས་དང་།
།མི་སྣང་མི་སྲིད་ཆོས་ལས་འདས་སོ་ཅོག
།ཐམས་ཅད་ཡེ་ནས་དབྱིངས་སུ་གྲོལ་ཟིན་པས།
།ད་གཟོད་འབད་པས་སུས་ཀྱང་གྲོལ་མི་དགོས།
།དེ་ལ་འབད་རྩོལ་བྱས་ཀྱང་དོན་མེད་པས།
།མ་བྱེད་མ་བྱེད་རྩོལ་ཞིང་སྒྲུབ་མ་བྱེད།

Meditation is primordially liberated, liberated beyond objects of thought.

Existence and non-existence are primordially liberated, liberated without extremes.

Eternalism and nihilism are primordially liberated, liberated without ground or root.

Absolute purity is primordially liberated, liberated beyond the conceptualized intention.

What is not absolute purity is liberated, liberated beyond intellectual bias.

All deeds are primordially liberated, liberated without defilement.

Afflictions are primordially liberated, liberated without bondage or liberation.

Habitual inclinations are primordially liberated, liberated without a support or ground.

Ripening causes are primordially liberated, liberated without a ground of experience.

Antidotes are primordially liberated, liberated without anything to abandon,

Without duality of acceptance and rejection, liberated in vastness equal to the sky.

Liberation is primordially liberated, liberated without entrapment.

Non-liberation is primordially liberated, liberated with neither liberation nor entrapment.

Looseness is primordially liberated, liberated without a cause of looseness.

Complete settling is primordially liberated, liberated without a cause of settling.

To summarize, all appearing and all existent phenomena,

As well as non-appearance and non-existence, all that is beyond phenomena,

Everything is liberated from the beginning in space,

So that there is no need for anyone to be liberated by endeavor now.

To all of this, it is meaningless to apply effort and endeavor;

So don't do it! Don't do it! Don't try to accomplish by endeavor!

།མ་ལྟ་མ་ལྟ་ཡིད་ཀྱི་ཆོས་མ་ལྟ།
།མ་བསྒོམས་མ་བསྒོམས་བློ་ཡི་ཆོས་མ་བསྒོམས།
།མ་དཔྱད་མ་དཔྱད་ཡུལ་སེམས་རྗེས་མ་དཔྱད།
།མ་བསྒྲུབས་མ་བསྒྲུབས་རེ་དོགས་འབྲས་མ་བསྒྲུབས།
།མ་སྤངས་མ་སྤངས་ཉོན་མོངས་ལས་མ་སྤངས།
།མ་ལེན་མ་ལེན་ཡང་དག་ཆོས་མ་ལེན།
།མ་འཆིང་མ་འཆིང་རང་གི་རྒྱུད་མ་འཆིང་།
།ཐམས་ཅད་གྲུམ་ལོག་གང་ལའང་ཡུལ་མེད་པས།
།ཁྲིགས་དང་ཆོས་མེད་དམིགས་གཏད་ངོས་གཟུང་མེད།
།གཞི་ལོག་ལམ་ལོག་འབྲས་བུའི་ཆོས་ལོག་པས།
།ལེགས་ཉེས་ཤོར་གོད་རྩལ་ཙམ་དམིགས་སུ་མེད།
།གྲུམ་གྲུམ་གྲུང་ཆད་ཡེ་ཆད་སྣང་སྲིད་ཆད།
།འཁོར་འདས་རུ་ལོག་དབྱིངས་ཀྱི་སོ་ན་མེད།
།གང་ཡིན་ཅི་ཡིན་འདི་ཡིན་གཏད་སོ་མེད།
།ཅྲིད་ཅག་ཅི་བྱུང་ནི་གང་ན་འདུག
།སྤྱིར་ཤུལ་དམེད་འདི་ལ་སུས་ཅི་བྱ།
།ཧ་ཧ་འདི་འདྲ་མཚར་ཆེ་དགོད་རེ་བྲོ།
།སྣང་སྲིད་སྣོད་བཅུད་འཁྲུལ་པ་རུ་ལོག་པས།
།ཉིན་མཚན་ཡེ་སངས་རང་སངས་ནམ་མཁའ་སངས།
།ཞག་དང་ཆོས་སངས་ལོ་ཟླ་བསྐལ་པ་སངས།
།གཅིག་སངས་ཀུན་སངས་ཆོས་དང་ཆོས་མིན་སངས།
།འཁོར་འདས་འཁྲུལ་གཞི་གདོད་མའི་དབྱིངས་སུ་སངས།

Don't look! Don't look! Don't look at intellectual phenomena!

Don't meditate! Don't meditate! Don't meditate on conceptualized phenomena!

Don't analyze! Don't analyze! Don't analyze traces of mind and its objects!

Don't try to accomplish! Don't try to accomplish! Don't try to accomplish the fruition of hope and fear!

Don't reject! Don't reject! Don't reject the activity of the afflictions!

Don't accept! Don't accept! Don't accept the true, pure Dharma!

Don't be trapped! Don't be trapped! Don't trap your natural continuum!

Everything reverts into evenness, without objects for anyone,

So without orderliness and without phenomena, there are no reference points to identify.

The ground falls apart, the path falls apart, and the fruition falls apart;

Therefore, one cannot imagine even an atom of good or evil, loss or decline.

Completely even, decisively resolved, primordially decreed, appearance and existence are severed.

The division between the falling apart of samsara and nirvana also does not exist in its natural place.

What is — whatever is — is not a reference point of "this is it."

What are you all going to do? Where am I?

Past traces do not exist now. What can anyone do about this?

Ha! Ha! What a great surprise. It makes me laugh!

The illusion of appearance and existence, the universe and its inhabitants, falls apart;

So day and night are primordially awakened, self-awakened, sky-awakened;

Day-and-date-awakened, year-month-and-eon-awakened;

One-awakened, all-awakened, phenomena-and-non-phenomena-awakened.

The illusory ground of samsara and nirvana is awakened in primordial space.

།དབྱིངས་ཞེས་ཐ་སྙད་བློ་ཡི་ཆོས་སངས་པས།
།གང་སྒྲུབ་ཅི་འབད་ད་ནི་ཅི་ཞིག་གཉེར།
།འདོད་བློའི་འཁྲིས་ཟད་ནམ་མཁའ་ཡ་མཚན་ཆེ།
།ཆོས་མེད་སྤྲང་པོའི་རང་བཞིན་དེ་འདྲར་ཟད།
།ས་གཞི་རིན་ཆེན་ནམ་མཁའ་བར་སྣང་སྟོང་།
།རྗེན་མེད་ཡེ་གྲོལ་དགོངས་པར་ལྷུན་གྲུབ་པས།
།སྲིད་གསུམ་སྣོད་བཅུད་ཡུལ་མེད་ཆེན་པོར་གྲོལ།
།ཕྱོགས་མེད་ཕྱོགས་སུ་འཛིན་པས་བཅིངས་པ་རྣམས།
།རང་བཞིན་མ་ཤེས་རང་གིས་རང་བསླད་པས།
།རང་ལ་རང་སྣོངས་འཁྲུལ་པ་ཨ་རེ་འཁྲུལ།
།འཁྲུལ་པ་མེད་ལ་གཡང་སར་འཛིན་པས་འཁྲུལ།
།འཁྲུལ་དང་མ་འཁྲུལ་བྱང་ཆུབ་སེམས་ཀྱི་ཀློང་།
།བྱང་ཆུབ་སེམས་ལ་འཁྲུལ་གྲོལ་ཡེ་ནས་མེད།
།དེ་ལས་རོལ་པར་ཤར་ལ་འཛིན་པས་བཅིངས།
།དོན་ལ་འཆིང་གྲོལ་གཉིས་མེད་ཡུལ་སེམས་མེད།
།མེད་ལ་ཡོད་པར་འཛིན་པས་མ་བསླུ་ཞིག
།ཡེ་སངས་རྒྱས་པས་གྲོལ་བའི་རིག་པ་དེ།
།གཏད་འཛིན་ཆོས་ཀྱི་གཟེབ་ཏུ་མ་འཆིངས་ཤིག
།ཡེ་ནས་ཡུལ་མེད་རྣམ་ཀུན་དག་པའི་ཀློང་།
།མཁའ་མཉམ་བདེ་ཆེན་གཞི་རྩ་བྱང་ཆུབ་ཀློང་།
།དེ་ལ་འཁོར་བ་མི་སྲིད་གདོད་མའི་བབས།
།ཐིག་ལེ་ཉག་གཅིག་གྲྭ་ཟུར་མེད་པ་ལ།
།གཅིག་དང་ཐ་དད་འཛིན་པ་འཁྲུལ་པའི་སེམས།
།རང་བྱུང་ཡེ་ཤེས་རྒྱུ་རྐྱེན་མེད་པ་ལ།

Conceptual phenomena conventionally known as "space" are awakened.
So what is there to accomplish, strive for, or care for now?
Entangling thoughts of desire are exhausted — great, amazing space!
So one's natural state has become like that of an irreligious beggar.
The fortress of the precious ground and the space of the sky,
Without support, are spontaneously accomplished in the intention of primordial liberation.
So the three existences, the universe and its inhabitants, are liberated in the great objectless state.
Those who grasp to partiality where there is no partiality are bound.
One corrupts oneself by not understanding the self-nature,
So one is confusing oneself — how deluded a delusion!
There are no delusions, but seeing them as an abyss, one is deluded.
Delusions and non-delusions are the expanse of compassionate mind.
The compassionate mind has no delusion and no liberation from the beginning.
Grasping to whatever arises as the display, from that, one is bound.
In truth there is neither bondage nor liberation; there are neither objects nor mind.
Don't be deceived by grasping what does not exist as existing.
Since this awareness of liberation is primordially awakened,
Don't be bound in the cage of fixating on and grasping at phenomena.
At all times, in the primordially objectless, ever-pure expanse, equal to the sky,
The great bliss, the basic root, is the expanse of compassion.
In that, it is impossible for samsara to exist. It is the primordial state.
As the single essence is without corners or edges,
Grasping at same or different is deluded mind.

།འཁོར་བའི་ལམ་དུ་འཛིན་པ་བྱང་ཆུབ་གེགས།
།ལྷུན་གྲུབ་ཕྱོགས་མེད་མཐའ་དང་བྲལ་བ་ལ།
།ཕྱོགས་ལྷུའི་མཐའ་ལ་ཞེན་པ་སླེམ་བྱེད་བདུད།
།དངོས་མཚན་མེད་པའི་སྟོང་པ་འགག་མེད་ལ།
།ཡོད་མེད་སྣང་སྟོང་འདོགས་པ་ལོག་པའི་བློ།
།དེས་ན་གང་འདོད་ཕྱོགས་རིས་གཟེབ་བོར་ལ།
།ལྷུན་གྲུབ་ཕྱོགས་མེད་ནམ་མཁའ་ལྟར་ཤེས་གྱིས།
།སྣང་གྲགས་མཐོང་ཐོས་ཚོགས་དྲུག་ཅི་ཤར་ཡང་།
།ཐམས་ཅད་རང་གསལ་དབྱེ་བསལ་མེད་པའི་ཀློང་།
།ཡེ་གྲོལ་མཉམ་པའི་ཀློང་དུ་ལ་བཟློས་ཤིག
།མཉམ་ཉིད་གཅིག་ལ་ཅིར་སྣང་འབྱུང་བས་དབྱིངས།
།ཡོན་ཏན་ཐམས་ཅད་སྐྱེད་པར་བྱེད་པས་གཞི།
།ཐམས་ཅད་བྱ་བྱེད་མེད་པར་གྲོལ་བས་ཀློང་།
།ཀུན་འབྱུང་སྙིང་པོར་ཤར་བས་བྱང་ཆུབ་སེམས།
།མཁའ་འདྲ་གདོད་ནས་དག་པར་ཤེས་པར་བྱ།
།རང་བྱུང་ཡེ་ཤེས་གཞི་ཀློང་ཡངས་པ་ལ།
།ཡེ་ནས་དྲི་མེད་འཁོར་བས་མ་གོས་བྱང་།
།ཡོན་ཏན་ལྷུན་གྲུབ་རྒྱུ་འབྲས་འདས་པས་ཆུབ།
།རང་རིག་སྙིང་པོ་འོད་གསལ་དག་པས་སེམས།
།བྱང་ཆུབ་སེམས་སུ་ཀུན་འདུས་རྣམ་པར་དག
།རྩལ་ལས་རོལ་པར་ཤར་བའི་རང་ངོ་ལ།
།རྟོགས་པས་གློ་བུར་ཡང་སངས་རྒྱས་པ་དང་།
།མ་རྟོགས་མ་རིག་འཁྲུལ་པའི་ཚོགས་ཤར་བས།
།ཀུན་གཞི་ལས་མཆེད་ཚོགས་བརྒྱད་ཡུལ་དང་བཅས།

As self-originated primordial wisdom is without causes or conditions,
Grasping it as the path of samsara is a hindrance to perfection.
As the spontaneously accomplished is without partiality and free from extremes,
Attachment to a biased, limited view is the demon of arrogance.
As unobstructed emptiness is without substantial characteristics,
Labeling existence and non-existence as appearance and emptiness is misguided thought.
Therefore, abandon whatever is desired, the trap of bias and partiality.
Understand like the sky, spontaneously accomplished, without partiality.
Whatever arises in the six senses, such as seeing sights and hearing sounds,
Everything is naturally clear in the expanse of no division and no distinction.
Cross the pass in the expanse of primordially liberated equanimity.
Since all that arises arises within a single state of equality,
It is the ground that produces all qualities.
It is the liberated expanse, as everything is without acting or action.
Since the origination of everything arises as the essence, it is compassionate mind.
One must understand that it is primordially pure, like the sky.
As to the vast expanse of the ground, self-originated primordial wisdom,
Since it is undefiled by samsara from the beginning, it is pure.[73]
Because its qualities are spontaneously accomplished beyond cause and effect, it is perfect.[74]
Because self-awareness, the luminous essence, is pure, it is mind.[75]
Within compassionate mind, everything is gathered and always pure.
As to the selfnature of display arising from the potential,
By realization, there is sudden reawakening.

།སྣང་སྲིད་སྣོད་བཅུད་རོལ་པར་ཅི་ཤར་ཡང་།
།བྱང་ཆུབ་སེམས་ཀྱི་ཀློང་ལས་གཡོས་པ་མེད།
།སེམས་ཀློང་མ་གཡོས་མཉམ་པའི་ངང་གནས་ན།
།འཁོར་འདས་ཁྱབ་ཆུབ་དགོངས་ཀློང་ཡངས་པར་གྲོལ།
།གཉིས་ལ་འཁོར་འདས་མི་སྲིད་རང་བཞིན་བབས།
།བཟང་ངན་བླང་དོར་མི་སྲིད་རང་བཞིན་བབས།
།སྤྱངས་ཐོབ་གཟུང་འཛིན་མི་སྲིད་རང་བཞིན་བབས།
།དུག་ལྔའི་ཉོན་མོངས་མི་སྲིད་རང་བཞིན་བབས།
།རྒྱུ་ཆད་ཕྱོགས་ལྷུང་མི་སྲིད་རང་བཞིན་བབས།
།རྩལ་དང་འཆར་བ་མི་སྲིད་རང་བཞིན་བབས།
།ཕྱོགས་ཚམ་བཏགས་པ་མི་འགོག་རང་བཞིན་བབས།
།རང་བྱུང་ཡེ་ཤེས་ཆོས་ཟད་མིང་མེད་ལ།
།རྩལ་དང་རོལ་པ་ཅི་ཤར་གཞི་མེད་ཉིད།
།འཆིང་གྲོལ་མེད་པ་གནས་ལུགས་རང་བཞིན་བབས།
།གྲོལ་ཞེས་བརྡར་བཏགས་རང་ཡལ་རྗེས་མེད་ཙམ།
།ཀུན་ཡིན་ཀུན་མིན་བརྟགས་པར་མི་འགལ་བས།
།ཡེ་ནས་གྲོལ་ཞེས་ཚིག་ཏུ་བརྗོད་པ་ཡིན།
།དབྱེ་བསལ་མེད་དོ་ལྷུན་གྲུབ་ཀློང་དུ་གྲོལ།
།འདུ་འབྲལ་མེད་དོ་ཐིག་ལེའི་ཀློང་དུ་གྲོལ།
།ཅིར་ཡང་འཆར་རོ་ངེས་མེད་ཀློང་དུ་གྲོལ།

Due to the manifestation of the unrealized heap of deluded ignorance,
From the all-ground proliferate the eight assemblages[76] and their objects.
Whatever arises — the display of appearance and existence, the universe and its inhabitants —
Is unmoved from the expanse of compassionate mind.
If, without moving, the expanse of mind remains in the continuum of equanimity,
All at once, samsara and nirvana are perfected and liberated in the vast expanse of the intention.
In reality, samsara and nirvana are impossible in the natural state.
Good and evil, acceptance and rejection, are impossible in the natural state.
Abandoning and obtaining, grasper and grasped, are impossible in the natural state.
The afflictions of the five poisons are impossible in the natural state.
Limited boundaries and falling into partiality are impossible in the natural state.
Energy and appearance are impossible in the natural state.
Merely labeling is unobstructed in the natural state.
As to self-originated primordial wisdom, non-labeled phenomenal exhaustion,
Whatever energy and display arise are just groundless.
Without bondage or liberation is the reality of the natural state.
So-called liberation is just a labeling word. There is merely self-disappearance without a trace.
Since labeling it as "it is everything" or "it is nothing" is not contradictory,
So-called primordial liberation is just a verbal description.
There is no division and no distinction — liberated in the spontaneously accomplished expanse.
There is no gathering and no separating — liberated in the expanse of the essence.
Whatever arises is liberated in the expanse of uncertainty.

།གཟུགས་སུ་སྣང་ངོ་སྣང་བ་རང་སར་གྲོལ།
།སྒྲ་རུ་གྲགས་སོ་གྲགས་པ་རང་སར་གྲོལ།
།དྲི་རུ་ཚོར་བ་ཚོར་བའི་དབྱིངས་སུ་གྲོལ།
།རོ་མྱོང་རིག་པ་རང་སའི་ངང་དེར་གྲོལ།
།དྲན་རིག་བྱུང་ཚོར་གཞི་རྩ་རྡེན་མེད་གྲོལ།
།གཅིག་ཏུ་གྲོལ་ལོ་ཆོས་ཉིད་ཀློང་དུ་གྲོལ།
།གཉིས་སུ་མེད་དོ་ཡུལ་སེམས་མཉམ་པར་གྲོལ།
།རང་བྱུང་གྲོལ་ལོ་ཡེ་ཤེས་ཀློང་དུ་གྲོལ།
།ལྷུན་གྲུབ་གྲོལ་ལོ་གཞི་དབྱིངས་དག་པར་གྲོལ།
།སྣ་ཚོགས་གྲོལ་ལོ་ཉག་གཅིག་ཀློང་དུ་གྲོལ།
།ཕྱོགས་མེད་གྲོལ་ལོ་ལྷུན་གྲུབ་ཀློང་དུ་གྲོལ།
།ཐམས་ཅད་གྲོལ་ལོ་སྙིང་པོའི་ཀློང་དུ་གྲོལ།
།འོད་གསལ་གྲོལ་ལོ་ཉི་ཟླའི་ཀློང་དུ་གྲོལ།
།ཆོས་ཉིད་གྲོལ་ལོ་ནམ་མཁའི་ཀློང་དུ་གྲོལ།
།ཆོས་ཅན་གྲོལ་ལོ་རྒྱ་མཚོའི་ཀློང་དུ་གྲོལ།
།མི་འགྱུར་གྲོལ་ལོ་རི་རྒྱལ་ཀློང་དུ་གྲོལ།
།གདོད་ནས་གྲོལ་ལོ་སྐྱེ་མེད་ཀློང་དུ་གྲོལ།
།ཕྱམ་གཅིག་གྲོལ་ལོ་ཡེ་སངས་ཀློང་དུ་གྲོལ།
།ཡོངས་གྲོལ་གྲོལ་ལོ་ཡེ་རྒྱས་ཀློང་དུ་གྲོལ།

།ཆོས་དབྱིངས་རིན་པོ་ཆེའི་མཛོད་ལས།   །ཆོས་ཐམས་ཅད་བྱང་ཆུབ་སེམས་སུ་ཡེ་ནས་གྲོལ་བའི་རང་བཞིན་བསྟན་པའི་ལེའུ་སྟེ་བཅུ་གཉིས་པའོ།།

Whatever appears as a form, appearance itself, is liberated in its own place.
Whatever is heard as a sound, sound itself, is liberated in its own place.
Whatever odor is smelled is liberated in the space of smell.
Whatever taste is experienced through contact is naturally liberated in its own place.
Whatever mindfulness, awareness, or feeling originates is liberated without support of a basic ground,
Liberated as one, liberated in the expanse of the nature of phenomena.
Without duality, object and mind are evenly liberated.
Self-origination is liberated, liberated in the expanse of primordial wisdom.
Spontaneous accomplishment is liberated, liberated in pure, basic space.
Variety is liberated, liberated in the expanse of total certainty.
Impartiality is liberated, liberated in the expanse of spontaneous accomplishment.
Everything is liberated, liberated in the expanse of the essence.
Clear luminosity is liberated, liberated in the expanse of the sun and moon.
The nature of phenomena is liberated, liberated in the expanse of the sky.
All phenomena are liberated, liberated in the expanse of the ocean.
The unchanging is liberated, liberated in the expanse of the king of mountains;
Primordially liberated, liberated in the expanse of the unborn;
Evenly liberated, liberated in the expanse of the primordially awakened.
Total liberation is liberated, liberated in the primordially blossoming expanse.

From The Precious Treasury of Phenomenal Space, showing that all phenomena are liberated in the nature of compassionate mind, the twelfth chapter, is completed.

།ཆོས་རྣམས་ལྷུན་གྲུབ་བྱང་ཆུབ་སྙིང་པོ་ལ།
།འབད་རྩོལ་མེད་པའི་གནད་ཀྱིས་གོམས་བྱས་ན།
།ཡེ་སངས་རྒྱས་ལ་ཡང་སངས་རྒྱས་འབྱུང་སྟེ།
།འདི་ནི་བླ་མེད་རྡོ་རྗེ་སྙིང་པོའི་དོན།
།རིམ་དགུའི་སྙིང་པོ་བྱང་ཆུབ་ཀློང་ཆེན་ཡིན།
།མཁའ་དཀྱིལ་ཉི་ཟླའི་དཀྱིལ་འཁོར་འོད་གསལ་ཡང་།
།མ་རྟོགས་སྤྲིན་ཆེན་སྙིང་པོས་ཡོངས་བསྒྲིབས་པས།
།མི་སྣང་བྱང་ཆུབ་རང་ལ་ཡོད་པའི་ཚུལ།
།སྤྲིན་ཆེན་དབྱིངས་སུ་བཞག་པས་རང་དེངས་ལྟར།
།འབད་རྩོལ་མེད་པས་རྒྱུ་འབྲས་སྤྲིན་བྲལ་ནས།
།མཁའ་དཀྱིལ་བྱང་ཆུབ་སྙིང་པོ་རང་ལ་འཆར།
།དབང་པོའི་རིམ་པས་ཐེག་པ་ཐ་དད་ལ།
།ངོ་བོ་ཉི་བཞིན་ཆོས་དབྱིངས་ཀློང་ན་གསལ།
།རྩལ་ལས་ཟེར་བཞིན་ཀུན་ཤར་རིས་མེད་པས།
།ས་དང་རྒྱ་མཚོར་ཟྲོད་ཀྱིས་ཁྱབ་པ་ན།
།ཀླངས་ལས་སྤྲིན་གྱི་རོལ་པར་ཤར་བ་ཡིས།
།ངོ་བོ་ཉིད་དང་རྩལ་ཡང་བསྒྲིབས་པ་བཞིན།
།ངོ་བོ་ཉིད་ལས་རང་རྩལ་མ་དག་པའི།
།རོལ་པས་སྙིང་པོའི་དེ་ཉིད་རང་ངོར་སྒྲིབ།
།སྣང་སྲིད་སྣོད་བཅུད་འཁྲུལ་སྣང་བསམ་མི་ཁྱབ།

13

From *The Precious Treasury of Phenomenal Space*, all phenomena that are primordially enlightened in compassionate mind are shown here as reawakened without effort or endeavor, the thirteenth chapter.

As to the perfect essence, all phenomena are spontaneously accomplished.
If one becomes familiar with the technique of non-effort and non-endeavor,
In the original enlightenment, enlightenment originates again.
This is the meaning of the unsurpassable vajra essence.
This is the essential, perfect, great expanse of the nine yanas.
Even though in the midst of space, the mandala of the sun and moon is luminously clear,
Great clouds of ignorance completely obscure the essence,
So the way the perfect essence exists within is not manifest.
Just as great clouds left alone in space dissolve by themselves,
The perfect essence, the mandala of space, appears to oneself
Without effort or endeavor, free from clouds of cause and effect.
In accord with gradations of understanding, there are different vehicles.
The essence, like the sun, appears in the expanse of phenomenal space.
The potential, like the rays of the sun, arises impartially everywhere;
And when the heat of the rays pervades the ground and oceans,
From the resulting vapor there arises a display of clouds;
And by that display, the essence itself, as well as its potency, is obscured.
Likewise, from the essence itself, the play of one's own impure potency
Obscures its own face, the suchness of the essence;
So that there are inconceivable appearances of illusion, such as appearance and existence, the universe and its inhabitants.

།ཉི་ཟེར་རྩལ་ལས་རླུང་བསྐྱོད་སྤྲིན་དེངས་ལྟར།
།རང་ངོ་རྟོགས་ལས་རོལ་པ་རྒྱན་དུ་ཤར།
།འཁྲུལ་པ་ཡེ་གྲོལ་རང་སར་རང་གྲོལ་བས།
།འཁྲུལ་སྣང་འཁྲུལ་འཛིན་མ་སྤངས་དབྱིངས་སུ་ཞི།
།ཀར་སོང་ཆ་མེད་དྭངས་པའི་ནམ་མཁའ་ལ།
།སྐུ་དང་ཡེ་ཤེས་ལྷུན་གྲུབ་ཉི་མ་ཤར།
།གཞན་ནས་མ་འོངས་རང་སྣང་དག་པ་ཙམ།
།གཉིས་སྐྱེས་སྒོང་ངའི་ནང་ནས་འདབ་རྒྱས་པ།
།སྒོང་རྒྱས་འཐུམས་ལྟར་ད་ལྟར་མི་སྣང་ཡང་།
།སྒོང་རྒྱ་རལ་བས་མཁའ་དཀྱིལ་ལྡིང་བ་ལྟར།
།གཟུང་འཛིན་འཁྲུལ་རྟོག་ཟག་པ་སྤུར་ཟད་ཀྱང་།
།ཟག་འབྲས་ལྷག་བཅས་སྒོང་རྒྱ་རལ་མ་ཐག །
།ལྷུན་གྲུབ་རིག་པ་རང་གསལ་རང་ལ་འཆར།
།སྐུ་དང་ཡེ་ཤེས་སྣང་བས་མཁའ་དབྱིངས་ཁྱབ།
།རང་ངོ་ཤེས་པས་ཀུན་བཟང་ཀློང་དུ་གྲོལ།
།ཕྱོགས་བཅུར་ཐུགས་རྗེའི་རོལ་པ་ཚད་མེད་ལས།
།སྤྲུལ་པ་འཕྲོ་བས་འགྲོ་བའི་དོན་ཀུན་བྱེད།
།འཁོར་བ་ཇི་སྲིད་མཛད་པ་ཉེ་བར་སྟོན།
།འདི་ནི་རང་བཞིན་བབས་ཀྱི་ངོ་བོ་ལས།
།རྩལ་གྱི་ཐུགས་རྗེ་ཕྱོགས་མེད་ཤར་བ་སྟེ།
།རོལ་པས་གཞན་དོན་ཕུན་སུམ་ཚོགས་པ་ཡིན།

From the potential of the sun's rays, as winds blow and clouds disperse,
By realizing self-nature, display arises as an ornament.
Confusion is primordially liberated, self-liberated in its own place;
So, without abandoning anything, illusory appearance and illusory grasping are pacified in space,
Without knowledge of where they have gone.
In the clear sky, the kayas and primordial wisdoms are spontaneously accomplished, and the luminous sun arises,
Not coming from anywhere else, just pure self-appearance.
The wings of the twice-born bird[77] develop inside the egg,
But as the eggshell covers the bird, this does not appear.
However, when the eggshell is broken, it soars in the midst of space.
Like that, illusory defiled thoughts of grasper and grasped are already completely exhausted;
However, when the eggshell — the remaining result of delusion[78] — is broken,
Naturally clear, spontaneously accomplished awareness appears to oneself.[79]
All the space of sky is pervaded by the appearance of the kayas and primordial wisdoms.
By knowing self-nature, one is liberated in the expanse of All-Good.
From the measureless display of compassion in the ten directions,
By sending forth emanations, all benefit for beings is performed.
Until the end of samsara, activities will be accordingly shown.
From the essence of the natural state,
The energy of compassion arises without partiality.
By this display, benefit for other beings is auspiciously perfected.

།མ་དག་ཆ་བཅས་རོལ་པ་ཉེར་ཞི་ཡང་།
།མ་དག་འགྲོ་ལ་སྤྲུལ་པ་སྣང་བ་ནི།
།སྟོན་པའི་ཧེ་བཞིན་-ཤུགས་ཀྱི་ཐུགས་རྗེ་དང་།
།འགྲོ་སེམས་གཙང་མའི་ལས་སྨོན་དག་པས་འཆར།
།དེ་ཚེ་ཞིང་ཀུན་སྤྲུལ་པ་ཚད་མེད་ཅིང་།
།མཐའ་ཡས་འགྲོ་བ་བྱང་ཆུབ་འདྲེན་མཛད་ཀྱང་།
།སྟོན་པའི་ཆོས་སྐུ་དབྱིངས་ལས་མི་གཡོ་སྟེ།
།རང་བྱུང་ཡེ་ཤེས་རྟག་ཆད་ཕྱོགས་ལྷུང་མེད།
།དབྱིངས་ལས་རང་ཤར་སྟུག་པོ་བཀོད་པར་ནི།
།རིག་འཛིན་མཁའ་འགྲོས་བསྐུའི་སེམས་དཔའ་ལ།
།ལོངས་སྤྱོད་རྫོགས་པའི་བཀོད་པ་བསམ་ཡས་སྣང་།
།དེ་ཡང་དབྱིངས་ལས་སྟོན་པའི་ཐུགས་རྗེ་དང་།
།གདུལ་བྱའི་མོས་དགོས་ལྷུན་གྲུབ་རང་དོར་སྣང་།
།ཆོས་སྐུའི་ངོ་བོ་རང་བྱུང་ཡེ་ཤེས་ཏེ།
།རོལ་པར་ཐམས་ཅད་མཁྱེན་པའི་ཡེ་ཤེས་མཆོ།
།གདོད་མའི་དབྱིངས་ན་ཐིག་ལེ་གཅིག་ཏུ་བཞུགས།
།ལོངས་སྐུའི་ངོ་བོ་རང་བཞིན་ལྷུན་གྲུབ་སྟེ།
།རོལ་པར་རིགས་ལྔ་ཡེ་ཤེས་རྣམ་པ་ལྔ།
།ནམ་མཁའི་དབྱིངས་ཀུན་གང་བར་སྣང་བ་ཡིན།
།སྤྲུལ་སྐུའི་ངོ་བོ་ཐུགས་རྗེའི་འཆར་གཞི་སྟེ།
།རོལ་པར་གང་ལ་གང་འདུལ་དེར་སྣང་ཞིང་།
།ཕྲིན་ལས་ཆེན་པོས་མདའ་དབང་འགྱུར་པ་ཡིན།

Even the slightest impure display completely subsides.
Nonetheless, the appearance of emanations to impure beings
Is as is shown, due to the force of compassion,
And it appears only to beings with pure karma and aspirations.[80]
At that time, in all fields, there are countless emanations,
And limitless beings are led to perfection;
However, the dharmakaya of Buddha is unmoved from space.
Self-originated primordial wisdom is free from the bias of eternalism or nihilism.
Naturally arising from space, the Densely Ornamented Pure Land
Appears as an inconceivable array of perfect enjoyment
To vidyadharas, dakinis, and bodhisattvas on the tenth bhumi.
An inconceivable array of perfect enjoyments appears.
That is also the compassion of the teacher from space.
By the virtue and devotion of disciples to be tamed, it appears to their spontaneously perfected self-nature.
The essence of dharmakaya is self-originated primordial wisdom.
Its play, the ocean of wisdom of all-knowing,
Settles in primordial space as a single sphere.
The nature of the sambhogakaya is spontaneously accomplished.
Its display, the five families and five primordial wisdoms,
Appears everywhere in space, filling the sky.
The essence of the nirmanakaya is the ground of arising of compassion.
As display, it appears according to various needs.
By great enlightened activities one achieves sovereignty.

།འདི་དག་རྒྱུ་འབྲས་རྩོལ་བས་མ་བསྒྲུབས་ཏེ།
།ཡེ་ནས་ལྷུན་གྲུབ་ཅོག་གཞག་ངང་ལ་སྣང་།
།མཆོག་གསང་རབ་ལ་ཚེ་འདིར་སྣང་བ་སྟེ།
།དེ་ལས་གཞན་དུ་བར་དོར་མི་བསླུ་བས།
།རྡོ་རྗེ་སྙིང་པོ་རྩེ་མོའི་ཐེག་པ་ནི།
།རྒྱུ་འབྲས་ཐེག་པ་ཀུན་ལས་ཁྱད་པར་འཕགས།

།ཆོས་དབྱིངས་རིན་པོ་ཆེའི་མཛོད་ལས། །ཆོས་ཐམས་ཅད་བྱང་ཆུབ་ཀྱི་སེམས་སུ་ཡེ་སངས་རྒྱས་པ་ལ་རྩོལ་བ་དང་སྒྲུབ་པ་མེད་པར་ཡང་སངས་རྒྱས་པར་བསྟན་པའི་ལེའུ་སྟེ་བཅུ་གསུམ་པའོ།།

All these are not accomplished by endeavor or cause and effect.

From the beginning, spontaneously accomplished, they appear in the continuum of complete resting.

By great beings, the supreme secret is seen in this lifetime.

For others it will be unfailing in the intermediate state.

Thus, the highest path, the vajra essence

Is much more exalted than all the vehicles of cause and effect.

From *The Precious Treasury of Phenomenal Space*, all phenomena that are primordially enlightened in compassionate mind are shown here as reawakened without effort or endeavor, the thirteenth chapter, is completed.

།དེ་ལྟར་ཆོས་ཉིད་རྡོ་རྗེ་སྙིང་པོའི་གླུ།
།མཁའ་མཉམ་གདོད་ནས་དག་པའི་རང་བཞིན་འདི།
།མི་འགྱུར་གཞི་རྩ་བྲལ་བའི་གནས་ཉིད་དུ།
།རང་ཤར་འཕོ་འགྱུར་མེད་པའི་རོལ་པར་ཤར།
།ཡེ་མཉམ་ཕྲུམ་གདལ་ཀློང་ཆེན་ཡངས་པའི་དོན།
།གང་ཡང་མ་ཕྱིན་གདོད་མའི་རང་བཞིན་དང་།
།མི་གཡོ་ལྷུན་གྱིས་གྲུབ་པའི་ཆོས་ཉིད་ལ།
།རྒྱུ་ཆད་མེད་ཅིང་ཕྱོགས་ལྷུང་བྲལ་བར་གྱུར།
།དོན་རྣམས་ཇི་བཞིན་མཁའ་མཉམ་ཡངས་པའི་དཀྱིལ།
།གང་དུ་རང་བྱུང་ཀློང་ཆེན་རྒྱལ་པོ་ནི།
།རྟག་ཏུ་མི་གཡོ་སྣ་ཚོགས་རང་སར་གྲོལ།
།འདི་ཞེས་མི་མཚོན་དབྱིངས་རུམ་ཡངས་པར་ཕྱིན།
།རྟོགས་པའི་དུས་ངེས་མཁའ་འདྲའི་རྣལ་འབྱོར་པས།
།རང་ཉམས་ཕྱོགས་གཅིག་ལུང་དོན་མཐུན་པ་ནི།
།རྩ་བའི་སེམས་ལུང་ཉི་ཤུ་རྩ་གཅིག་དང་།
།ཀློང་གསུམ་མན་ངག་སྡེ་བཞི་མཐུན་པར་བཀོད།
།དགེ་བ་འདི་ཡིས་མ་ལུས་འགྲོ་བ་ཀུན།
།མ་འབད་བཞིན་དུ་གདོད་མའི་སར་ཕྱིན་ནས།
།ཀུན་བཟང་ས་ལ་འཕོ་འགྱུར་མེད་པ་ཡི།
།དོན་གཉིས་ལྷུན་གྲུབ་ཆོས་ཀྱི་རྒྱལ་པོར་ཤོག

From *The Precious Treasury of Phenomenal Space*, the conclusion.

Such is the song of the vajra essence, the nature of phenomena.
Equal to the sky, this nature of primordial purity,
Unchanging in its own place, free from ground or root,
Appears as a self-arising display, free from change and transformation.
The meaning of the primordially even, all-pervading great vast expanse
Has not gone anywhere. In the continuum of the primordial nature,
As to the unmoving, spontaneously accomplished nature of phenomena,
It has no restrictions, and it is free from bias.
All meanings as they are — the center of the vast equal sky,
In which the great expanse, the self-originated king,
Is always unmoved, all variety liberated in its own ground —
Cannot be indicated as "this," gone to the vast womb of space.
Certain about his own moment of realization, the sky-like yogi
Has written some of his own experience,
Which is in accord with the meaning of the twenty-one root mind transmissions,
The three expanses, and four instructions.
By this merit may all beings without exception,
Without endeavor, reach the primordial state.
And in the unchangeable ground of the All-Good,
May they all spontaneously accomplish the two benefits and become victorious kings of Dharma.

།ཕྱོགས་རྣམས་ཀུན་ཏུ་བདེ་དཔལ་འབྱོར་པ་ནི།
།དག་པའི་ཞིང་བཞིན་འདོད་དགུ་ལྷུན་གྲུབ་ཅིང་།
།ཆོས་རྔ་སྒྲོགས་པས་ཐར་པའི་རྒྱལ་མཚན་འཛུགས།
།དམ་ཆོས་མི་ནུབ་བསྟན་པ་རྒྱས་པར་ཤོག
།ཆོས་དབྱིངས་རིན་པོ་ཆེའི་མཛོད་ཅེས་བྱ་བ།
།ཐེག་པ་མཆོག་གི་རྣལ་འབྱོར་པ་ཀློང་ཆེན་རབ་འབྱམས་
ཀྱིས་གངས་རི་ཐོད་དཀར་གྱི་མགུལ་དུ་ལེགས་པར་
བཀོད་པ་རྫོགས་སོ། དགེའོ།། དགེའོ། དགེའོ།།

At all times and in all directions, with happiness and wealth,

As it is in a pure land, may all desires be spontaneously accomplished.

By sounding the drum of Dharma, raise the victory banner of liberation.

May the holy Dharma not wane, and may the teachings spread and flourish.

This work, entitled *The Precious Treasury of Phenomenal Space,* was written in the neck[81] of White Skull Snow Mountain by the *Yogi* of the highest path, Longchen Rabjam.

Virtue! Virtue! Virtue!

From the Heart Essence of the Great Expanse

The Most Secret Guru Yoga Having the Seal of the Essence

ༀ༔ ༔ཀློང་ཆེན་སྙིང་གི་ཐིག་ལེ་ལས༔ ཡང་གསང་བླ་མའི་སྒྲུབ་པ་
ཐིག་ལེའི་རྒྱ་ཅན་བཞུགས༔

ༀ༔ ༔གུ་རུ་ཨ་བྲ་ཧི་ཏ་མ༔ ཡང་གསང་བླ་མའི་སྒྲུབ་པ་ནི༔ ཤིན་ཏུ་དབེན་ཞིང་ཡིད་མཐུན་པར༔ མཚལ་ཚོམ་བུ་ལྔ་པའི་སྟེང༔ ཧྲཱིཿཧཱུྃ་དུམ་བུ་གསུམ་པའི་ནང༔ རིག་འཛིན་འདུས་པའི་སྒྲོག་འཁོར་དང༔ སེལ་མེད་དམ་རྫས་ཨ་མྲི་ཏ༔ རིན་ཆེན་སྨན་དང་འབྲུ་སྣས་བཀང༔ སྟེང་ནས་དར་དམར་ཕྱིང་གུར་དབུབ༔ མདུན་དུ་གཏོར་ཚོགས་སྤྱི་མཐུན་བཤམས༔ བདེ་བའི་སྟན་ལ་བག་ཕབ་སྟེ༔ དང་པོ་སྐྱབས་སུ་འགྲོ་བ་ནི༔

ཧཱུྃ༔ ངོ་བོ་རང་བཞིན་ཐུགས་རྗེའི་ཚུལ༔
སྐུ་གསུམ་ཆེན་པོར་ལྷུན་རྫོགས་པའི༔
རང་རིག་དོན་གྱི་བླ་མ་ལ༔
འཛིན་མེད་ངང་ནས་སྐྱབས་སུ་མཆི༔

ལན་གསུམ༔ གཉིས་པ་སེམས་བསྐྱེད་ནི༔

ཧོ༔ སངས་རྒྱས་མེད་ལ་སེམས་ཅན་མེད༔
ཡིན་པ་མེད་ལ་མིན་པ་མེད༔
སོ་སོ་རང་གདངས་ལྷུག་པའི་གདངས༔
རང་གྲོལ་ཆེན་པོར་སེམས་བསྐྱེད་དོ༔

ལན་གསུམ༔

From the Heart Essence of the Great Expanse[82]
The Most Secret Guru Yoga Having the Seal of the Essence

Jigme Lingpa

Guru Ah Gra Hi Nama ༔

As for the most secret Guru yoga, in an extremely solitary but agreeable place, on a mandala of five heaps,[83] is a bhandha having three divisions[84]; in it is the life force mantra wheel of all the awareness-holders.[85] It is filled with immaculate samaya substances,[86] nectar,[87] precious medicine, and various grains. Above, it is covered with a red canopy. In front, the usual set of torma[88] offerings is arranged. While remaining at ease on a comfortable seat, first, go for refuge.

HUNG ༔ The essence, nature, and power of compassion ༔

Are spontaneously perfect as the three great kayas. ༔

To the absolute Guru of self-awareness, ༔

I go for refuge in the continuum of non-grasping. ༔

Repeat three times. Second, generate compassionate mind.

HOH ༔ There are no buddhas; there are no sentient beings; ༔

There is nothing that is; there is nothing that is not. ༔

The freshness of self-manifestation is manifestation of natural ease. ༔

In the great self-liberation, I generate compassionate mind. ༔

Repeat three times.

གསུམ་པ་མཚམས་གཅོད་ནི༔

ཧྲཱིཿ གདོད་ནས་འཁོར་འདས་གཉིས་མེད་ལ༔
བགེགས་དང་བར་ཆད་མིང་ཡང་མེད༔
འོད་གསལ་སྒྱུ་འཕྲུལ་དྲྭ་བའི་ངང་༔
རྣམ་རྟོག་བག་ཆགས་མཚམས་གཅད་དོ༔
རྐྵ་ན་བཛྲ་རཀྵ་ཧཱུྃ༔

བཞི་པ་བྱིན་དབབ་མཆོད་རློབ་ནི༔

ཧཱུྃ༔ སྟོང་ཉིད་དབྱིངས་ལས་ཐུགས་རྗེའི་རྩལ༔
མཁའ་ལ་འཇའ་ཚོན་ལྷ་བུར་ཤར༔
དཀྱིལ་འཁོར་མཆོད་པའི་རྫས་རྣམས་ཀུན༔
རང་གྲོལ་ཆེན་པོར་བྱིན་གྱིས་རློབས༔
ཛྙཱ་ནཱ་བཛྲ་ས་མ་ཡ་ཡཾ་ཡཾ༔
ཨོཾ་ཨཱཿཧཱུྃ༔

ལན་གསུམ་བརྗོད་པས་མཆོད་རྫས་བརླབ༔ ལྔ་པ་དཀྱིལ་འཁོར་བསྐྱེད་པ་ནི༔

ཧཱུྃ༔ རིག་སྟོང་ཆོས་ཉིད་མངོན་སུམ་དབྱིངས༔
དྲན་རྫོགས་ཉམས་སྣང་གོང་འཕེལ་སྐུ༔
རིག་པ་ཚད་ཕེབས་དོན་གྱི་ལྷ༔
ཆོས་ཟད་མ་བཅོས་ཀློང་ཆེན་པ༔

བི་མ་ལ༔ ཞེས་ཀྱང་བསྒྱུར་ཆོག་པ་རྩ་བའི་མན་ངག༔

Third, sealing the boundaries.

From the beginning, since there is no duality of samsara and nirvana, ༔
Not even the names of obstructing spirits and obstacles exist. ༔
In the continuum of the luminous, magical net ༔
Conceptual thoughts and habits are cut off. ༔
JYANA VAJRA RAKSHA HUNG ༔

Fourth, invocation and blessing the offerings.

HUNG ༔ From the space of emptiness, the power of compassion ༔
Arises like a rainbow in the sky. ༔
The mandala and all the offering substances ༔
Are blessed as the great self-liberation. ༔
JYANA VAJRA SAMAYA PHEM PHEM ༔
OM AH HUNG ༔

By saying that three times, bless the offering substances. Fifth, visualizing the mandala.

HUNG ༔ Emptiness-awareness is the actual state of phenomena itself. ༔
In perfect mindfulness, appearance and meditative experience intensify as the body of the deity. ༔
Reaching the ultimate measure of awareness is reaching the absolute deity. ༔
Exhaustion of phenomena is the unfabricated Longchenpa.[89] ༔

In the root instruction it is stated that you can replace Longchenpa with Vimalamitra.

ཞི་འཛུམ་པདྨ་ཏ་ཡི་ཆས༔
སེམས་ཉིད་དལ་གསོའི་ཕྱག་རྒྱ་ཅན༔
སྣང་ལ་རང་བཞིན་མེད་པའི་ངང༔
སྐུ་གསུམ་ཞིང་ཁམས་ཐམས་ཅད་རྫོགས༔
གནས་གསུམ་ཡི་གེ་གསུམ་གྱིས་མཚན༔
དེ་ལས་འཕྲོས་པའི་འོད་ཟེར་གྱིས༔
དུས་གསུམ་བདེ་གཤེགས་རྩ་བ་གསུམ༔
རིག་འཛིན་མཁའ་འགྲོ་རྒྱ་མཚོ་བཅས༔
མ་ལུས་སྤྱན་དྲངས་དབྱེར་མེད་བསྟིམ༔

དྲུག་པ་སྤྱན་འདྲེན་བྱ་བ་ནི༔

ཧཱུྃ༔ རྣམ་རྟོག་བྲལ་བའི་ཕོ་བྲང་ནས༔
གདོད་མའི་མགོན་པོ་གཤེགས་སུ་གསོལ༔
ཕྱོགས་ལྷུང་མེད་པའི་ཕོ་བྲང་ནས༔
དུས་གསུམ་བདེ་གཤེགས་གཤེགས་སུ་གསོལ༔
འཇའ་ལུས་ཟང་ཐལ་ཕོ་བྲང་ནས༔
དཔལ་མགོན་བླ་མ་གཤེགས་སུ་གསོལ༔
རིག་པ་སྐུ་རུ་སྨིན་པ་དང༔
འོད་ལུས་འགྲུབ་པར་བྱིན་གྱིས་རློབས༔
མནྟ་གུ་རུ་ཛྙཱ་ན་ས་མ་ཡ་ཛཿཛཿ

Peaceful and smiling, in the style of a pandita,[90] ༔

With the mudra[91] of resting the mind, ༔

In the continuum of appearances without inherent nature ༔

The three kayas and the pure lands are perfected. ༔

The three places are marked with the three syllables.[92] ༔

From these, light rays emanate, ༔

Inviting the sugatas of the three times, the three roots, and the ocean of awareness-holders and dakinis. ༔

All these without exception dissolve inseparably in oneself. ༔

Sixth, inviting.

HUNG ༔ From the palace free from discursive thoughts, ༔

I invite the primordial protector. ༔

From the palace free of partiality, ༔

I invite the sugatas of the three times. ༔

From the palace of the transparent rainbow body,[93] ༔

I invite the glorious lord Guru. ༔

Please bless me so that awareness ripens as the kayas ༔

And I attain the rainbow body. ༔

MAHA GURU JYANA SAMAYA JAH JAH ༔

བདུན་པ་བཛྲ་ཕྱག་འཚལ་བ་ནི༔

ཧོཿ ལྷ་དང་རང་སེམས་དབྱེར་མེད་དང་༔
དམ་ཡེའི་འཛིན་པ་དག་པའི་ཕྱིར༔
བསམ་བརྗོད་བྲལ་བའི་བླ་མ་ལ༔
སྤང་བླང་མེད་པར་ཕྱག་འཚལ་ལོ༔
ཨ་ཏི་པུ་ཧོཿ
པྲ་ཏཱིཙྪ་ཧོཿ

བརྒྱད་པ་མཆོད་པ་བྱུ་བ་ནི༔

ཧཱུྃ༔ ཚོགས་དྲུག་ཡུལ་གྱི་རྒྱལ་སྣང་ཀུན༔
ཕྱི་ནང་གསང་བའི་མཆོད་སྤྲིན་དུ༔
ཕུལ་བས་ཞེན་འཛིན་རྣམ་རྟོག་ཀུན༔
འོད་གསལ་ཆེན་པོར་དག་པར་སྨོལ༔
ཨོཾ་བཛྲ་ཨརྒྷཾ། པཱདྱཾ། པུཥྤེ། དྷཱུ་པེ། ཨཱ་ལོ་ཀེ། གནྡྷེ།
ནཻ་ཝི་དྱ། ཤབྡ། རཱུ་པ། ཤབྡ་གནྡྷེ། རཱ་ས་སྤརྴེ་མ་ཧཱ་པཉྩ་ར་ཀྵ་བ་ལིཾ་ཏ་ཁཱ་ཧི༔
མ་ཧཱ་སུ་ཁ་ཛྙཱ་ན་ཏ་པཱུ་ཛ་ཧོཿ

Seventh, the gesture of homage.

HOH ༔ In the continuum of the inseparability of one's mind and the deity, ༔
To purify grasping at the deities of samaya and primordial wisdom,[94] ༔
I will make prostration, without accepting or rejecting, ༔
To the inexpressible and inconceivable Lama. ༔
ATI PU HO ༔
PRATĪCCHA HOH ༔

Eighth, making offerings.

HUNG ༔ All the appearances of the potential, objects of the six senses, ༔
I offer as outer, inner, and secret offering clouds. ༔
By this, may all discursive thoughts of attachment and grasping ༔
Be purified as the great luminosity. ༔

Say from
OM VAJRA ARGHAM ༔
to
RUPA ༔
SHABDHA ༔
GANDHE ༔
RASA ༔
SPARSHE ༔
MAHAPANYCAMRITA ༔
RAKTA ༔
BALINGTA ༔
KAHI ༔
MAHASUKHA DHARMADHATU PUJA HOH ༔

དགུ་པ་དོན་དམ་བསྟོད་པ་ནི༔

ཧྲཱིཿ མ་བཅོས་སྤྲོས་བྲལ་འོད་གསལ་ཆོས་སྐུའི་ངང་༔
རྣམ་མང་རྒྱུད་སྤྱི་རྒྱ་མཚོའི་དཀྱིལ་འཁོར་རྫོགས༔
སྐུ་གསུམ་འདུ་འབྲལ་མེད་པའི་བླ་མ་ལ༔
ཀུན་རྫོབ་སྒྱུ་མ་ཙམ་དུ་བསྟོད་པར་བགྱི༔

བཅུ་པ་ཛཔ་ཀྱི་དགོངས་པ་ནི༔

ཐུགས་ཀར་ཐིག་ལེ་འོད་ལྔའི་ཀློང་༔
ཡེ་ཤེས་སེམས་དཔའ་ཀུན་ཏུ་བཟང་༔
མཐིང་གསལ་མཉམ་གཞག་ཕྱག་རྒྱ་ཅན༔
དེ་ཡི་ཙིཏྟའི་གུར་ཁང་དབུས༔
པདྨ་ཉི་ཟླའི་གདན་གྱི་སྟེང་༔
ཧཱུྃ་ཡིག་མཐིང་གའི་མཐའ་བསྐོར་དུ༔
རིག་འཛིན་འདུས་པའི་སྲོག་སྔགས་ཀྱིས༔
བསྐོར་བའི་འོད་ཟེར་ཕྱོགས་བཅུར་འཕྲོས༔
དུས་གསུམ་བདེ་གཤེགས་ཐམས་ཅད་དང་༔
ཁྱད་པར་འོད་གསལ་རྫོགས་ཆེན་གྱི༔
རིག་འཛིན་བརྒྱུད་པའི་ཐུགས་རྗེ་བསྐུལ༔
ཚུར་འདུས་བདག་ལ་ཐིམ་པ་ཡིས༔
མཆོག་ཐུན་དངོས་གྲུབ་ཐོབ་པར་དམིགས༔
ཨོཾ་ཨཱཿཧཱུྃ་མ་ཧཱ་གུ་རུ་ཛྙཱ་ན་སིདྡྷི་ཧཱུྃ༔

རྩ་སྔགས་ཡིག་འབྲུ་བཅུ་གཉིས་པ༔

Ninth, the absolute praise.

HRIH ༔ In the continuum of luminous dharmakaya, free from fabrication and elaboration, ༔

The mandala of the manifold ocean of tantra is perfected. ༔

To the Lama who is the inseparability of three kayas, ༔

I offer praise in mere relative illusion. ༔

Tenth, the principle of the recitation.

At my heart, in an expanse of circles of the five lights,[95] ༔

Is the wisdom deity All-Good,[96] ༔

Clear blue, having the meditation mudra.[97] ༔

In the heart of that deity is a canopy. Under the canopy, in the middle, ༔

On a lotus, sun, and moon seat, ༔

Is a dark blue HUNG syllable, and surrounding that ༔

Is the life-force mantra of all the awareness-holders. ༔

Surrounding that again are light rays emanating in the ten directions. ༔

They invoke the compassion of all the sugatas, ༔

Especially that of the awareness-holders of the lineage of the Great Perfection. ༔

They are gathered back, and by their dissolving into myself, ༔

I visualize that the blessings of the supreme and ordinary accomplishments[98] are attained. ༔

OM AH HUNG MAHA GURU JYANA SIDDHI HUNG ༔

Recite this twelve-syllable root mantra 100,000 times.

འབྲུ་འབུམ་དག་ཏུ་བསྙེན་པར་བྱ༔

བསྙེན་སྒྲུབ་ལས་གསུམ་∫འོད་ཟེར་འཕྲོས་པས་བདེ་གཤེགས་མཆོད་པ་བསྙེན་པ། སེམས་ཅན་གྱི་སྡིག་སྒྲིབ་སྦྱངས་ཤིང་ལྷར་སྒྱུར་བ་སྒྲུབ་པ། ཚུར་འདུས་ནས་བདག་ལ་ཐིམ་པས་སྒོ་གསུམ་གྱི་སྒྲིབ་པ་བྱང་ཞིང་དངོས་གྲུབ་ཐོབ་པ་སྒྲུབ་ཆེན། དམིགས་པ་མཉམ་པ་ཉིད་དུ་བཞག་པ་ལས་སྦྱོར་རོ། །མཆན།) ཚིག་ཚོད་ཡིན༔ ཉམས་དངོས་རྨི་ལམ་མ་ངེས་པར༔ ཞལ་མཐོང་གསུང་ཐོས་རིག་རྩལ་འབབ༔ གླེགས་བམ་ཆར་རྒྱུན་འབབ་པ་དང༔ སེང་གེ་གླང་ཆེན་ཞོན་སོགས་རྨི༔ ཁྱད་པར་ཉམས་རྟོགས་རྩོལ་མེད་འཆར༔ མ་བསླབས་ཆོས་ཀྱི་གཏེར་མཛོད་རྡོལ༔ དེ་ཚེ་དངོས་གྲུབ་བླང་བར་བྱ༔ ས་མ་ཡ༔ རྒྱ་རྒྱ་རྒྱ༔

ཨེ་མ༔

ཤིན་ཏུ་ཡང་ཟབ་དགོངས་པའི་གཏེར༔
ཡང་གསང་ཐིག་ལེའི་རྒྱ་རྟགས་ཅན༔
གདོད་མའི་མགོན་པོ་ཀློང་ཆེན་པས༔
དཔལ་གྱི་བསམ་ཡས་མཆིམས་ཕུ་རུ༔
ཁོ་བོའི་སྙིང་གི་དབུས་སུ་སྦས༔
ལོ་ལྔའི་བར་དུ་གསང་རྒྱ་བྱས༔
ད་ལྟ་དུས་ངན་སྙིགས་མའི་ཚེ༔
ཟབ་རྒྱ་གྲོལ་བའི་སྣོད་དཀོན་ཡང༔
གདུག་པ་ཞེ་སྡང་སྦྲུལ་གྱི་ལོར༔
ལྷ་བ་དཀར་པོའི་ལྗོང་གུར་ནང༔
ཡེ་ཤེས་དབྱིངས་ཀྱི་མཁའ་འགྲོ་མས༔
འདི་ནས་ལོ་གསུམ་འདས་པ་ན༔
ཐུགས་ཀྱི་སྲས་མཆོག་གསུམ་ཡང་འབྱུང༔
བཛྲའི་མིང་ཅན་སྙིང་སྟོབས་ཆེ༔
ཛྙ་ནའི་མིང་ཅན་གྲུབ་པའི་གཙོ༔
རིགས་ལྔའི་མིང་འཛིན་སླན་ངག་མཁན༔
དེ་དག་རྣམས་ལ་ཆོས་སྒོ་འབྱེད༔

Service, worship, and activity[99] *are completed all at once.*

Uncertain whether it is in waking experience or a dream, the face is seen, the speech is heard, and the power of awareness increases.[100] *A rain of volumes continuously descends, and one dreams one is riding lions or elephants. In particular, meditation experiences and realizations effortlessly arise. Even if you have not studied, Dharma treasures naturally come forth. At that time one should receive accomplishment. Samaya, GYA GYA GYA* ༔

How marvelous! ༔
This most extremely profound mind-treasure, ༔
The secret essence, which has the sealed sign of the essence, ༔
Was hidden in the center of my[101] heart, ༔
In glorious Samye Chimpu, ༔
By the primordial protector Longchenpa. ༔
It was kept confidential for five years. ༔
At the present time of the dark age, ༔
Though suitable vessels for spreading this profoundly sealed teaching are rare indeed, ༔
In the year of the malevolent, aggressive snake, ༔
In a white woolen canopy, ༔
The dakini of primordial wisdom space prophesied: ༔
After three years from this time, ༔
There will be three heart sons. ༔
One with great strength of heart will have an indestructible name. ༔
One who prioritizes accomplishment will have a primordial wisdom name. ༔
One, a poet, will hold a name of the five families. ༔

ཅེས་པའི་ལུང་བསྟན་ཇི་བཞིན་དུ༔
བརྒྱུད་འཛིན་སླིང་གི་བུ་རྣམས་དང་༔
ཀོང་སྨྲོན་སྲས་པའི་རྣལ་འབྱོར་གྱིས༔
བསྐུལ་ངོར་ཟབ་དོན་བཀའ་རྒྱ་བཀྲོལ༔
སྨན་བཙུན་ཚེ་རིང་མཆེད་ལྔ་དང་༔
གཟའ་རྒོད་སྲོག་གི་སྤུ་གྲི་ཡིས༔
ཐུབ་པར་སྲུངས་ཤིག་དམ་ཚིག་རྒྱ༔
ལས་ཅན་རྣམས་ཀྱི་དཔལ་དུ་ཤོག༔ ༔

To these the gates of the teachings will be opened. ༔

In accord with this prophesy, ༔

In response to the entreaties of these lineage-holder heart sons ༔

And the hidden yogi, the madman of Kong, ༔

The seal of this teaching of profound meaning was released. ༔

By the healing deities, Tsering Chenga, ༔

And the protector, the planetary deity Rahula, ༔

May it be capably guarded. Samaya sealed. ༔

May there be glory for those of good fortune. ༔

Glossary

abyss, *g.yang sa* (Tib.): A potentially dangerous place of straying or going wrong, a great gap or discontinuity between samsara and nirvana. From the beginning, all phenomena are the great equality of samsara and nirvana, so in ultimate reality, there is no dangerous abyss or precipice between them.

afflictions, *nyon mongs* (Tib.), *kleśa* (Skt.): Emotions stained with attachment, aversion, and ignorance, which produce negative karma.

all at once, *phyam gcig* (Tib.): Simultaneously, instantly, all-inclusively.

all-encompassing, *phyam gdal* (Tib.): All-pervading, continuous, open, in equanimity, even minded, spread-out.

All-Good, *kun tu bzang po* (Tib.), *Samantabhadra* (Skt.): The dharmakaya Buddha and the meditational deity that personifies the experience of the Great Perfection within fundamental phenomenal space. This realization is fundamentally good, beyond all concepts of good and bad.

all-inclusive, *kun 'dus* (Tib.): The universal essence, the nature of phenomena, emptiness, includes within it all that there is. The nature of phenomena is also the nature of enlightened mind, in which all phenomena are subsumed or gathered.

antidote, remedy; *gnyen po* (Tib.): A method in Buddhist practice used to counteract obstacles to enlightenment, such as disturbing emotions. For example, in the Hinayana vehicle, contemplation of the disgusting aspects of the physical body is used as an antidote for carnal lust. In the Mahayana vehicle, contemplation of emptiness is used as an antidote for mistaken belief in a truly existing selfhood of phenomena. Ati emphasizes practice without antidotes, since realization of buddhahood is unconditionally self-existing and all-inclusive.

Anu: See nine vehicles.

appearance and existence, *snang srid* (Tib.): The delusive appearance of conditioned manifestation or samsaric existence.

as it is, *rang sor* (Tib.): The freshness of one's original, natural state.

Ati, *a ti* (Tib.), *ati* (Skt): Ati means supreme. The third of the three inner tantras, and the pinnacle of Buddhist teachings, it holds that liberation is attained through realizing the nature of primordial enlightenment, free from accepting and rejecting, hope and fear. An equivalent term for Ati is Great Perfection, *dzogchen* (Tib.). See nine vehicles.

awareness, *rig pa* (Tib.): In ordinary usage, it refers to the insightful awareness of ordinary people. In Ati, it refers to enlightened awareness of things as they are.

awareness-holder, *rig 'dzin* (Tib.), *vidyādhara* (Skt.): Indicates one who is accomplished in tantra and constantly abides in the state of pure awareness (*rig pa*).

basic ground, *gzhi rtsa* (Tib.): Another common translation is "ground and root." See ground.

beyond characterization as "this," *'di 'o mtshon las 'das* (Tib.): The denial of the absolute validity of linguistic assertions. In reality, one experiences instantaneous phenomena of perception and memory only in one's own mental continuum and only in the present moment. The alleged characterization of dualistic, external objects rests on a host of assumptions that cannot be substantiated, and thinking that linguistic assertions can serve as a basis for logical certainty about them is a delusion. For example, one could succeed in identifying an object as "this," only if there are separate, dualistic objects of experience that persist through time and which, along with their qualities, are perceivable by many different beings. Since in reality, all phenomena are the instantaneous experiences of a particular apprehender, such alleged identification is impossible, and so, all phenomena are beyond characterization as "this."

bodhicitta: See compassionate mind.

bodhisattva, *byang chub sems dpa'* (Tib.): Strictly speaking, a bodhisattva is someone who, on the five paths, has reached at least the path of seeing, but has not yet attained complete buddhahood. Along with the buddhas, they are called noble ones. There are ten levels of the bodhisattva path, and one of the ten perfections (paramitas) is emphasized on each level. Sometimes the term "bodhisattva" is used more loosely to signify anyone who practices the bodhisattva vehicle, the Mahayana, which advocates a compassionate attitude aspiring to bring all sentient beings to enlightenment.

Buddha, *sangs rgyas* (Tib.): The Tibetan term consists of two words, awake and expanding. Purifying dark ignorance and obscuration, one is awakened. For the higher vehicles, purity is attributed to realization of emptiness, as described in the Madhyamaka. "Expanding," or "blossoming," refers to realization of the limitless positive qualities of enlightenment within emptiness. These are the phenomena of the kayas, primordial wisdom, buddha qualities, and so forth.

carefree, *rgya yan* (Tib.): Since realization in Ati is free from conceptions altogether, it is free from all codified constraints of conduct. There are no absolute prerules for what is to be done or achieved and not done or avoided. Free from preoccupation with such things, the yogin is carefree.

causal and resultant vehicles, *rgyu 'i theg pa dang 'bras bu 'i theg pa* (Tib.): The causal vehicles of Hinayana and Mahayana regard the practice of the path as the cause that leads to, and produces the result of, buddhahood. In the resultant vehicle of Vajrayana, fruition is indivisible from the path. The Vajrayana sees the ground as inherently present in our experience from the beginning. The teacher helps to bring flashes of such experience into full awareness, and this makes it possible to begin treading the path. The path is the process of becoming increasingly familiar with that basic state and its many aspects. The result is experiencing that in its fullness.

compassion, *snying rje, thugs rje (hon.)* (Tib.): Compassion for all beings is a distinguishing feature of the Great Vehicle, the Mahayana. In Ati, compassion is equivalent to the power of manifestation, the form kayas, rupakaya, which produce benefit for others and bring them to dharmakaya, benefit for oneself. In Ati, the

Great Perfection, bodhicitta is the absolute mind of enlightenment, more or less equivalent to awareness, *rig pa*. Within that, nothing faulty and nothing dualistic can exist. Phenomena subsumed within it are cleansed as aspects of absolute truth, and from that perspective bodhicitta can be regarded as a cleansing energy.

complete settling/resting, *cog gzhag* (Tib.): The meditative practice of letting go into natural, uncontrived resting of body and mind, rather than trying to achieve artificial concentration through action and effort.

concept, *rtog pa* (Tib.): Concept(ion), or perceiving things in terms of concepts. From the viewpoint of Ati, conceptual statements may be true in a relative, practical sense, but they are empty of absolute truth. Therefore, realized experience of things as they are in Ati Yoga is said to transcend description by concepts.

Conqueror, *rgyal ba* (Tib.): A buddha who has fully conquered the two obscurations of afflictive emotions and dualistic fixations of the knowable.

contemplation like that of the gods, *lha lta bu 'i bsam gtan* (Tib.): According to the Buddhist teachings in general, the gods are adept in meditational states like the four concentrations. They have overcome most of the afflictions, but they have not overcome attachment to their own accomplishments, nor have they overcome obscurations of the knowable by realizing emptiness. Therefore, their meditation is inferior to that of accomplished Buddhist practitioners of the Great Perfection.

continuum of natural origination, *rang byung ngang* (Tib.): The experienced continuum of the Great Perfection is unconditioned and naturally present from the beginning. It is not a conditioned result produced through practice. Though it is said to be naturally originating or self-arising, it is an intrinsic aspect of the way things are, and, in that sense, there is actually no time when it arises. In another sense, it is said to arise in experience when enlightenment is attained.

continuum, *ngang* (Tib.): Examples in ordinary experience are the spatial continuum of points within the sky or the temporal continuum of a being's personal experiences. The continuum of absolute truth is dharmadhatu, phenomenal space within which all phenomena appear to arise, endure, and cease.

cross the pass, *la bzla* (Tib.): A figure of speech meaning "to resolve a problem decisively," as in phrases such as "cross the pass of cause and effect" or "cross the pass into the equality of samsara and nirvana." According to the lower teachings of the causal vehicles, to attain the fruition of enlightenment we must strive diligently on the path, employing skillful, causal means. In this way, the defiled and deluded continuum of a sentient being in samsara can be transformed into the undefiled, undeluded continuum of an enlightened being. For the higher teachings of the fruition vehicles, including Ati, the conceptual duality of such an approach becomes a major obstacle. This problem can never be solved as long as the rigid dichotomies of a struggle between right and wrong persist. The problem is resolved only when we realize, within the Great Perfection, the equality of all conceptualized projections of samsara and nirvana as emptiness. The actual meaning of "crossing the pass" is closer to the idea of avoiding or eliminating a pass, rather than going over it. In terms of the path, "crossing the pass" might be experienced as a leap into space. But this leap is grounded in the understanding that there was never anything but space, so the leap is more like a surrendering to how things are and have always been. The obstacles we imagine never really existed.

crown anointment, *spyi blugs* (Tib.): Originally this was a vase used in the coronation of kings. Symbolically it refers to the self-existing empowerment of the Great Perfection, with which the practitioner is said to be crowned as a "king of dharmakaya."

Dakini, *mkha' 'gro* (Tib.): Literally, a lady who goes in the sky. Usually, a dakini refers to a female tantric deity of the five families who guards, serves, presents, and embodies the tantric teachings and is a consort of a heruka, a male tantric deity. They are generally wrathful or semi-wrathful. They symbolize compassion, emptiness, and wisdom; the basic fertile space from which everything arises; and the tricky and playful aspects of empty phenomena. The higher dakinis are primordial wisdom deities of the five tantric families who give basic inspiration to seek enlightenment or cut through distortions of the teachings.

deed, action; *byed pa* (Tib.), *bya ba byed pa* (Tib.): Produced by action. Action in this case is purposeful, dualistically conceptualized action within samsara. Such action is delusory, and so no such action occurs in the realization of Ati. Instead there is non-dual Buddha activity beyond concept.

deity, divine, god; *lha* (Tib.), *deva* (Skt.): Buddhism is not a religion devoted to worship of a god or gods regarded as separate from or superior to oneself. Buddhism accepts Hindu cosmology, with its various kinds of beings, including the gods. Though the gods are the highest class of temporal beings, they are not worshipped as superior. On the contrary, these gods are typically attached to their own virtues and lack realization of emptiness. Therefore, it is said that buddhahood can only be attained by human beings, since humans are capable of complete non-attachment and realization of emptiness. The deities of tantric practice — yidams, protectors, buddhas and bodhisattvas (such as Samantabhadra) — are sometimes supplicated through offerings, mantras, etc., as beings having personal existence; however, they are generally regarded as principles of the energies of mind and phenomena. For example, in *The Precious Treasury of Phenomenal Space*, Samantabhadra and Vajrasattva are symbolized aspects of the Great Perfection. In any case, for Ati practitioners, deities, like everything else, are ultimately empty of essence. Ati is said to be beyond the use of deities in practice, though such practice is involved in other aspects of the Nyingma path. It is also said that buddhahood is eternal, but that Samantabhadra was the first to realize it. Doing so, Samantabhadra ceased to be merely personal. We too can experience the same realization.

Densely Ornamented Pure Land, *stugs po bkod pa 'i zhing khams* (Tib.), *gandavyūha* (Skt.): Synonymous with the pure realm of Akanishta. It is the form of the vision of the sambhogakaya realm that realizes and enjoys the pure perceptions and energies of omniscient wisdom. It is also aesthetic perception of phenomena as an ornament. This field is dense, not only because it is elaborate, but also because of its infinite matrix of interdependent arising, in which everything is connected to, and reflected within, everything else. In this endless, boundless net of pure vision, everything encompasses everything else, so independent absolutes of time, space, and objects are nowhere to be found.

development and completion/perfection stages, *bskyed rim, rdzogs rim* (Tib.), *utpattikrama, sampanakrama* (Skt.): In tantric liturgy practice, the developing stage involves recitation and visualization of the deities, palace, and so forth. One makes praises and offerings to them and recites their essence mantras. This is done to realize that the phenomenal world is a pure environment and its inhabitants are the mandala of deities. The completion stage consists primarily of formless practice, such as resting in emptiness. However, yoga practice of the winds, channels, and essences is also considered completion stage practice. The direct realization of Ati is beyond the techniques of these two stages.

Dharma, *chos,* (Tib.), *Dharma* (Skt.): The term has many meanings. In these texts the most relevant are: 1. Dharma (capitalized), the Buddhadharma, usually means the teachings of Buddha. In Ati, the vision of realization is called "the Dharma." If the Guru transmits this vision, it is called "giving the Dharma." 2. dharma (not capitalized), Phenomena knowable by the mind, whether or not they are known as they really are.

dharmadhatu, *chos dbyings* (Tib.), *dharmadhātu* (Skt.): Space, source, or realm of phenomena.

dharmakaya, *chos sku* (Tib.), *dharmakāya* (Skt.): See three kayas.

direct(ly present), *zang(ma) thal, thad drang* (Tib.): Direct experience is fully and completely experienced. This raises the question, what sort of experience would be incomplete and indirect? By definition, mere experience, all experience, is experienced fully and completely. Questions about degrees of directness and completeness arise only when experiences are conceptualized as experiences of some real event, beyond the experience itself. For Ati practitioners, all such conceptualizations are deluded. Therefore, from that viewpoint, the degree to which experience is regarded as direct corresponds to the degree to which our experience is free from such dualistic conceptualization. When we are completely free from conceptual attachment, the Great Perfection is spontaneously and directly realized in its fullness.

display, play; *rol (pa)* (Tib.): 1. Play like that of children, without the need of serious purpose, not a fixed activity. 2. Display (such as play of a fountain), sport, or art. 3. Manifestation of phenomena altogether. 4. For realization, play is pure appearance or primordial wisdom. Due to emptiness, it is free of defilements.

distinct self-awareness, *so so rang rig* (Tib.): Also commonly translated as discriminating awareness. Enlightened awareness realizes the great equality of all phenomena in the essence that is emptiness, but also realizes the individual qualities of phenomena without mixing them up.

disturbance, *rnyog pa* (Tib.): Also commonly translated as turbidity, as in muddy water.

dullness and discursive thoughts, *bying rgod* (Tib.): Common problems resulting from being under- or over-energized in meditation practice.

effort and endeavor, *rtsol zhing sgrub pa* (Tib.): Since the Great Perfection is established primordially, there is no need to make an effort to establish it again. See deed, action above.

eight assemblages, *tshogs brgyad* (Tib.): The eight consciousnesses. They are the five sense consciousnesses; mind consciousness (memory and conception); afflicted mind consciousness; and allground consciousness.

eight extremes, *mtha' brgyad* (Tib.): birth and cessation, eternalism and nihilism, going and coming, one and many (same and different).

emanating and dissolving, gathering and dispersing, elaborating and dissolving, diffusion and absorption; *'phro 'du* (Tib.): Typical contexts are the mind's emanating and dissolving of phenomena altogether, particularly of discursive thoughts, or phenomena of the deities, the palace, and so on, as visualized in tantric practice of the developing stage.

empowerment, *dbang* (Tib.): The conferring of power or authorization to practice certain Vajrayana teachings, the indispensable entrance door to tantric practice. Empowerment gives control over one's vajra body, vajra speech, and vajra mind and confers the authority and ability to regard forms as deity, sounds as mantra, and thoughts as wisdom.

empty (-iness), *stong pa (nyid)* (Tib.): Nagarjuna is said to have established emptiness through reasoning by showing that no concept can be instantiated, because inherent contradictions are involved, as with instantiation of a round square. At the time of fruition, and in realization of Ati, emptiness is realized more fully as a direct experience of the inseparable naturelessness of all phenomena, "nothing whatever and so it arises as all there is." This non-dual emptiness is sometimes called emptiness possessing all the supreme aspects.

encompassing, *gdal ba* (Tib.): For example, dharmadhatu is the all-encompassing space of phenomena.

energy, power, potential; *rtsal* (Tib.): Power, energy, skill, dexterity, manifestation in general in some cases. As an Ati technical term, energy is the mind's intrinsic power to give rise to luminous manifestation that does not depart from its essence, emptiness. When contrasted with play, energy is what produces the play of manifestation. In one approach, energy is regarded as incorruptible, like the essence itself. Energy is more the ground of arising of manifestations than the manifestations themselves. Jigme Lingpa says: "phenomena have arisen as the play of the energy of the mind." Thus, for example, the sun and its rays are regarded as changelessly pure, but capable of being concealed by the play of obscuring clouds. Longchenpa says, "The essence of awareness is like a mirror. Its energy is like the clarity of the mirror. From that, the play of manifestation arises like reflections in the mirror. At the time it arises, it does not move from the essence of mind, dharmakaya. So this manifestation is also dharmakaya." Sometimes energy is said to be pure and play to be defiled, as when it is said that energy manifesting as the play of samsara is like a rope being wrongly seen as a snake. Much of the difficulty with this term comes from its having such multiple senses. Longchenpa brings these together in the following passage from his commentary on *The Precious Treasury of Phenomenal Space*: "The self-clarified energy of bodhicitta is like a spotlessly transparent jewel. Within it is the appearance of buddhahood, free from stains of incidental conceptualizations. It goes nowhere beyond appearing as awareness itself. By non-realization of that, it becomes the vessel and essence of ignorant and confused sentient beings with the eight consciousnesses. But these too do not go beyond the state of awareness."

equanimity, equality; *mnyam pa nyid* (Tib.): All phenomena are equal in not going beyond the essence of phenomena, emptiness. Phenomena are also equal in not going beyond the enlightened experience of them as empty, even though they also have distinct phenomenal natures. How are the two meanings connected? Since everything is equally the complete fulfillment, or great bliss, of enlightenment, experience by enlightened beings has the emotional quality of equanimity.

essence, *ngo bo, snying po, thig le* (Tib.): "Essence" (*ngo bo)* is commonly used in the context of characterizing the three kayas as empty essence, luminous nature, and all-pervading compassion respectively. (Heart-)essence (*snying po*) can have a similar meaning, with overtones of the quintessence of reality and realization. Statements like "a banana tree has no heart" (*snying po*) assert emptiness as explained in Madhyamaka. The essence of the Thus-gone One (*de bzhin gshegs pa'i snying po,* Tib., *tathāgatagarbha,* Skt.) is the suchness of appearance/emptiness, as realized in the Prajnaparamita and Madhyamaka. The essence of the Bliss-gone One (*bde bar gshegs pa'i snying po,* Tib., *sugatagarbha,* Skt.) is emptiness possessing all the supreme aspects of the kayas, primordial wisdoms, and buddha qualities of sambhogakaya (*longs spyod rdzogs pa'i sku*) with its intrinsic quality of perfect enjoyment (*longs spyod*) or great bliss (*bde ba chen po*). Sphere or seed-essence (*thig le)* commonly occurs in the context of yoga, where it refers to vital energy within the body. It is also used to describe the sexual essences, which are concentrated and transmuted to a higher form in yoga practice. However, in *The Precious Treasury of Phenomenal Space,* it occurs most commonly in contexts like, "without corners or edges, the essence (*thig le*) is circular." *Thig le, bindu* (Skt.), can mean dot or circle. For example, the red dot that Hindu women display on their foreheads is called a bindu. In these passages *thig le* is used as both a metaphor and its meaning. As a circle is without divisions of corners, the essence of phenomena is without divisions of conceptual complexity. The meaning aspect is similar to the meanings of *ngo bo* and *snying po.*

eternalism and nihilism, *rtag chod* (Tib.): Eternalism asserts that some or all phenomena have a real, changeless, and independent nature. Nihilism asserts that some or all phenomena have no real nature and do not truly exist. Longchenpa accepts that all such assertions are refuted by Madhyamaka philosophy. What then of statements by Longchenpa and other advocates of Madhyamaka that non-dual emptiness is the changeless essence of all phenomena, or that the delusive phenomena of samsara never existed and never will, because they are essentially natureless? Are they self-refuting? Ultimately they are, but not on the conventional level on which they are being used. These assertions are made within limited contexts of discourse for particular practical purposes of teaching and acting. They are specifically qualified by saying that they have no absolute significance. The same is true of the eminently effective theories of natural science and all the practical wisdom of ordinary life. As Mipham says, "Not all assertions of 'eternal' are proclamations of eternalism. Not all assertions of 'nothingness' are proclamations of nihilism. ...The wise proclaim what is and is not, just as it is." And Mipham also asserts that someone who does not accept some such position and maintains without qualification that all assertions are self-refuting will be unable to present that position coherently or even say, "This is the system of my tradition."

even, *phyal ba* (Tib.): Even, level, uninterrupted, without any highlights. Things are all equally revelations of the empty essence of buddhahood, the goal, oneself, etc.

evenly pervaded, *phyam gdal* (Tib.): All phenomena constitute an even continuum because they are pervaded by emptiness.

exaggeration (glorification) and deprecation, *sgro 'dogs dang skur 'debs* (Tib.): Misconception, reification, superimposition, projections. The literal meaning is "to apply feathers and cast aspersions." Anyone who makes assertions of doctrine thinking that they are absolutely true commits errors of exaggeration and deprecation. However, teachers who know that their teachings can never be absolutely true still teach in order to bring beings to realization of how things are. It has been said, "Absolute truth is hard to see at first, and so we put feathers on it so that students know where to look."

examples of illusion, *sgyu dpe* (Tib.): Examples of illusion are reflection of the moon in water, optical illusion, mirage, dream, echo, city of the gandharvas, hallucination, rainbow, lightning, bubbles on water, and reflection in mirror.

expanse, *klong* (Tib.): Expanse can be differentiated from phenomenal space (dharmadhatu) just as the space of ultimate mind can be differentiated from that of the universal ground. Phenomenal space involves experience of vastness, like contemplating the horizon from the seashore. Expanse is beyond reference points of vastness and constraint; like a single dot, it is a limitless expanse with a single nature apprehended all at once.

extreme, *mtha'* (Tib.): A one-sided, rigidly conceptualized viewpoint that confuses concepts with reality. Concepts are useful in various kinds of practical situations, but to think they have absolute validity, independent of the context in which they are used, invariably leads to mistakes, according to Madhyamaka. The four and eight extremes, discussed in separate entries, are lists of extremes that should be avoided. Thus, if one understands the conventions and limits of words, one can use them to talk about the world and the teachings without falling into extremes. Mipham says, "Not every assertion of existence asserts extreme existence. Not every assertion of non-existence asserts extreme non-existence."

faulty and hollow phenomena, *ra ri zab zeb chos* (Tib.): When realization occurs, the seemingly solid phenomena of one's former delusion are realized both intellectually and experientially to be invalid and delusional.

five paths, *lam lnga* (Tib.): The paths of accumulation, preparation, seeing, meditation, and fulfillment. 1. Accumulation: Practitioners accumulate merit and wisdom and avoid confusion and evil deeds, so that eventually they can escape the lower realms and enlightenment will manifest. The four foundations of mindfulness are practiced and developed through tranquil resting meditation, *zhi gnas* (Tib.), *śamatha* (Skt.). This leads to clear-seeing meditation, *lhag mthong* (Tib.), *vipaśyana* (Skt.), which clearly comprehends emptiness. 2. Preparation (unification): Further developing vipashyana, one sees through the fallacies of grasper and grasped and consequently develops a deep understanding of the four noble truths, cutting the root of the desire realm. 3. Seeing: The practitioner comes to understand the unsatisfactory nature of all the realms of form, including the god realm. Emptiness is directly and experientially seen. This conveys the essence of liberation, and one enters the first bodhisattva ground, Supremely Joyful. 4. Meditation:

Practicing meditation and relating to the phenomenal world through the successive perfections, one attains the second through tenth grounds. This culminates in realization of non-dual luminosity and primordial wisdom. 5. Fulfillment or No More Learning: Attaining the vajra-like absorption, the practitioner enters the eleventh ground, the omniscient luminosity of buddhahood.

five poisons/afflictions, *dug lnga, nyon mongs lnga* (Tib.): The five afflictive emotions: attachment, aversion, ignorance, pride, and jealousy.

five primordial wisdoms, *ye shes lgna* (Tib.): The mirror like wisdom, wisdom of equality, wisdom of individual discrimination, all-accomplishing wisdom, and dharmadhatu wisdom.

four extremes, *mtha' bzhi* (Tib.): For a certain concept, its assertion, negation, both, and neither. For example, the four extremes of existence are existence, non-existence, both, and neither.

free from elaboration, *spros bral* (Tib.): Free from the elaboration of generating conceptual thoughts and conceptualized phenomena. The complexity of one's mental continuum increases as one generates an overwhelming multiplicity of discursive thoughts. Elaboration also refers to fragmentation of the original unity of the Great Perfection into a delusive variety of separate entities believed to exist separately from the mind with real natures of their own.

freedoms and favorable conditions, *dal 'byor* (Tib.): The eight freedoms are freedom from being born in hell, as a hungry ghost, as an animal, as a long-lived god, as an ignorant barbarian, as a person with wrong views, in a time without buddhas, or as a person who cannot understand speech. The ten favorable conditions, according to Longchenpa, are as follows: "I was born in the human realm, and in the central country. Also, I am sound in all my faculties, not having gone wrong in my actions beyond what can be corrected; I am properly faithful in the objects of faith. Thus the five holy favors regarding oneself are complete. The Buddha has come and he has taught the Dharma. Moreover, at this time the teachings still remain. So that they may continue, people still follow them. Others treat us with kindness and concern. Thus the five favors regarding others are complete."

garuda, *khyung* (Tib.), *garuda* (Skt): A bird of Indian mythology that is said to hatch fully grown, so that it can fly effortlessly as soon as it leaves the egg. Therefore, it symbolizes self-existing buddhahood. The garuda's overcoming of the nagas (poisonous serpent-beings dwelling in dark caverns) symbolizes overcoming the darkness, confinement, and toxic nature of samsara. It is said that when the garuda first appeared, his luster frightened the Hindu gods who thought it was Agni, the god of fire. Its brilliance symbolizes the radiant luminosity of enlightenment.

grasper and grasped, *gzung 'dzin* (Tib.): The fixating, grasping mind and the fixated, grasped object. Both are illusory, samsaric fixations postulating independent, truly existing subject and object. The true, enlightened object is the three kayas, emptiness possessing all the supreme aspects. The true, enlightened subject is awareness, primordial wisdom. They are inseparable, non-dual self-insight.

Great Perfection, *rdzogs chen* (Tib.): The way things are for buddhahood, as described by Ati Yoga. According to Nyingma lineage of Longchenpa, the highest of the nine vehicles of attaining enlightenment. *The Precious Treasury of Phenomenal Space* explains its nature and qualities in detail.

ground, *gzhi* (Tib.): Fundamental nature or state of being. For example, dharmakaya is the ground of enlightened reality, the all-ground is the ground of samsaric reality, and dharmadhatu is the ground of reality altogether. In the trio of ground, path, and fruition, from the viewpoint of Ati, ground is apprehension of basic reality, path is working with phenomena to see their relation to that reality, and fruition occurs when one succeeds in seeing all phenomena as aspects of the ground.

grounds, *sa* (Tib.), *bhūmi* (Skt.): Various levels of the path, such as the eight shravaka grounds and ten bodhisattva grounds.

hopeless and immeasurably painful, *tshi chad nad* (Tib.): The literal meaning is a painful, debilitating disease.

ignorance, *ma rig pa* (Tib.): Ignorance, as opposed to *rig pa*; awareness, understanding, insight. It is cognitive inability to apprehend things as they are because of the duality of grasper and grasped involved in the obscuration of knowables. Ignorance, *gti mug*, is an afflictive emotion that is one of the three defiling poisons of attachment, aversion, and ignorance. This type of ignorance reacts to phenomena that are neither desirable nor harmful by regarding them as irrelevant or insignificant.

immaculate, *dri med* (Tib.): As experienced by the realization of Ati, all phenomena are empty, and therefore all defilements of the afflictions are likewise empty, and phenomena are pure of them from the beginning (*ka dag*, Tib.). This is like saying "pure from the letter A."

impartial, directionless; *phyogs med* (Tib.): According to Ati, when there is no conceptual bias or partiality, there is nirvana — and freedom from the duality of samsaric delusion. With impartiality, the inseparability of the two truths, appearance and emptiness, is naturally seen.

in its own place, *rang sar* (Tib.): Naturally, spontaneously, its own condition; in itself; as it is.

included, gathered, subsumed; *'dus pa* (Tib.): The term may refer to inclusion under any category or within any realms of experience, enlightened or otherwise. In this text it usually refers to phenomena being included within the realm of the Great Perfection or within the scope of the essence, emptiness. Also, gathering a visualization into emptiness.

indefinite, uncertain, unpredictable; *ma nges, nges med* (Tib.): In ordinary thought and experience, uncertainty usually has a negative connotation. In Ati, the connotation is often positive, referring to freedom from conceptual restriction in enlightened experience.

independence, *rang dbang* (Tib.): Freedom, mastery. A quality of the Great Perfection.

independent reality, *rang mtshan* (Tib.): Also translated intrinsic characteristics.

indestructible, *'jig med, rdo rje* (Tib.), *vajra* (Skt.): The essence of phenomena, emptiness, is changeless, and hence uncreated and indestructible. In Ati, when this is realized as what one really is, indestructible bodhicitta and so forth, one is said to gain the indestructible vajra body.

indifferent, unbiased; *ris med* (Tib.): Great impartial equanimity, without distinction. For example, the Great Perfection is unbiased about, or has no attachment to, samsara or nirvana.

intended meaning, *dgongs don* (Tib.): For example, the intended meaning of the Buddha's teachings on emptiness is not nihilism, nor a recommendation to abandon language, but advocates transcendence of attachment to concepts and asserts that absolute truth transcends expression in conceptual terms.

interdependence, *rten (par 'brel bar) 'byung ba* (Tib.): Interdependent arising, e.g., as a rainbow appears from the interconnection of sunlight, rain, air, the sense faculty of sight, and the perceiving mind. The rainbow is not the appearance of any one of these or of all of them together; and at the same time, it is not the appearance of something else either. In Madhyamaka, interdependent arising is equated to emptiness, because interdependence entails the absence of independent self-nature.

intrinsic characteristic, *rang mtshan* (Tib.): Specific, or individuating characteristics that things would have if they were independent, individual entities existing in their own right. Ati accepts Madhyamaka claims to establish the impossibility of such characteristics.

intrinsically clear, *rang gsal* (Tib.): Natural, clearly as it is; intrinsic clarity, radiance; brilliance; naturally awake; self-cognizing.

karma, *las* (Tib.), *karma* (Skt.): Habitual patterns of dualistic grasper and grasped and the resulting afflictions of the three poisons, etc., ceaselessly accumulate in the continuum of a sentient being and determine future experience by their power. Since the causality of karmic seeds in beings' continuums persists even after death, karma determines the circumstances of a being's series of rebirths in the different realms of samsara.

kaya, *sku* (Tib.), *kāya* (Skt.): Kaya is an honorific term for "body," as a fundamental aspect or embodiment of reality.

King of Mountains, *ri'i rgyal po* (Tib.): This refers to Mount Meru, which according to Hindu and Buddhist cosmology is at the center of the disk-shaped world realm and is so tall that it reaches into the heavens, where celestial bodies circle around it.

Kriya, *bya rgyud* (Tib.), *Kriyā* (Skt.): See nine vehicles.

label (mere), *btags pa (tsam)* (Tib.): In Ati, conceptions are said to be mere labels because what they attempt to describe is ultimately without nature and empty of true existence. Such assertions depend on the terminology and reasoning of Madhyamaka philosophy, though that terminology is also used to point out the ineffable, realized experience of empty phenomena.

Lama, *bla ma* (Tib.): Can be used to refer to any monk. References to the "the Lama," especially when capitalized, refer to a revered principal teacher in Vajrayana. In that case, the term is synonymous with Guru.

leave/rest as it is, *rang bzhag* (Tib.): Self-rested, self-established.

luminous (luminously clear), *'od gsal* (Tib.): The phenomena of enlightened awareness are said to be empty in essence and luminous by nature. The empty essence is associated with the basic space of dharmakaya and dharmadhatu, in which empty phenomena manifest. The luminous nature of phenomena is associated with the kayas of form, the phenomenal display of sambhogakaya and nirmanakaya. Enlightened experience does indeed involve striking brilliance and splendor, but it should be noted that postulating luminosity as its essential quality is somewhat abbreviated and metaphorical. For one thing, only visual phenomena can be literally apprehended as luminous, yet there are many other modes of phenomena, sensory, mental, and otherwise. What point is being made, then, by speaking of luminosity? First, enlightened phenomena are clear, in the sense of being fully and directly perceived without conceptual intermediaries and restrictions (cf. direct). Secondly, phenomena so perceived have freshness, vivid intensity, and power that ordinary phenomena do not. That quality is very positive and is described in terms of universal goodness (all-good), transcendence of suffering, and great bliss.

magic show, *ltad mo* (Tib.): In Ati, since all that appears is empty of true existence, it is like a magical appearance of illusory horses, elephants, and so forth conjured by a magician. Cf. examples of illusion.

Maha, *Mahā* (Skt.): See nine vehicles.

mandala, *dkyil 'khor* (Tib.), *mandala* (Skt.): Literally, center and border. The mandala of a deity has that deity with customary accoutrements at the center. Around the central deity are the retinue and attendants. The central deity will be of one of the five families and the attendants are divided into the four families other than that of the deity. Around that are the palace, vajra fence, charnel grounds, and other environmental symbols. Altogether they symbolize in detail the particular modes of being, action, and awareness of that particular deity. Ati does not rely on contrived practices of visualizing deities, so the term "mandala" usually refers to self-existing aspects of enlightened experience, such as the mandala of the three kayas or mandala of the four directions.

mantra, *sngags* (Tib.): A word or series of words that are recited with magical effect, such as OM MANI PADME HUM. Included are seed syllables used to invoke deities. In tantra, even individual letters are regarded as having mantric power, and the Sanskrit alphabet may be recited as a mantra. Since realization is self-existing in Ati, it does not need to be invoked by mantras.

meditation, *mnyam bzhag,* (Tib.) (in contrast to post-meditation, *rjes thob,* Tib.): Activities and experiences engaged in during a session of meditation in contrast to breaks between sessions. In particular, it may refer to the direct intuition of emptiness in the formless meditation of the noble ones (as opposed to their apprehension of illusion-like appearances in post-meditation). Since the realization of Ati is self-existing and is not dependent on techniques of meditation, it transcends distinctions of sessions of meditation and breaks in between.

mind, *sems* (Tib.): 1. Mind in general (neutral sense). 2. Dualistic mind (pejorative sense). 3. The nature of mind, mind itself (*sems nyid,* Tib.), bodhicitta (positive sense, as it appears, for example, in the titles of Ati tantras).

mind itself, nature of mind; *sems nyid* (Tib.): 1. The nature of mind, emptiness, which is the same as the nature of phenomena. 2. Mind itself, what mind really is, the enlightened perceiver, can become deluded and go astray in samsara and then reawaken to the enlightened state. In either case, mind and it contents are ultimately non-dual dharmadhatu.

miraculous display, *cho 'phrul* (Tib.): Magical display, apparition, illusion, emanative power, miracle.

miraculous illusions, *ngo mtshar sgyu ma* (Tib.): The phenomenal world consists of amazing, illusory appearance of what does not truly exist. These are the miracles of the play of phenomena that ultimately guide sentient beings to enlightenment.

Mount Meru, *ri rgyal rab* (Tib.): The King of Mountains. In Indian cosmology, Mount Meru is at the center of the world surrounded by four continents. Of these we inhabit the southern continent, Jambudvipa (Jambuling).

naga, *klu* (Tib.), *nāga* (Skt.): Water spirit, serpent (deity). Living in low watery places and caverns, they are often associated with the lower aspects of the human situation, especially those that are dark, evil, and poisonous. Thus they are associated with skin diseases such as leprosy. In this aspect, nagas are the enemy of the garuda. However, higher nagas are also said to have great wealth and to have received the wisdom of the prajnaparamita sutras from the Buddha, guarding them until Nagarjuna could receive them. Also the nagas protected Buddha from attacks of the maras on the night before his enlightenment.

nameless state beyond labels, *ming med* (Tib.): To say that something is "*ming med*" is to say not only that it does not exist, but that even the name for it does not truly exist. In Madhyamaka and Ati this is true for all phenomena, because reality transcends conception and labels.

Natural Great Perfection, *rang bzhin rdzogs pa chen po* (Tib.): Nature of the Great Perfection or great, naturally perfect nature. 1. Perfect, in the sense that everything begins and ends at just the right time. 2. Complete, e.g., the task is done; the mandala, which is never arranged but is always complete. 3. Exhausted, because fixations, hopes, and fears are all used up. These three senses are tied together, as the exhaustion of confusion reveals the perfection of the awakened state. Complete exhaustion of obscurations completes the task of coming to see completeness, another word for perfection. Moreover, the essence of the perfection is emptiness. Exhaustion of relative limitation is the freedom of liberation. "Completion" comes closest to the meaning, but it lacks a sense of sacredness and wonder. Therefore "perfection" is used, except in cases where "exhausted" seems obviously closer to the primary meaning.

natural (origination), *rang byung* (Tib.): Natural; naturally occurring or arising; self-arising, spontaneous. For example, hunger naturally arises when one does not eat. A shape like a face found on a rock is called a "self-arising" sculpture. Impromptu verse is described as "self-arising."

natural place, own place; *rang sa* (Tib.): Phenomena are said to be in their own or proper place when experienced as they really are — as empty, luminous, and unceasing. Sometimes emotions are said to be in their proper place when directed toward the right objects. Ordinary dualistic passion, anger, and pride directed at others are afflictive emotions. Passion for enlightenment and a virtuous life, anger at the suffering caused by ignorance and delusion, and pride in having the nature of the deity are called the corresponding vajra emotions and are considered excellent virtues.

natural state, the way things are; *gnas lugs (tshul)* (Tib.); and natural, *rang (bzhin) babs* (Tib.): Occurring as it is, what is, natural(ness), natural flow, natural state, spontaneous, naturally occurring. These are synonymous with suchness and the Great Perfection.

nature, *rang bzhin* (Tib.): Actuality, natural expression, natural, intrinsic, inherent. In relation to sambhogakaya, nature refers to the luminous manifestation, as distinct from the empty essence of dharmakaya. See the three kayas.

nature of phenomena, *chos nyid* (Tib.), *dharmatā* (Skt.): The nature of phenomena is emptiness, so in phenomenal space (dharmadhatu), the nature of phenomena (dharmata) is what is seen. In Ati, this is the great emptiness beyond conceptualizations of emptiness and non-emptiness, things as they are.

nine vehicles or yanas, *theg pa dgu* (Tib.): The first three are the vehicles of causes and characteristics: 1. Shravaka vehicle of Hinayana, in which the "hearers" achieve personal liberation. 2. Pratyekabuddha vehicle of Hinayana, in which practitioners typically realize personal liberation from samsara by themselves, without a teacher. 3. Bodhisattva vehicle of Mahayana, in which practitioners aspire to attain enlightenment in order to benefit all sentient beings. The next three are the outer tantras of Vajrayana: 4. Kriya focuses on purity, and the deity is regarded as a king. 5. Upa focuses on conduct, and the deity is regarded as a master. 6. Yoga focuses on meditation, and the deity is regarded as one's own nature. The final three are the inner tantras of Vajrayana: 7. Mahayoga emphasizes the visualization of deities and mandalas of the developing stage. 8. Anu emphasizes the yogic techniques of the completion stage. 9. Ati, as described in this text, is the pinnacle of the Buddhist teachings, enlightened manifestation of things as they are.

nirmanakaya, *sprul sku* (Tib.), *nirmanakāya* (Skt.): See three kayas.

nirvana, *mya ngan las 'das pa* (Tib.), *nirvāna* (Skt.): Enlightenment. Enlightenment in Ati is said to be beyond samsara and nirvana, in order to differentiate it from the conceptualized partial notions of enlightenment found in the lower vehicles, which from the viewpoint of Ati are not completely free from bias and attachment. Preconceived programs of accepting and rejecting only obscure the naked, boundless condition that Longchenpa presents as true enlightenment, the Great Perfection.

non-duality, *gnyis med* (Tib.): The non-existence of grasper and grasped. The grasper is the perceiver of samsara and the grasped is delusory objects. They are misperceived as separate entities, and so they are seen as dualistic. As they are delusory, neither grasper nor grasped truly exist from the viewpoint of Ati.

not departing from space, *dbyings las mi g.yo* (Tib.): Phenomena do not go beyond the space of the empty essence, in the sense of becoming something with a truly existent nature. In Ati, there may be actual experience of phenomena as space.

not produced, *ma bskyed* (Tib.): Not purposely produced, developed, or cranked up. Hence, self-existing, natural.

nothing exists, but everything is manifest, *cir yang ma grub cir yang 'char ba ste* (Tib.): In Ati, the assertion that nothing exists is based on the viewpoint of Madhyamaka, where existence has a very specific sense of a thing with a completely independent nature of its own. However, such things could not be produced or perceived through causal interactions. If that is what a "thing" is, then no thing exists. Nevertheless, phenomena undoubtedly appear in manifestation.

obscuration, *sgrib pa* (Tib.): A factor that obscures awareness, in particular the two obscurations: the cognitive obscurations, which involve the dualistic apprehension of grasper and grasped, and the emotional obscurations, which lead to attachment. These result in karma and rebirth in the sufferings of samsara. They are the primary obstacles to omniscience and the pure vision of non-dual luminosity, in which one transcends karma and suffering. The realization of Ati is beyond the two obscurations.

ornament, adornment; *rgyan* (Tib.): In the Great Perfection, several points are made when it is said that phenomena arise as ornaments of space. First, in the Great Perfection, space exemplifies emptiness, the essence of all things, and phenomena are seen as mere decorative ornaments. Given that phenomena are inseparable from essential space, ultimately they are insubstantial and without essence, without intrinsic significance. Second, as phenomena adorn space, they also illuminate space. The directly experienced insubstantiality of phenomena demonstrates that the space of mind is not obstructed by phenomena, as it seems to be for samsaric beings. Third, luminous phenomena are wondrous and delightful, like the sight of a Christmas tree seen by a small child for the first time. All variety, in which good qualities are ultimately victorious, is due to phenomenal space. Finally, in the Great Perfection, when all-fulfilling enlightenment is attained, adornments are the phenomena of the kayas and primordial wisdoms. These are nothing other than the ornaments of space.

outer, inner, and secret, *phyi nang gsang* (Tib.): Outer concerns the external world, inner the body, and secret the inner life of thoughts, feelings, etc.

outer tantras, *phyi rgyud* (Tib.): The outer tantras understand luminosity and emptiness to be beyond conception, but unlike Ati, they believe that the fruition is established by stages through effort.

own nature, own face; *rang ngo* (Tib.): One's own nature, original face, true nature, self-nature.

own place/bed, *rang mal* (Tib.); own/natural/proper place, *rang sar* (Tib.): To "keep to one's own place" is to not be distracted from the state of meditation. It is also letting things rest as they naturally are, not trying to achieve enlightenment by effort, and not looking for it somewhere other than within oneself.

path, *lam* (Tib.): The practitioner's way to enlightenment as taught by the Buddha. Ati rejects the notion of the path as a process of achieving fruition apart from one's own nature by stages involving action and effort. It is sometimes said that the path in Ati is a process of becoming increasing familiar with and confident about enlightenment as one's own nature.

perfections, *pha rol tu phyin pa* (Tib.), *pāramitā* (Skt.): Achieved by the perfection practices of the bodhisattva path. The six perfections are generosity, discipline, patience, diligence, meditation, and wisdom. The first five become perfect or transcendent when practiced from the perspective of the sixth, the wisdom of emptiness. For example, generosity is perfect when there is no thought of giver, gift, and receiver — of any action of giving. Then the giving is pure and spontaneous. Similarly, in Ati all phenomena are perfect when seen as aspects of the essence, emptiness.

personal experience, *rang snang* (Tib.): One's own experience. When delusive, it has a sense of false appearance, one's own projection. When positive, it can mean the natural self-appearance of things as they are, in particular, of objects appearing merely as one's own experience and not as solid, external entities.

phenomena: See dharma.

phenomenal exhaustion, *chos zad* (Tib.): On the level of self-originated primordial wisdom, all phenomena are directly experienced as empty of true existence and free from valid conceptual labeling. This is called the state of phenomenal exhaustion.

phenomenal space, *chos dbyings* (Tib.), *dharmadhātu* (Skt.): The non-dual, fundamental space in which mind experiences objects. Here all phenomena of enlightenment and delusion arise, abide in experience, and subside. As the source of all phenomena, phenomenal space is called the womb or treasury of phenomena. It is said to be a "precious" treasury in two ways. First, experience of phenomena over countless lifetimes, slowly but inexorably, develops ignorant beings into enlightened ones. From that viewpoint, phenomena, skillful means, compassion, and compassionate mind (bodhicitta) are equated. Phenomenal space is therefore precious as the source of all goodness. Second, beings that have let go of all obscurations to realization of how things are experience phenomenal space fully, as enlightened mind (also bodhicitta.) This realization is precious in fulfilling all wishes of beings.

pool, *'khyil (ba)* (Tib.): The usual sense is one of ongoing inclusion. It is less like rivers flowing together and more like the state of a lake into which they flow. No effort is needed to gather together the pooled space of bliss, nor is any effort required to maintain it. In *The Precious Treasury of Phenomenal Space* it says, "Whatever arises is the true nature of phenomena, without effort and endeavor, pooling in the single blissful expanse." Since all phenomena are included in the empty space of the essence, they are naturally gathered within it, as the embodiment of that essence and its power. An alternate, dynamic sense of the word — "swirl (together)," *gcig tu* — does describe an action of coming together. From the *Treasury*, "It is one, single expanse without duality, the swirling, blissful expanse."

Pratyekabuddha, *rang rgyal* (Tib.): See nine vehicles.

Precipice: See abyss.

primordial, from the beginning; *ye, gdod nas* (Tib.): For example, the Great Perfection is primordial because it is unchangeably the nature of things, what is.

primordially pure, *ye dag, gdod nas dag pa* (Tib.): Since the essence of the Great Perfection is emptiness, it is always empty, or pure, of all defilements and obscurations.

pure land/buddhafield, *(sangs rgyas) zhing* (Tib.): 1. Realms of particular buddhas where sentient beings attain enlightenment. For example, Jambudvipa, which is the buddhafield of the Buddha Shakyamuni. The infinity of buddhafields is a major theme in such tathagatagarbha sutras as the *Gandavyuha* and *Avatamsaka*. 2. Pure land or realm, where pure refers to pure appearance on the level of sambhogakaya.

real/substantial thing, *dgnos po* (Tib.): Usually pejorative, this refers to a thing, conceptualized as something solid and real with a fixed, independent essence. Realization in Ati is beyond conceptual distinctions between real things and non-things.

recognizing the display (of the essence), *rol par ngos bzung ba* (Tib.): Phenomena are recognized as the display of the essence when they are experienced as not straying from that essence, which is emptiness, and therefore as participating in the great equanimity of phenomenal space.

reference point, *gza 'gtad* (Tib.): In the Tibetan, *'gtad* means something trusted and relied on. *Gza* means planet and suggests taking one's bearings from a star or relying on a systematic framework like a calendar. Thus, applying a reference point to the experience of phenomena involves identifying them in terms of one's conceptual system based on grasper and grasped. The realization of Ati is free from reference point, because it is the non-conceptual experience of primordial wisdom.

reflection, *gzugs brnyan* (Tib.): In Buddhism, one of the eight examples of illusion, used as figurative evocations of emptiness. Ordinarily we think of a reflection as an image of something that is not itself a reflection, such as the moon in water. But here, all phenomena are "reflections" of each other, because they arise interdependently. The external moon that is unreflectively accepted by ordinary beings as real is here regarded as a projected, false conception of a truly existent thing, which is actually empty of true existence. Whatever arises is experientially realized as empty, just like the way we experience the moon in water or the way we experience a dream when we know we are dreaming.

rest freely, *rang yan* (Tib.): 1. Rest freely, let be as it is, abandon, regard casually. 2. Free, wild, "ownerless, like deer in a meadow," as Marpa says. 3. Free from care, like a gypsy child who has never known the law.

sadhana, *sgrub thabs* (Tib.), *sādhana* (Skt.): literally, a means of spiritual accomplishment; hence, spiritual practice in general. In Tibetan, the word generally refers to practice liturgies, particularly those of Vajrayana.

Samantabhadra, All-Good; *kun tu bzang po* (Tib.), *Samantabhadra,* (Skt.): Samantabhadra literally means total or universal goodness. In Mahayana, Samantabhadra is one of the eight main bodhisattvas, an emanation of Vajrasattva. In tantric liturgies the environment is purified as pure appearance by the Samantabhadra offerings, in which offerings of desirable things of the five sense objects are visualized like clouds filling the whole of space. In Ati, Samantabhadra is the first, primordial buddha, who spontaneously achieved understanding of his own nature as universal enlightenment. His consort is Samantabhadri. Usually he is blue, she is white, and they are naked. She symbolizes the primordial space of the empty essence, dharmadhatu and Prajnaparamita. He symbolizes pure arising in that space of phenomena that do not go beyond its nature. Samantabhadra does not exist as an ego or individual being, but is buddhahood, one's own true nature. Therefore, all who are enlightened are said to be equal to him. Samantabhadra and consort may be considered the essence of all that is sacred.

samaya, *dam tshig* (Tib.), *samaya*, (Skt.): The tantric vows. There are many particular samayas, such as performing prescribed practices, respecting and obeying the vajra master, and so forth. These will vary in detail with different methods. Samaya in general means maintaining sacred outlook, or enlightened vision. Since the realization of Ati is indestructibly self-existing, it is said that there is no guarding of samaya.

samsara and nirvana, *'khor (ba dang mya ngan las) 'das (pa)* (Tib.): Literally, samsara is repeated cycling (in the sufferings of conditioned existence) and nirvana is transcendence of that suffering. The lower vehicles say that we should try to abandon samsara and achieve nirvana. Ati Yoga, the Great Perfection, says that by abandoning all conceptions of rejecting defilements and accepting virtues, we experience enlightenment as it is.

self, self- (prefixing compounds), one's own; *rang* (Tib.): Spontaneously, intrinsically, natural, (only) as it is, merely within one's own experience (and hence unreal), acting on itself. Multiplicity of meaning can make self- compounds very difficult to translate. Often more than one sense is relevant.

self-awareness, *rang rig* (Tib.): All experience has to be the mind's experience of itself, because there is nothing else to be experienced. When one understands that this mind is changeless, eternal, and naturally blissful, letting go of attachments to the incidental waves on the great ocean of mind, one loses hope and fear about samsara and nirvana and becomes enlightened. In Ati, insight is self-apprehending insight, and the luminous manifestations of the nature are actually of the essence of insight and do not go beyond it. Self-awareness is the experience of equanimity on the level of self-awareness primordial wisdom.

self-existing, *rang gnas* (Tib.): Naturally indwelling.

self-liberating, *rang grol* (Tib.): The thing liberates itself, like a knot tied in a snake.

self-luminous, naturally luminous/clear; *rang gsal* (Tib.): Similar to luminosity, but this term points out that luminosity is the true nature of phenomena.

self-subsiding, *rang yal* (Tib.): Subside, disappear, fade away by itself.

Shravaka, *nyan thos* (Tib.), *śrāvaka* (Skt.): See nine vehicles.

six realms, *'gro drug* (Tib.): The six realms of samsaric rebirth are gods, jealous gods, humans, animals, hungry ghosts, and hell beings. The first three are the higher realms, and rebirth there is due to good karma. The last three are the lower realms, and rebirth there is due to bad karma.

space, *dbyings* (Tib.), *dhātu* (Skt.): Field, realms, (basic) space, expanse, totality, continuum, source.

spontaneous(ly accomplished), *lhun grub* (Tib.): Self-existent. Having the sense of something that is naturally so and does not need to be created.

straying; *gol ba, gol sa* (Tib.): Deviation, misunderstanding; place where these can occur, for example, in clinging to bliss, clarity, and non-thought. Dilgo Khyentse Rinpoche said, "Misunderstanding the great primordial emptiness, one labels mind with conceptual negation. This is known as straying into the realm of conceptual emptiness. Not having faith in the ground and fruition of ordinary mind within oneself, one hopes for a new acquisition of the fruition of dharmakaya elsewhere. This is known as straying in regard to the path. Misunderstanding the way of self-liberation, one seeks antidotes somewhere other than in the afflictions themselves. This is known as straying in regard to the antidote. Thinking that all phenomena of apparent existence, samsara and nirvana, are mere emptiness, one is stuck in a fixation of nihilism. This is known as straying into labeling." Since Ati accepts the reality of all phenomena as they are within emptiness, there is no straying or anywhere to go astray.

suchness, thusness; *de bzhin nyid* (Tib.): Emptiness, things as they are.

sun and its rays, *nyi ma dang nyi ma 'i 'od zer* (Tib.): The sun and its rays are a common example of the relationship of the empty essence and luminous nature of phenomena. The example will be clearer if we understand some aspects of how Tibetans have thought of the sun. They believe it to be eternal and of a pure, incorruptible nature. Moreover, the ever-present solar rays are said to participate in that nature. Therefore, it is natural in Tibetan Buddhism to use the sun to exemplify the changeless essence of phenomenal emptiness and the sun's rays to exemplify the inseparable rays of the sun, which ceaselessly arise with the same nature as the sun itself.

Sugata, *bde gshegs pa* (Tib.), *sugata* (Skt.): The literal meaning is bliss-gone. One who courses in suchness (emptiness, things as they are) with an emphasis on the intrinsic fulfillment of that state. Cf. Tathagata, *de bzhin gshegs pa* (Tib.): The literal meaning is thus-gone. One who courses in suchness, with an emphasis on directness beyond conceptual superimposition. Both terms refer to buddhas.

ten directions, *phyogs bcu* (Tib.): The four main directions of north, south, east, and west; the four intermediate directions of northeast, southeast, northwest, and southwest; and above and below. That is, everywhere.

ten natures, *rang bzhin bcu* (Tib.): View, samaya, buddha activity, mandala, empowerment, path, levels of realization, conduct, wisdom, and self-perfection.

ten virtues, *dge ba bcu* (Tib.): Renunciation of the ten non-virtues: 1. Not destroying life. 2. Not stealing. 3. Refraining from improper sexual activity. 4. Not telling lies. 5. Not using abusive language. 6. Not slandering others. 7. Not indulging in meaningless speech. 8. Not being covetous. 9. Not being malicious. 10. Not holding wrong beliefs.

three existences, *srid pa gsum* (Tib.): The realms of desire, form, and formless.

three kayas, *sku gsum* (Tib.), *trikāya* (Skt.): dharmakaya, sambhogakaya, and nirmanakaya. Dharmakaya is the essence of buddhahood, the benefit for oneself, unborn primordial insight, awareness devoid of content, like space. It is called dharmakaya because it embodies the essence and fruition of the teachings. Dharmakaya is sometimes used in the sense of non-dual dharmakaya. In that case it includes all the phenomena of all three kayas, in the sense of none going beyond its essence. Among the three kayas, dharmakaya is associated particularly with the essence, emptiness. Sambhogakaya and nirmanakaaya are the two rupakayas or form bodies, which manifest for the benefit for others. Sambhogakaya is the realm of realization and enjoyment of pure form. This includes visions of the teachers and pure lands (e.g., Samantabhadra, *Akanishtha*, etc.) and the entire realm of form. It is associated with the vision of luminosity, the nature. Since nothing needs to be accomplished within the Great Perfection, the realization of sambhogakaya has a tone of appreciation and fulfillment, called the All-Good and the great bliss, and the associated activity is celebration. Nirmanakaya is associated with the play of appearance of this dualistic, material world and so forth, which arises from the power of compassion to ripen beings for enlightenment. Longchenpa points out that, strictly speaking, the two rupakayas should be regarded as the ground of arising of their respective form phenomena, rather than as those phenomena themselves. Otherwise confusion may arise from regarding dharmakaya, which is essentially non-apparent, and the various apparent phenomena of the rupakayas as having the same essence.

three poisons, *dug gsum* (Tib.): Attachment, aversion, and ignorance. These are the three root defilements that produce samsara. Ati is beyond them all.

transcendental wisdom, *shes rab* (Tib.), *prajñā* (Skt.): Literally, supreme knowledge. Intelligence, discriminating knowledge in general, and in particular knowledge of emptiness as presented in the perfection of transcendental wisdom (Prajnaparamita) scriptures, the reasoning of Madhyamaka, etc.

twice born bird, *gnyis skyes* (Tib.): Birds are said by the Tibetans to be born twice, once when the egg is laid and once again when it hatches.

two accumulations, *tshogs gnyis* (Tib.): The accumulations of merit and primordial wisdom. When they are completed, enlightenment and realization of the Great Perfection are attained.

uncertain, *nges med* (Tib.): Not ascertained as anything in particular, not fixed, unpredictable.

uncompounded, unconditioned; *'du ma byas* (Tib.): In the lesser vehicles, phenomena are postulated as separate independent entities, each with its own self-nature and characteristics. Compounded entities are constructed by combining a number of such entities into another more complex entity. Conditioned phenomena are those arising and functioning due to causal relationships with other phenomena or defined in terms of logical relationships with other phenomena. All samsaric phenomena are conditioned, because all worldly phenomena arise from causes and conditions, and defining them linguistically depends on their logical relationships with various other kinds of phenomena. The realization of Ati is beyond all conditioned phenomena.

universe and its inhabitants, *snod bcud* (Tib.): Literally, the vessel and contents (essence).

unmixed, unconfused; *ma'dres* (Tib.): 1. In primordial wisdom, the extent of phenomena, all the different, individual things are clear and distinct. They do not get mixed up with each other or confused. 2. Unadulterated. Wisdom is not mixed, adulterated with samsaric fixation and grasping.

unobstructed, *thogs med* (Tib.): Has the sense of unstopped, and also can mean ceaseless. The enlightened insight of Ati is said to be unobstructed.

unsupported, *rten med* (Tib.): If one compares ordinary notions of perception of objects in the external world with perception of objects in a dream, the former are perceptions caused by external objects, while the latter are not. The difference is expressed by saying that the former have a ground or support, and the latter do not. Ati accepts the terminology of the Mahayana philosophical schools that claim to establish that there are no external objects with real and independent natures of their own. This is the basis for saying that seeming appearances of real objects are without ground and support, like a dream.

vajra, *rdo rje* (Tib.): 1. The diamond, prince of stones. 2. Indestructible, adamantine. 3. The thunderbolt, weapon of Indra.

vajra conditions, *rdo rje rkyen* (Tib.): The phenomenal world by means of which enlightenment is actualized.

vajra holder, *rdo rje 'dzin* (Tib.): Level of a vajra holder.

Vajradhara, *rdo rje chang* (Tib.): Personifies the state of primordial buddhahood. His function in the Kagyü schools is rather like that of Samantabhadra in the Nyingma.

vajradhatu, *rdo rje dbyings* (Tib.): Indestructible space, the vajra-like aspect of ultimate space.

Vajrasattva, *rdo rje sems dpa'* (Tib.): A buddha of the vajra family, white in color and associated with purity. Also the sambhogakaya buddha.

vehicle, *theg pa* (Tib.): A systematic presentation of the Buddha's teachings as a means for attaining enlightenment. See nine vehicles.

vehicles of cause and characteristics, *rgyu mtshan theg pa* (Tib.): In particular, the first three of the nine vehicles, which present enlightenment as a causal process. However, all the vehicles, with the exclusion of Ati, have characteristics that are to be abandoned and qualities that are to be attained by causal means.

vidyadhara, *rig 'dzin* (Tib.): Literally "awareness-holder." It indicates someone who constantly abides in the state of pure awareness (rigpa).

vividly clear; *sal gyis gsal, sal le ba* (Tib.): Vividness. Ego fixation draws on the energy of the natural state to produce blockage and obscuration. By comparison, experience of things as they are is one of vivid splendor and immensity. Cf. luminosity.

wisdom (primordial), *ye shes* (Tib.): Literally pristine or primordial awareness, knowledge, or cognition. Direct intuition of absolute reality beyond conception.

world and beings, *snod bcud* (Tib.): The vessel and essence (as metaphor). The container as the external world and the experience of beings within it are compared to a bottle containing liquid, the liquid being the essential part of the two. Sometimes rendered "the environment and inhabitants" (of the phenomenal world).

Yoga (vehicle): See nine vehicles.

Zogpa Chenpo (Tib.): Alternative spelling for Dzogpa Chenpo (Highest realization).

Endnotes

1 Three sections or divisions of Dzogchen: Mind Section, Space Section, and Instruction Section; three divisions of the 6,000,400 Ati Yoga verses.

2 The nine expanses of the space section:, three white, three black, and three variegated.

3 Longchenpa.

4 The other two are Sakya Pandita and Tsongkhapa.

5 Yogins who have renounced ordinary activities.

6 The is the pure, spacious, all-pervasive, empty essence of mind and phenomena, the state of enlightened mind.

7 The luminous dimension of complete enjoyment, beyond dualistic limitations and beyond space and time.

8 The manifestation of the dynamic energy of emptiness. It is the display of amazing illusions, emanated by compassionate mind to bring beings to enlightenment.

9 Commonly refers to the state of beings between death and rebirth in another life, characterized by visions and hallucinations.

10 Innermost teaching of Ati Yoga is known as Yangti, meaning "innermost Ati."

11 The relevant context seems to be a list of three kinds of ignorance. They are described as follows by Sera Khandro, a teacher of Chatral Rinpoche: Awareness that grasps an "I" is ignorance that regards individual selfhood as a cause. This develops into awareness that grasps object and perceiver as separate, called co-emergent ignorance. Developing from that again, the displays of external and internal phenomena of the world are labeled with names as separate things. They are grasped as separate objects. Grasping phenomena as separate, solid things is called the ignorance of conceptual labeling.

12 Samsara is the deluded, unenlightened state of ignorance and suffering. Nirvana is enlightenment.

13 The six qualities are: 1. Insight is elevated above the basis of confusion from the beginning. 2. The essence shines forth, appearing as one's own nature. 3. The essence discriminates the particulars of individual, personal insight. 4. It liberates into the sphere of discriminating wisdom. 5. Its fruition is self-manifesting and not dependent on anything other than itself, e.g. other persons, conditions, or scriptures. 6. Samantabhadra naturally abides, as the way things are, primordial liberation in which all six qualities are directly known.

14 The development and completion stages (see glossary).

15 A mandala is a symbolic depiction with an overall circular form of a deity with its retinue and environment. It may also refer to a circular plate of offerings organized like a mandala. The term can be used more loosely. For example, the mandala of the four directions is the physical world and the mandala of wisdom is the sphere of realization.

16 Samantabhadra (Skt.), Kuntuzangpo (Tib.), the primordial buddha, which represents the absolute, sky-like, primordial purity of the essence of mind. Samantabhadra means "all good" or "unchanging goodness." This realization is fundamentally good, beyond concepts of good and bad.

17 The peak of vehicles is Ati, the Great Perfection. The Nyingma school of Tibetan Buddhism has nine vehicles, which are organized systems of teachings and practices leading to enlightenment.

18 In Buddhist cosmology, the King of Mountains is Mount Meru, at the center of the four continents and the rotating circle of heavenly bodies.

19 Mount Meru is so tall that it reaches above the world into the heavens, where the sun, moon, and stars rotate around it.

20 The three inseparable aspects of enlightened mind: dharmakaya, sambhogakaya, and nirmanakaya.

21 The mind's emanation and dissolution of phenomena, particularly of discursive thoughts.

22 Ornaments of space are unceasing, like a circle without beginning or end.

23 The six realms of samsara are those of the gods, jealous gods (asuras), humans, animals, hungry ghosts (pretas), and hell beings.

24 From womb, egg, heat and moisture, and miracle.

25 The dualistic fixation of subject and object.

26 The basic space in which all phenomena and awareness are subsumed, and the empty ground from which they arise. This basic space is the subject of this treatise.

27 The sambhogakaya, the dimension of complete enjoyment and the field of total enrichment, beyond dualistic limitations.

28 The nirmanakaya.

29 The precipice is a metaphor for dangerous places to go astray, such as illusions of solidity that give rise to afflictions.

30 In particular, the two accumulations of merit and wisdom.

31 If eternalism were true, everything would be permanent. If nihilism were true, there would only be nothingness.

32 The realms of desire, form, and formlessness.

33 A sambhogakaya pure land, such as the western paradise of Amitabha, where one sees purely and can hear the teachings of realized beings.

34 In the Mahayana, bodhicitta often refers to the wish for enlightenment for the benefit of all beings. In the Ati vehicle it usually refers to compassionate enlightened mind itself.

35 Dharmata (Skt.), suchness, or thusness, is a synonym for emptiness or the nature of things. It is the state of being "as it is."

36 The fortress represents an impenetrable defense against attacks of afflicting emotions and delusion.

37 The Tibetan for "essence" here is *thig le*, which can also mean circle or dot.

38 "Perfection of enjoyments" is sambhogakaya.

39 Potency, also translated as "power" or "energy," is the power of awareness to produce a display of phenomena.

40 A "nail" is a central point that holds everything together. Here, the three nails are example, sign, and meaning.

41 All-Good is Samantabhadra, and Indestructible Enlightened Mind is Vajrasattva.

42 In Indian mythology, gandharvas are celestial musicians dwelling in castles in the sky.

43 Forms are "empty" in that they do not exist in the way they appear. The lower vehicles establish emptiness through intellect; in the Ati vehicle the empty essence of things is experienced directly.

44 Potential is the capacity of awareness to reflect a display of phenomena.

45 Though substance and characteristics appear to exist from their own side in a fixed way, in the ultimate nature they do not truly exist like that.

46 The mind's gathering and dispersing of phenomena, particularly of discursive thoughts.

47 In ancient India, the crown anointment was a ritual for the coronation of a king. Symbolically, it refers to the self-existing empowerment of the Great Perfection, in which the practitioner is crowned as a king of dharmakaya.

48 The literal meaning is bliss-gone. One who courses in suchness (emptiness, things as they are) with an emphasis on the intrinsic fulfillment of that state.

49 Samaya are vows or commitments associated with Vajrayana empowerments. They involve such things as maintaining a daily practice and behaving respectfully toward the vajra master and sangha members. The profound samaya is to maintain awareness at all times and to see the world and all beings with pure perception.

50 With the body: refraining from killing, stealing, and sexual misconduct; with speech: not lying, slandering, talking harshly, or engaging in gossip; with the mind: not being covetous, malicious, or holding wrong views.

51 The primarily monastic "hearers" of the foundation vehicle of Hinayana.

52 Hinayana practitioners who typically realize personal liberation from samsara by themselves, without a teacher or group environment.
53 Practitioners of the Mahayana vehicle who seek enlightenment in order to benefit all sentient beings.
54 The three outer tantras of Vajrayana. Kriya focuses on purity, Upa on conduct, and Yoga on meditation. A deity is regarded as a master in Kriya, a friend in Upa, and one's own nature in Yoga.
55 The three inner tantras of Vajrayana. Mahayoga emphasizes the visualization of deities and mandalas of the developing stage. Anu emphasizes the yogic techniques of the completion stage. Ati is the pinnacle of the Buddhist teachings, the Great Perfection, as explained in this text.
56 The three bodhis (Skt.), the three levels of enlightenment of Hinayana, Mahayana, and Vajrayana. The first two constitute the causal vehicles, and the last, the resultant vehicle.
57 Oxen, having big bodies, represent practitioners who are overblown with pride. Both oxen and conceited practitioners are obscured by ignorance.
58 Prajna (Skt.), the sixth paramita.
59 Ordinary consciousness has seemingly "clear" perception of delusive grasper and grasped; but awareness in the Great Perfection is truly clear, because it does not have delusions of grasper and grasped.
60 The objects of the five senses.
61 Attachment, aversion, ignorance, pride, and jealousy.
62 Spoken sacred formulae such as Om Mani Padme Hum.
63 View, samaya, buddha activity, mandala, empowerment, path, levels of realization, conduct, wisdom, and self-perfection.
64 Body, speech, and mind.
65 The first, original, or primordial Buddha is Samantabhadra.
66 The garuda is a bird from Indian mythology that is able to fly as soon as it hatches from the egg.
67 "Great universal expanse" in Tibetan is Longchen Rabjam, the pen name by which Longchenpa is most commonly known.
68 "Self-liberated variety" in Tibetan is Natsok Rangdrol, another pen name for Longchenpa.
69 The main directions are north, south, east, and west; the intermediate directions are southeast, southwest, northeast, and northwest.
70 The three times are past, present, and future.
71 Here, "white and red" signify all the variety of appearances.
72 Shamatha (Skt.) "with an object" consists of focusing the mind one-pointedly on an object. Shamatha "without an object" consists of resting the mind without

trying to control it. Experiences that arise are noted; however, if attachment or aversion arises, it is cut off and one returns to the basic meditation.

73 Purified: byang (Tib.) Here Longchenpa explains the meaning of the words that make up the Tibetan term for compassionate mind, *byang chub sems.*

74 Perfect: chub (Tib.)

75 Mind: sems (Tib.)

76 The assemblage of phenomena perceived by the five senses; the mental sense; the repository of remembered sense phenomena tainted by the three or five poisons; and the all-ground consciousness, the state of consciousness that is mere clarity and knowing, which has not developed into active sense cognition of a multiplicity of individual objects. That develops in the all-ground, the universal ground of dualistic phenomena that is the support of habitual tendencies.

77 The mythical garuda, which develops fully in the egg. "Twice born" refers to birds in general, which are "born" once within the egg and again when they hatch.

78 The result of delusion, the body, remains, as in buddhahood with remainder.

79 Buddhahood without remainder.

80 It is possible for impure beings to have some pure karma and aspirations.

81 As the peak of the mountain is referred to as the "head," the area immediately below the peak is referred to as the "neck."

82 Longchen Nyingthig (Tib.).

83 A mandala is made of five small heaps, for example, of rice, in the four directions and center.

84 A bhandha (Skt.) is a skull-cup. It may have differing numbers of lines, one, three, five, etc., corresponding to the sutures where the skull bones are joined. Three is an auspicious number for these.

85 The mandala is not in any special place, but is simply added with the other offering substances.

86 Various special offering substances, as prescribed elsewhere.

87 Amrita (Skt.), originally the immortality-producing food or drink of the gods. In tantra practice, a liquor offering that symbolizes the practitioner being spiritually "intoxicated" into a state of timeless realization. It is commonly said that in that case, ordinary liquor is blessed as amrita.

88 A food offering; in particular, roughly conical forms made of barley flour mixed with butter, colored, and decorated in different ways according to the type of deity with which they are associated.

89 These four are known as the four appearances of Ati Yoga.

90 A learned person. Here one can visualize, Longchenpa, Vimalamitra, or one's own teacher, as desired.

91 Ritual gesture used in sadhana practice and so forth, for example, in the mudra of resting the mind mentioned here.

92 The three places are the head, throat, and heart. The three syllables are OM AH HUNG.

93 The rainbow body is attained when, at the time of death of a practitioner who has reached the exhaustion of grasper and grasped through Dzogchen practice, the five gross elements that form the physical body dissolve back into their essences as five-colored rainbow light, leaving no corpse or only the hair and nails.

94 In many sadhana practices, deities of samaya and primordial wisdom are distinguished. The first consists of one's visualization in ordinary consciousness according to the samaya to perform the practice. Then one visualizes that primordial wisdom deities descend and transform one's visualization into primordial wisdom. Ideally, such a transformation actually occurs. In the realization of Ati, all experiences are aspects of primordial wisdom from the beginning, so there is no need for a transformation.

95 Of the five colors: white, blue, yellow, red, and green.

96 Samantabhadra (Skt.)

97 The two hands with the palms placed facing upward, the fingers of the right hand on top of those of the left, with the tips of thumbs touching. Usually done in cross-legged posture with the forearms resting on the thighs.

98 The ordinary accomplishments are various miraculous abilities, such as knowing the minds of others or flying in the sky. The supreme accomplishment is enlightenment itself.

99 Author's note: Regarding service, worship, and activity, service consists of making offerings to the sugatas by emanating light rays. Worship is purifying the evil deeds and obscurations of sentient beings and becoming the deity. Having gathered back the light rays and dissolving them into oneself, purifying obscurations of the three doors, and attaining accomplishment constitute great worship. Resting in the principle, equanimity, is the application of activity.

100 Such manifestations of the Guru occur.

101 "My" refers to Jigme Lingpa.